MW01105855

Letters On Artillery

LETTERS ON ARTILLERY

BY

PRINCE KRAFT ZU HOHENLOHE INGELFINGEN

TRANSLATED BY

COLONEL N. L. WALFORD, R.A.

WITH SIX FOLDING PLATES

THIRD EDITION

LONDON: EDWARD STANFORD

26 & 27 COCKSPUR STREET, CHARING CROSS, S.W.

1898

PREFACE

THE following translation of the *Letters on Artillery* was originally issued in the *Proceedings of the Royal Artillery Institution*, and I desire to express my sincere thanks to the Committee of that Institution for their kind permission to publish them.

The reception of the letters by the officers of the Royal Artillery has been so favourable, and so many inquiries have been made as to the possibility of the supply of copies to officers of the other arms, that I have felt myself justified in reprinting them.

I have further to acknowledge, with my most grateful thanks, the extreme courtesy which I have received from the Author and from his Publishers, Messrs. Mittler of Berlin.

N. L. W.

SHOEBURYNESS,
    September 1888.

CONTENTS

LETTER IX

ON THE RENEWAL OF AMMUNITION IN TIME OF WAR

LETTER X

HOW THE ARTILLERY "SAVED" ITSELF DURING THE LAST WAR

LETTER XI

GENERAL VON HINDERSIN

LETTER XII

PRINCIPLES FOR THE FUTURE EMPLOYMENT OF FIELD ARTILLERY

LETTER XIII

CONCERNING THE PROPOSAL "THAT ARTILLERY FIRE SHOULD NOT
COMMENCE AT AN EARLIER MOMENT THAN SHORTLY BEFORE THE
INFANTRY FIGHT; BUT THAT IT SHOULD THEN AT ONCE BEGIN
AT SUCH A RANGE THAT ITS EFFECT WILL BE ANNIHILATING."

LETTER XIV

SHOULD ARTILLERY AVOID IN FUTURE THE ZONE OF INFANTRY
FIRE?

LETTER XV

LETTER XVI

LETTER XVII

THE ANSWER OF THE CORRESPONDENT, GIVING A SUMMARY OF THE PRECEDING LETTERS

LETTER XVIII

ANSWERS TO VARIOUS QUESTIONS

1. Opening fire at a range of 5500 yards.
2. Should the artillery be taken from the divisions?
3. As to the temporary silence of the artillery of the defence.
4. Horse Artillery in a cavalry action.
a. The authority over the artillery of generals commanding troops.
b. Details of the formation of, and of the sequence of command in, a mass of artillery.
c. The position for the main mass of the artillery of the attack— Artillery firing over the heads of infantry.
d. How far is it advisable to " lay back " ?

LIST OF PLANS

LETTER I

THE USE MADE OF FIELD ARTILLERY IN THE WAR OF 1866

YOU quietly, my dear friend, put to me a very grave question when you ask me:—" What is the reason that our artillery, which in the campaign of 1870-71 did such excellent service, failed altogether four years before, in the war with Austria, to answer to the expectation excited by the effect which it produced at Düppel in 1864, and this although its matériel was with but few exceptions the same, while it was under the command of the very same men?" This question has been briefly answered by drawing attention to the fact that the Prussian artillery, though nearly equal in number to that of the Austrians, had in each group of 16 batteries, only 10 which were armed with rifled guns, while our adversaries had condemned all their S.B. guns; and, it was added, smooth-bore guns cannot compete with rifled guns.

This answer is not exhaustive nor is it quite accurate, for the Austrian pieces of 1866 were rifled muzzle-loading guns which, on account of the complicated system of their rifling, of their difficult and

B

slow service, of the uncertain bursts of their percussion shell, and of the doubtful effect of their shrapnel, were altogether inferior, as regards accuracy and effect of fire, to the rifled breech-loading Prussian pieces. If each side had been equally skilled as regards the employment of its artillery and the accuracy of its fire, 10 Prussian guns might well have been expected to balance 16 Austrian, so superior were the former to the latter in point of construction. Therefore the 6 S.B. batteries which each Prussian army-corps possessed, over and above its 10 rifled batteries, should be considered as constituting for us a surplus of artillery which should have turned the scale of the artillery combat in our favour. The rifled guns of the Austrians were, it is true, superior, as regards accuracy of fire, to the Prussian 12-pr. S.B., but this superiority was not so great but that the latter might have been capable of holding their ground against them, above all if a sufficient number of them had been brought into action.

At Schweinschädel the 3d battery of the Horse Artillery of the Guard held its ground, with its six 12-pr. S.B. guns, against 16 Austrian rifled guns ; and many other S.B. batteries (for example the batteries under Schmelzer and Theiler at Königgrätz) took a glorious and active part in the general combat of artillery, and this sometimes even when they were isolated, in which case they boldly approached to within such a distance of the enemy as was necessary to attain the desired effect. If then, while searching for the solution of the problem, account be taken of the factor of matériel only, we shall be inclined to admit that, in the war of 1866, the Prussian artillery should have shown itself superior to that of the Austrians.

The fact that this was not the case authorises your question—" What was the reason of this ?" It was long before I could bring myself to seek for the solution of this question, for as soon as one sets to work to inquire why such and such a thing was not done when it might have been done, or why an undertaking has failed, or at least has not succeeded as well as one had a right to expect, it is found as a rule that somebody has committed a fault, and it is then necessary to declare, " It was this or that officer who was the cause of the failure." And this is true apart from the fact that the general public has a very natural tendency, when anything unpleasant happens, to seek for a scapegoat, as was well shown by the tragic fate of Bazaine. But the mere finding of a scapegoat proves nothing ; its only effect is to heap hatred and contempt on some individual, who is perhaps not so guilty as is believed, and who may possibly be altogether innocent. This is sufficient for the crowd, but no one gets any good from it.

But the more I worked at the problem, the more certain I felt that there could be no question of making any one person responsible for the disappointment of our hopes, or of being compelled to accuse any individual in my altogether impartial endeavour to solve it. You yourself, by the manner in which you state your question, are evidently of the same opinion, since at the end you draw attention to the fact that the same officers commanded the artillery in 1870 as in 1866. It is true that a certain number of the colonels of 1866 commanded in 1870 the artillery of an army-corps ; some of the commandants who in 1866 led brigades,[1] were in 1870 in command of regiments ; a proportion of the captains of batteries found themselves in charge of brigades, but many commandants and captains commanded in 1870 the same force which they had led in 1866.

On the other hand, the study of the causes in question has led me to examine some newly established principles of the employment and tactics of Field Artillery, so that I am compelled, in order to answer you, to enter fully upon the vast domain which this arm includes, since I shall find myself obliged to speak of the successive developments which led to the mode of proceeding that obtained in 1870. We shall draw truths from this study which will lose nothing of their value, even though the sphere of action of firearms be still further enlarged by new inventions. While seeking, then, a careful and well-reasoned answer to your question, we shall not only study the history of the past, but shall also arrive at conclusions with a practical value. Not having, therefore, in order to find an answer to your question, to accuse any person whatever, and believing that I

---

[1] A Prussian Regiment of Artillery, at this time and during the war of 1870, was made up of 4 "Abtheilungen." I have ventured to translate this word as "Brigade." Three of these brigades consisted of 4 Field batteries each, while the fourth was composed of 3 batteries of Horse Artillery.

To each of the two Divisions of which a Prussian army-corps was constituted a brigade of Field Artillery was apportioned, while the remainder, with the exception of such H.A. batteries as might be attached to the cavalry, formed that which in 1866 was called the "Reserve artillery," but in 1870 received the name of "Corps artillery."

The batteries were commanded by captains, the brigades by commandants, and the regiment by a colonel.—*N.L.W.*

can also lay down practical rules which may be useful in the future, I will gladly devote myself to this study. But you must be exceedingly patient.

As the subject which I am about to treat is a very large one, I must devote to it more than one letter. It will, besides, take me some time to sub-divide it and set it in order ; you will therefore only receive my letters from time to time. You must allow me to again invite you to follow me over almost all the fields of battle of 1866, 1870, and 1871. Even that will not be sufficient ; I shall find myself obliged to introduce you into the cabinet where, in time of peace, is carried out the elaboration of all that concerns the artillery, at the risk of wearying you with details which may interest you but little, since you do not belong to that arm. But this is necessary in order to give you an answer to your question.

The data which my own past offers, if they do not embrace the whole subject, are at least very numerous. Not only have I, as an officer of that arm, followed very closely the action of the artillery in our last four campaigns, in 1864, 1866, 1870, and 1871, but I have also been in close communica-tion with the men who had the principal part in all affairs which regard the arm, and I have been fre-quently desired to assist in the modifications which it has undergone. I cannot therefore excuse myself from owning, in what follows, the weaknesses and errors of which we gunners were guilty before 1866 ; and perhaps, my friend, you will be inclined to ironi-cally compare the cross-examination to which I shall subject myself to "The confession of a beautiful

soul " out of *Wilhelm Meister*.   But I shall not
mind that, for the result at which I shall arrive will
be very different ; Goethe's heroine improves and
perfects herself only inwardly, while our improvements have declared themselves outwardly and
visibly.

You will admit to one who felt the matter bitterly,
that there was widespread discontent in 1866 at the
action of our Field Artillery.   This discontent was
founded upon facts so well known that each of us
gunners was obliged, however clear was his own
conscience, however sure he felt that he had himself
done his duty as well as any officer of the other
arms, to acknowledge it as well founded.   The public
in general for its part judged only by results, and it
was our duty, as gunners, to find out the cause of
the evil, and the ways and means to remedy it.
The results obtained in the campaign of 1866 told
most unfavourably against the artillery.   If we study
them by the light of the work of the General Staff,
we shall see in 1866 our artillery, on almost every
occasion, entered upon the scene far too late and
with far too small a number of guns.   In the course
of all the engagements the infantry found itself
exposed to the murderous fire of an artillery very
superior in number to ours, and in order to reply
and to defend itself had to have recourse to its own
fire of musketry.

Let us begin with the combat of Trautenau,
fought on the 27th of June 1866.

At the beginning of the engagement one battery,
Trautenau.   it is true, advanced through Trautenau in
order to take up a position on the right

bank of the Aupa ; it was reinforced by 2 guns from the detachment on the right ; but very soon, after a little more than an hour, the 3 batteries of the advanced guard which had passed the river were brought back to the left bank, in order that they might from the northern heights cover the retreat, should that become necessary. After 1 P.M. Böhnke's battery came into action with the 44th and 45th regiments of infantry to the south of the Aupa. Twenty-four hostile guns obliged it to retire. One hour and a half after Böhnke's advance, 2 batteries (12 guns), under Major Noak, engaged these 24 Austrian pieces on the south of Trautenau, and at least drew away from the infantry the murderous fire of this artillery. But Major Noak had to leave a battery in reserve at the western outlet of the village of Trautenau, for the reason that it had S.B. guns, which would not carry far enough.

When at 3.30 P.M. the enemy, reinforced by fresh troops, advanced once more to the attack, the 2 batteries of Major Noak were, and continued to be, the only artillery which supported the infantry on the left bank, though there were near it (i) the 12-pr. battery which had been left at the western outlet of Trautenau, (ii) Böhnke's battery, and (iii) the 3 batteries posted to the north of Trautenau, which had been reinforced by 2 others taken from the reserve ; in all therefore 42 guns. Major Noak's 2 batteries likewise left their position between 4 and 5 P.M. From this moment the infantry carried on the fight without the assistance of any artillery, while the enemy increased his to 40 guns. We do not hear that our artillery came into action again until 8 P.M. ;

this artillery, of the strength of 2 batteries, covered
the retreat by firing on the outlet of Trautenau from a
position to the north-west of Parschnitz, about 3 miles
(English) therefore in rear of the position of Major
Noak's batteries, of which we have spoken above.

On the side of the Prussians, then, no more than
6 batteries and 1 division or 38 guns took an active
part in the fight; but never more than 2 batteries
were in action at one time, namely, 8 guns at first,
then 6 others, and at last 12 others.   After that,
during 3 hours, the infantry, though hard pressed
by the enemy's infantry, remained without any
assistance from the artillery, and it was not until the
evening that 2 batteries came into action to cover
the retreat.   Can we then blame the infantry, who
knew that 96 guns were present with the army-corps, if
they asked with astonishment—"What has this mass
of artillery of ours done during all this long day?"

The day after the fight at Trautenau the Guard
corps, as we know, defeated the 10th
corps of the Austrian army, which had
been victorious the day before.   What
part did our artillery play on that occasion, and of
what assistance was it to the infantry?   At the
commencement one battery of the reserve artillery of
the Austrian corps fired on the head of the Prussian
troops, and on our part was opposed by the 1st 4-pr.
battery.   While the Austrian battery was reinforced
by several others who came into line in succession,
we find on the Prussian side the 1st[1] 6-pr. battery

Soor, or
Burkersdorf,
28th June 1866.

---

[1] The Prussian guns were at this time classed (4-prs. or 6-prs.) by
the weight of a spherical solid shot suited to their calibre.   They thus
threw a heavier shell than their names implied.—*N.L. W.*

coming into action in aid of that which was at first in position. The work of the Austrian staff tells us that, before the moment at which the infantry of the Prussian advanced guard carried out its attack against the clumps of trees to the east of Burkersdorf, the following batteries had been placed in position : the 9th, 5th, 8th, 10th, 3d, and 7th of the 3d corps, that is to say 6 batteries, and consequently 48 guns. This line of artillery was not reinforced during the course of the day.

At another point of the field of battle, to the north of Neu-Rognitz, the battery of Mondel's brigade (1st of the 3d corps) took part in the action, in addition to the battery of Wimpffen's brigade, which stood to the south of Hohenbrück. Of the 9 batteries (72 guns) which the 10th Austrian corps possessed, 8 (64 guns) were thus employed during the day, while 6 of these (48 guns) were in action from the first, in one and the same long line. The Prussian Guard corps, on the other hand, engaged at first only 2 batteries (12 guns); nor was this number increased, for though later on the 5th battery (12-pr.) took an active part in the fight, it merely relieved the 1st 4-pr. battery. Of 78 guns belonging to this corps, 18 only took part in the action, for the Horse Artillery battery had been, that day, detached with the Heavy Cavalry Brigade of the Guard to the 5th corps.

Our brave infantry of the Guard conducted its advance on that day with inimitable valour and self-sacrifice, and, in spite of the murderous fire of the enemy's guns, carried through its attack and won a brilliant victory. But it would have been impossible

to have blamed it, had it complained that it was not
supported by the sister arm, and had it angrily
asked, "Where were the 60 other guns?" On the
day of this engagement I had, very early in the
morning, left the bivouac which had been assigned
to me at Braunau with the reserve artillery of the
Guard, and in accordance with orders which I had
received, had marched by Politz and Hronow on
Kosteletz, which had been given me as my point.
I felt sure that we should find ourselves obliged to
fight immediately after passing the frontier, had
therefore hastened my march as much as possible,
and arrived at Kosteletz with the head of my column
at 10 A.M., having thus in a mountainous country
marched 18 (English) miles in 6 hours.

At Kosteletz I received an order to remain for the
present in reserve with some other troops, for the
reason that fighting was going on at Skalitz as well
as at Soor, and it was as yet undecided where
the reserve would be of most use. It was not until
5 P.M., when favourable news arrived of the fight
at Skalitz, that I received authority to endeavour to
rejoin my corps, and I then had to make a march of
several miles, with the defile of Eipel at the end of
it. After a troublesome march through this defile,
which is 3 (English) miles in length, and which was
rendered almost impassable by the ambulances carrying the wounded and by other carriages, I at length
reached, long after dark, the open country between
Ober-Raatsch and Staudenz where, in accordance
with orders, I bivouacked. The last battery did not
rest until after midnight.

At the break of day (between 3 and 4 A.M.),

some routed Austrian troops broke into my bivouac, and the battalion which I had received as escort (the 2d of the 1st Regiment of the Guard) after a short fight overpowered them. During the early part of the morning this happened several times before I was able to join the corps and its staff, in order to obtain my orders. As a matter of fact I thought that I had made superhuman efforts to come to the assistance of my comrades who were fighting. I was therefore very disagreeably surprised when, on marching in the direction of Königinhof, according to the order which I had received from the General commanding the corps, to take my place in the column at Burkersdorf, I was accosted by my comrades of the infantry, who were all old friends of mine, with the words—"Here you are at last! where in the world have you been? We had to allow innumerable guns of the enemy to overwhelm us with a hail of projectiles. We kept on looking to see if you were coming, but you did not come!" At the moment these reproaches drove me to despair; but when I now compare the figures which I have given above, which I have taken from the two official accounts, I am no longer astonished at them.

During the action at Trautenau another unforeseen fight took place at Nachod, the result of the meeting of the 5th Prussian corps with the 7th Austrian corps and the cavalry division of the Prince of Holstein. The Austrians had 12 batteries (96 guns). On the side of the Prussians General von Steinmetz had 15 batteries (90 guns) at his orders.

Nachod, 27th June 1866.

At the beginning of the action 2 batteries were

firing at each other. The Austrian battery (of Hertwek's Brigade) was obliged to retire, but it was soon reinforced by the battery of Jonak's Brigade, which two others afterwards joined, while on the Prussian side only one, the 1st battery of 4-prs. joined that at first engaged (the 5th 4-pr. battery), so that at this place 32 Austrian guns were engaged against 12 Prussian. About 11 o'clock the latter were increased to 18 by the arrival of a Horse Artillery battery.

It would appear that, during the interval, the Austrian line of artillery had been increased to 40 guns by the arrival of the battery of Solm's Brigade, for when, at midday, the reserve artillery of the Austrian corps came into action, at Kleny, with 40 additional guns, it is mentioned that 80 Austrian guns had opened fire. On the part of the Prussians, other batteries came up in succession to the field of battle. But the line of artillery was not even then strengthened, for the 2 batteries which had commenced the action (the 1st and the 5th 4-pr.) had been withdrawn, while the only Horse Artillery battery was destroyed as it unlimbered, and could not open fire.

It was not until between 4 and 5 o'clock in the afternoon, when the turning movement attempted by the Austrian cavalry and infantry against the Prussian right wing had failed (during which movement the second battery attached to an Austrian division seems to have come upon the scene, and to have brought the amount of their artillery up to 88 guns), not until this moment did the Prussian reserve artillery, 4 batteries of rifled guns, make its appearance, and then the 2 batteries of the advanced guard, which

had been ordered again to the front, joined themselves
to it. The fire of these 42 guns, and that of the
4th 12-pr. battery on the left flank, combined with
that of the 18 guns already engaged, giving a total
of 66 guns, seems to have decided the enemy to
renounce all idea of renewing the attack.

We see thus that in the action at Nachod up to
11 A.M. 12 Prussian guns were engaged with 32
Austrian; up to midday 18 Prussian against 32
Austrian; from noon to half-past 4, 18 Prussian
against 80 or 88 Austrian, and after 4.30, 66 Prussian
guns against the Austrian artillery, which was gradually reduced in number. We do not find that the
Austrians mention their rocket battery, which does
not appear to have taken any part in the action.

On the Prussian side the 1st 6-pr. battery had
during the day to retire, not being able to hold its
ground, while Ohnesorge's battery was put out of
action. I do not find the 3d and 4th 4-pr. batteries
mentioned in the official account; they may have
been brought into action, but have been obliged to
withdraw, on account of the superior fire of the enemy.
We find then that on the Prussian side 4 batteries
failed to co-operate in the action. On this occasion
also our brave infantry contrived to conquer in spite
of a hostile artillery superior to our own, a superiority
which up to 4.30 P.M. amounted to double or treble
our force.

With regard to the action at Skalitz, which followed that of Nachod, we may make the
same remark.

Skalitz,
28th June
1866.

According to our official account the
Austrian corps had 88 guns; according to the

Austrian account, it had only 64 at its disposal against 102 Prussian guns. We may consider the Austrian figures as correct, but, as in these 64 guns are not included the 8 of Schindlocker's brigade, we must allow that the Austrians had really 72 pieces available. Of these 72 the 40 of the reserve artillery of the corps were in position from the first, and had commenced firing when a battery of General Löwenfelds's detachment began a useless cannonade, which ceased on either side as the range was too great. But when, at 10.45, General von Steinmetz resolved to make a serious attack, isolated batteries only came into action on the Prussian side, with very poor results, so that our infantry had to suffer from the entire fire of the enemy's overpowering artillery. Even " the batteries specially attached to the advanced guard had remained in rear."

At noon 2 Prussian batteries came into action against the 40 guns of the reserve artillery of the Austrian corps, but the latter brought up also the 3 batteries of its brigades; it thus used the fire of 64 guns, in addition to those of Schindlocker's brigade, which fired from the other bank. It was not until 12.30 that the reserve artillery of the 5th Prussian corps reached the position of Kleny, from which since the early morning it had been distant no more than 2 (English) miles. In this position 9 Prussian rifled batteries were then massed, and they exercised a decisive influence on the artillery fight.

Thus we find that on the Austrian side almost every battery was engaged from the commencement; on the Prussian the principal mass of the artillery took no part in the action until after the infantry had been forced, during two whole hours, to undergo the very superior fire of the enemy's guns.

I have no intention of wearying you by analysing, from a gunner's point of view, the part played by the artillery in every engagement fought during the war of 1866. I propose, before mentioning the great decisive battle of Königgrätz, to make observations on only one other of our armies, in order to see if these characteristics were everywhere present. For this reason I beg of you to kindly follow me to the battle of Gitschin.

The 5th Division was accompanied by its 4 batteries. When its leading troops were received by the fire of the enemy's artillery, one of its batteries was, about 4 P.M., sent Gitschin, 29th June 1866.
to the front; to this shortly afterwards a second was added. The enemy replied with 48 guns. About 4.30 the Prussian artillery was increased to 18 guns. This was the total strength brought into action during the entire course of the engagement, for the account does not say that the 4th 12-pr. battery was employed at all. On the side of the Austrians, on the other hand, another battery was soon unmasked, while from the heights to the south of Dieletz other batteries opened fire. According to this, it would appear that, up to 5 P.M. there were 80 guns in action against the 5th Prussian Division.

But in addition the Saxon division of Stieglitz, and with it the reserve artillery of the Saxon corps, received the order to advance, and arrived at 6.30 P.M.

Following the *ordre de bataille*, the 1st Austrian corps was composed of 5 brigades of infantry, of which each had its battery of artillery; it had in addition a corps reserve of 7 batteries; in rear of them was Edelsheim's cavalry division with 3 batteries. Of these 5 brigades one, that commanded by General Piret, was posted at Eisenstadt; Poschacher's brigade was at Brada; Leiningen's was in rear of the latter; while Abele's and Ringelsheim's brigades took up a position at Prachow and Lochow. The batteries of these two last probably fired only on Werder's division.

All the reserve artillery of the corps, the battery of Poschacher's brigade, 2 batteries of Edelsheim's cavalry division, and 2 guns of Leiningen's brigade, in all 82 guns, fired from the first on the 5th division. At a later period, between 5 and 6 P.M., the batteries of Appel's cavalry brigade and of Piret's infantry brigade joined the others; there were thus, it would appear, 104 guns concentrated in action.

According to the Austrian official account, 2 batteries of Saxon brigades also reinforced the line at about 6.30, while a little later a battery of the Saxon reserve joined the others. From that moment the guns, in number 122, formed a powerful line of artillery, against which, on the Prussian part, 18 guns only could be brought into action.

Need we be astonished if, as we read of the battle in the Prussian official account, we come to the conclusion that the heroic infantry of the 5th Division was stopped in its advance by the enemy's artillery alone. Still less need we wonder if the infantry felt that it had not been sufficiently supported by its own artillery.

The situation was not altogether the same in the

action which Werder's division fought on the same day in front of Gitschin. The Prussians had there 3 batteries (18 guns) in action against 2 Austrian batteries of Abele's and Ringelsheim's brigades. It is true that the Prussian official account speaks of 3 Austrian batteries ("besides the battery already mentioned, which was posted to the west of the village, there were two others to the east of it"). But the Austrian official account speaks of 2 batteries only, and the Prussian work appears to found its statement on the reports of the Prussian troops which were engaged, who perhaps may have mistaken 2 half-batteries firing from two different spots for 2 whole batteries. It is hard to see, following the *ordres de bataille*, where a third battery on this part of the field can have come from. Consequently we find that for once the number of guns on the two sides was about equal, namely, 18 Prussian against 16 Austrian.

At the battle of Königgrätz the fight began by the advance of the different columns of the Prussian 1st army, and army of the Elbe, towards the Bistritz, which was **Königgrätz, 3d July 1866.** defended by the most advanced Austrian troops These columns were received with the fire of the enemy's artillery, to which they replied.

According to the Prussian official account, the army of the Elbe brought a battery into action at Nechanitz against a Saxon battery. In the 1st army Herwarth's division brought up 3 batteries on the right of the main road to Königgrätz; Horn's division, 3 others, on the left of the same road. Fransecky's division sent into action only 2 to the north of Benatek.

C

When, about 8 A.M., the advance was stopped
for some time, in order to await the arrival of the
remainder of the forces, there were 9 Prussian
batteries in action, or 54 guns which, with the
object of carrying out the preliminary action, were
spread over the whole Prussian front, about 7
(English) miles in length.

The enemy, according to the Prussian account,
received our troops, as they advanced from Nechanitz,
with the fire of one battery; another battery fired
upon us from the little wood of Sadowa, 4 batteries
from Dohalitzka, and one from the forest of Skalka.
At least 2 batteries in addition fired on us from
the heights of Maslowed and Horenowes.   Consequently at least one Saxon battery and 7 Austrian
(62 guns) fired on the heads of the Prussian columns.
Thus the official account speaks of the "numerous"
artillery which so directed their fire.

The Austrian official account, in contradiction to
this, says that up to 9 A.M. there were in action, on
the Austrian side, only the following batteries :—The
battery of Brandenstein's brigade on the right to the
south of Maslowed; in the centre the batteries of
Appiano's and Prohaska's brigades of the 3d corps,
with the 2 batteries of Knebel's brigade of the ·
10th corps; which makes up, including the Saxon
battery at Nechanitz, only 46 guns.   It is added
that up to this time, that is to say during an hour
and a half, this small number of Austrian batteries
had to hold its own, not only against a nearly treble
number of guns, but also against the advancing
hostile infantry.   However it may be, whether the
Austrian artillery, at this time, had 46 or 62 guns

against the 54 Prussian pieces, it is clear that the number of guns employed on either side to commence the action was not large, considering the mass of artillery which was present with the two armies. Between 8 and 11 A.M. the battle began to work out. During this time neither side made much use of its artillery in the combat carried on by the army of the Elbe, as it possessed itself of the line from Lubno to Hradek ; the fighting was not yet particularly fierce.

Far more serious was the struggle which the first army had to undertake when it had gained the passages of the Bistritz. From 11 A.M. General Fransecky was obliged to throw all his eleven battalions into the contest for the possession of the forest of Swip, where they had to hold their ground against 40 Austrian battalions supported by 11 others in reserve. Fransecky's infantry was assisted by only 24 guns. The infantry and the artillery were covered by a hail of projectiles from 128 hostile guns. The Austrians had thus an artillery five times more numerous than ours, without counting the reserve of 24 guns.[1]

The well-known reports from General Fransecky's

[1] Indeed, when I count the Austrian batteries, I find that they had 136 guns, for, in addition to the 96 which had opened fire from this place at 9.30, the following batteries came into action, viz., the battery of Thom's brigade, the 5th 4-pr. battery of the corps reserve, the 2 batteries of the cavalry divisions and the rocket battery of the reserve : in all 5 batteries or 40 guns. Perhaps the rocket battery has not been counted on account of the inefficiency of its fire. According to the *ordre de bataille* each of the two Austrian corps, which were fighting at this point, had 10 batteries or 80 guns. Consequently if only 128 guns were in action and 24 in reserve, one battery of 8 guns must have been detached. But in fact all this has only a relative importance.

infantry of the terrible effects of the fire of the enemy's artillery were indeed only too well founded.

In the centre, the three most advanced divisions of the 1st army seized, between 8 and 11 A.M., the passages of the Bistritz opposite to which they stood, and secured their conquest by occupying localities which lay immediately beyond these passages, namely, Mokrowous, Dohalitzka, Ober - Dohalitz, Unter - Dohalitz, and the Forest of Hola. On receiving an order to discontinue the advance, they had to content themselves for the moment with maintaining their hold on these points, and thus stood on the defensive. In this position they found themselves overwhelmed by the fire of a mass of artillery which crowned the edge of the heights running from Lipa to Stresetitz; of this mass the Saxon brigade Heydenreich, posted on the heights between Stresetitz and Tresowitz, formed the left wing.

It is probable that at this point there were 124 Austrian guns, for the Prussian official account says that in the whole line from Horenowes by Lipa to Stresetitz there were not less than 250 guns; and adds that 128 of these were firing on the forest of Swip.[1]

[1] If we examine the Austrian official account, it is impossible to gain an exact idea of the number of guns in action at this point. The 3d and the 10th corps were posted there, the former on the right, the latter on left. According to the *ordre de bataille* the 3d corps had 11 batteries, the 10th corps 10. Gablentz (10th corps) employed also the 3d Division (4 batteries) of the reserve artillery of the army, which when it had, at 2.30 P.M., expended its ammunition was relieved by the 4th Division; he also brought up 2 batteries of the 3d Division of the reserve cavalry. The mass of the artillery available at this point would thus amount to 26 batteries or 208 guns, from which indeed we must deduct a certain number of guns which had been lost by the 10th

Against this mass of artillery, on the side of the Prussians, up to 11 A.M., were brought into action the following: 3 batteries to the south of the forest of Skalka and 2 batteries which Werder's division threw across the Bistritz, while at this time the reserve artillery of the 2d corps were preparing to cross that river. There were thus at the most 30 pieces answering to the enemy's fire; for which reason the Prussian official account says: " However, these batteries did not succeed in diverting from the forest and attracting to themselves the excessively violent fire of the very numerous artillery of the enemy!" On this point, therefore, also the infantry (the 2d and 8th Divisions), who were engaged, were the mark of a truly infernal fire from the enemy's artillery, and felt themselves left in the lurch by the sister arm.

After 11 A.M. (I follow the chronological order adopted by the Prussian official account in describing these events) the 2d Prussian army came on the scene. In order to meet it the Austrian right wing had to be thrown back, facing to the north, and 40 Austrian pieces were posted on the height of Horenowes in order to cover this movement. The Austrian official account says that these were Nos. 1, 5, 7, 9, and 10 batteries of the 2d corps. Against them one after the other, up to noon, were brought into action the batteries of the 1st Division

corps at Soor. It is also doubtful—and the Austrian official account makes no distinct statement with regard to this—at what hour the mass of the artillery attained its greatest strength. At any rate the number of 120 guns, mentioned by the Prussian official account as having opened a simultaneous fire at this point, is the least which can be admitted.

of the Guard corps, which fired from the ground lying between Zelkowitz and Wrehownetz, and those of the 11th Division firing from the height which lies to the north-west of Racitz ; the total of the whole was 48 guns. A little later, about 12.30, this number was increased to 90 by the arrival of 5 batteries of the reserve artillery of the Guard and of 2 batteries of the 12th Division, who for some little time also fired on the height of Horenowes.

This is the only artillery fight during the whole of the battle of Königgrätz in which it can be shown that the Prussian artillery had a numerical superiority. It lasted a very short time ; the Austrian artillery soon fell back. We Prussian gunners thought at the moment that it retired before the superior effect of our fire, but it appears by the Austrian official account that it obeyed a categorical order from high authority to occupy the line from Chlum to Nedelist and the redoubts which lay in front of that line.

During this time the Prussian infantry continued without intermission to advance. The corps of the Austrian right wing fell back, the 2d in the direction of Lochenitz on the Elbe, while the 4th occupied the line from Chlum to Nedelist. There the batteries of the Austrian 4th corps, which had retired, were in position ; they were reinforced by the batteries of the 2d corps, as well as by two divisions (48 guns) of the reserve artillery of the army, and amounted, according to the Prussian official account, to 13 batteries, that is to say to more than 100 guns. I tried at the time to count these guns, and counted 120, including the artillery which was firing on our flank from the low ground. According to the

Austrian official account there were posted at this
point the following batteries, viz., the 1st, 8th, 4th,
10th, 9th, 7th, 11th, and 5th batteries of the 10th
corps, and Hoffbauer's 8 batteries, in all consequently
128 guns, without counting the batteries of the Austrian 2d corps or of the Tour-and-Taxis cavalry
division, which took us in flank for a moment from
the low ground through which the Elbe runs ; without counting also Gröben's battery which, the instant
that it commenced its attack against our infantry,
was destroyed at the southern extremity of Chlum.
At 2 P.M. the great line of artillery completed its
movement into position.   After having opened for a
short space of time an ineffective fire from the height
of Horenowes, 4 batteries of the reserve artillery of
the Guard placed themselves, at 2.30 P.M., on the
crest of the heights which run from Maslowed to
Nedelist ; on their right and left came up also 3
batteries of the 1st Division of the Guard.   There
were thus 42 Prussian guns against 128 Austrian,
for the S.B. battery of the 1st Division of the Guard
had remained in rear at the exit from Maslowed in
order to direct its fire from there against Cistowes,
while the batteries of the 6th corps and the 4th
H.A. battery of the Guard were advancing against
the 2d Austrian corps, which was posted in the low
ground through which the Elbe flows.

Thanks to the impetuosity and the rapidity with
which our infantry rushed to the front, the numerical
superiority of the enemy's artillery could not, for
want of time, produce at this phase of the struggle
such a tremendous effect as it did at other points and
at other moments in the course of the battle.   It

was no doubt on account of the very high corn, and
of the smoke produced by the rapid fire which it
kept up on our batteries, that the Austrian artillery
were not able to follow with the requisite attention
the advance of our foremost lines of skirmishers.   It
was these lines which, suddenly and at almost point
blank range, overwhelmed the enemy's guns with a
rapid fire and captured 68 guns of this long artillery
line (the 1st Division of the Guard took 55 and the
2d battalion of the 50th regiment 13 guns).   The
others succeeded in escaping.   I can still see clearly
every detail of the moment.   We had scarcely fired
two rounds, firing very slowly to pick up the range,
in reply to the rapid fire of the enemy, which made
a deafening noise, when we saw some of his limber-
boxes explode, and at once upon this the whole line
of the Austrian artillery ceased firing and disappeared.
We cheered at our success, and only learnt later on
—I own much to our annoyance—that these explosions were principally due to the explosive bullets of
the infantry.

At the commencement of this period of the battle
Fransecky's division had been obliged to hold its
ground against a force of the enemy whose numerical preponderance was enormous.   During the course
of the action it continued to be crushed under the
superior effect of the enemy's artillery, whose fire did
not begin to diminish until after noon.   It was not
until between 1 and 2 P.M. that it was perceived that
the attacks of the enemy were losing their vigour;
the fierce fight continued, and only at 2.30 P.M. was
the division freed from its most dangerous position.

In the centre, during this time, the 1st army had

felt more and more the superiority of the Austrian artillery. A great number of Prussian batteries had indeed come into action on the other side of the Bistritz; to the left (north) of the high road there was not room for more than 48 guns, but on the right (south-west) of the road and the forest of Sadowa, where there was more available space, 10 Prussian batteries were coming into line. But these batteries came up one by one, and several of them had to retire to repair damages, while others had expended all their ammunition, and were unable to find their ammunition column. At no time then at this point did the Prussian artillery attain to more than half of the effective strength of the Austrian, which besides occupied a very much more advantageous position. The Austrian artillery appears during the whole of this time to have possessed the complete number of guns of which I have spoken above as being present at 11 A.M., for the Prussian official account says that its force amounted to 200 guns. The same work mentions in what an awkward position our infantry thus found itself placed. It was only natural that it should consider itself abandoned by its artillery.

During this time, on that part of the field of battle where the army of the Elbe was engaged with the Saxon troops, up to 11 A.M. nothing had happened but a cannonade which had but little result, on account of the long range at which 24 Prussian guns were engaged with 34 Saxon. At 12.30 the line of Prussian artillery was reinforced to a strength of 11 batteries or 66 guns. About 3 P.M. these Prussian guns were advanced to the east of Ichlitz and also to near the forest of Popowitz, from which points, as the range was not so great, their fire was very effective, and these batteries, as also some S.B. batteries (Schmelzer and Theiler), took an energetic part in the infantry fight. But the Saxon artillery did the same, and it is impossible to say that there was on one side or the other any real superiority in the matter of artillery, with regard either to the number of guns or to the efficiency of fire. But 9 Prussian batteries, of which 5 were of the reserve artillery, were doing nothing at Nechanitz.

In the phase of the battle which followed, our infantry, and especially that of the 1st Division of the Guard, was once more overwhelmed by the fire of a superior artillery. This was at the moment when the Austrian reserves (1st and 6th corps) were set in motion against the above division. The latter found itself assisted in its fight, on the part of the artillery, by only the 4 batteries of the artillery reserve which were posted on the crest of the heights to the south of Chlum, and by the 5th 4-pr. battery (30 guns).

The Austrians prepared their counter-attack by bringing into action a very large mass of artillery. I counted at the time 120 guns (15 batteries) which converged their fire on us, being posted on the arc of a circle from Langenhof as far as Wsestar and Sweti and even farther up to Rosnitz.

The Austrian official account speaks only, it is true, of the battery of Appiano's brigade, of 4 batteries of the 1st Division of the reserve artillery of the army, of the reserve artillery of the 6th corps, and of the batteries of Rosenzweig's and Waldstät-

ten's brigades; a total of 12 batteries or 96 guns
which at this point opened fire on us. But the 1st
Division of the Guard in its advance had attacked
the 1st Austrian corps, and we may thus be permitted to suppose that this corps was also firing on
us with some part of its artillery; I believe that I
counted right. In any case the enemy's artillery
was more than three times superior in number to
ours, and this was to a great extent the reason that
the 1st Division of the infantry of the Guard had to
abandon Rosberitz.

After the Prussian infantry had won the victory,
and the Austrian army had found itself unable to
retrieve the battle by means of bold cavalry charges,
some few brigades of artillery did, it is true, support
the infantry who moved in pursuit of the enemy;
for instance Scherbening's 6 batteries at the foot of
the hill of Chlum, 7 others between Stresetitz and
Langenhof, and 9 batteries of the 6th corps on the
hill of Wsestar and Sweti.

But when, on the Austrian side, a number of
batteries had been established on the line Stosser,
Freihofen, and Ziegelschlag to Plotitz, these batteries,
with the assistance of the cavalry which covered
them, put an end to the pursuit for that evening,
and the Prussian batteries, which took up their
position at Charbusitz, Rosnitz, and Briza, could not
reduce the Austrian line to silence.

I will not weary you more to-day by quoting
other historical examples from the war of 1866.
Those which I have mentioned amply suffice to show
that the account of what occurred proves the truth
of the statement that the artillery, in this war, did

not come up to that which we thought we had a
right to expect, and that it never arrived at the point of
action in sufficient numbers.   For during one phase
only of the war, the moment when the 2d army appeared on the scene at the battle of Königgrätz, was it
superior in number to the enemy's artillery, while the
latter, on all other occasions, managed to bring into
action twice or three times, even four times, as many
guns as we, although the total number of guns of the
Austrians was no greater than that of the Prussians.
Other facts also have been proved : for example,
that our artillery did not shoot so well as we had
reason to anticipate, judging by the results obtained
on the practice-ranges and by its success against the
redoubts of Düppel ; again the renewal of expended
ammunition was carried out on no regular plan, so
that many batteries, owing to the want of ammunition, were not in a condition to injure the enemy ;
and batteries also constantly went out of action,
either on account of the enemy's infantry fire, or in
order to refit, when they would have done better to
have remained in their position.   But all this I
propose to enter upon with you at another time.

LETTER II

IN the campaign of 1870, the Prussian artillery
found itself, at the beginning of the war, in a much
better position than was the enemy's artillery, as regarded the question of matériel ; since all the Prussian
guns were rifled, and were, besides, constructed in
conformity with our technical progress, and with the
most recent inventions. The French guns, on the
other hand, were still the old bronze S.B. guns, which
had been altered on Lahitte's system. This alteration was a sort of half measure, out of which they
had made a system, and to which they held because
the guns had done good work in the war of 1859.
Their fire was very far inferior to that of the Austrian
guns in 1866. Moreover, the leaders of the Prussian
army knew in 1870 how to bring up their artillery
everywhere, at the exact moment, and in sufficient
numbers.

To the historical examples which I have borrowed
from the war of 1866, you might be tempted to
oppose this argument : in this campaign we fought
offensive battles only, the defender could thus more
easily than the assailant bring into action a consider-

able mass of artillery, since the latter had gradually
to change his order of march into the order of battle.
But this argument has an apparent value only ;
Nachod and Trautenau were chance encounters, in
which both adversaries had to similarly change their
formations, while at Königgrätz the 2d army, for its
part, was able as soon as it came on the scene to deploy
a mass of artillery superior to that of the enemy. How
was it then that the other armies could not do the
same?   Good generals ought to know how, even when
they take the offensive, to put into position at the desired
moment the necessary mass of artillery.   In 1870,
we fought hardly any but offensive battles, and the
leaders of the army knew perfectly how to satisfy
this condition.   I shall study only the battles which
were fought up to the 1st of September, for the
later engagements, being between seasoned and well
trained armies and newly raised and inexperienced
troops, cannot serve as a basis for establishing the
rules which should be observed in actions between
armies of an equal value.

    I shall once more follow the official account of
Weissenburg, the General Staff in its chronological order,
4th August and I shall therefore begin by the action
1870. at Weissenburg.   I read that the French
had not the least idea of the advancing movement of
the hostile troops until Bauer's Bavarian battery
opened fire on Weissenburg at almost the same
moment as the light infantry of the 10th battalion.
Later on this battery was reinforced by Wurm's
battery.   When this reinforcement had come up (at
8.30 A.M.) the preparation of the infantry fight was
commenced.   Both batteries were exposed to the fire

of the enemy's infantry. In a similar manner the advanced guard of the 5th corps opened the action by the fire of 2 batteries, which were reinforced by 2 batteries of the 11th corps. But very soon the 5th corps advanced its corps artillery also at a trot ; these, before 11 A.M., took up a position with 30 guns to the south of Windhof. At the last 66 guns supported the decisive attack. During this attack the artillery fired at the closest possible range while blowing in the gates of Weissenburg after the infantry had found itself unable to break them down ; again it went under a most deadly fire from the enemy's infantry, for the purpose of bombarding the Château of Geissberg, after the efforts of the infantry to take it by assault without waiting for the guns had completely failed. It appears that Haupt's and Kipping's batteries were used for this service, with the addition of the 3d heavy battery and the 2d brigade of Field Artillery, which stood on the hill crowned with poplars ; there were thus 42 guns in a half circle round the château. It is not easy to make out from the official account if all these had opened their fire when the defenders surrendered. We may add, finally, that after the action the artillery took part also in the pursuit.

It was natural that in this action, considering the enormous superiority of the Germans, they should employ more artillery than the French. But the fact that, though this superiority was equally marked as regards the infantry, 66 guns came into action against 18 in the preparation for the attack is characteristic, when we compare the use made of the artillery in the war of 1866.

Two days later the battle of Wörth was fought.

Wörth,
6th August
1870. The official account tells us that originally the General-in-Chief and his staff had not intended to fight on the 6th of August. The battle was the consequence of a reconnaissance, and the sound of the guns of the different corps decided them to go reciprocally to each other's aid. From this it resulted that partial and isolated movements were first made, and were after a certain time abandoned. The tendency to employ artillery early in the action was again characteristic of the battle. The first reconnaissance even, before the infantry had fired a single shot, was commenced by Gaspari's battery ; and when the noise of this cannonade decided General von Bothmer to advance, he also began with artillery fire. The sound of firing, which resulted from Bothmer's reconnaissance, led General von Kirchbach, not only to continue the reconnaissance which his advanced guard had been making (but which had been stopped), but also to direct a serious attack against the enemy's position. He deployed his artillery from the first, and brought at once into action every gun that was present with the corps ; he formed in combination with the 24 guns of the 11th corps (which at this moment had also opened fire from near Gunstadt) a continuous line of fire from Gorsdorf to Gunstadt. At this point then, after 9.30 A.M., 108 guns were in action, and this not only before the infantry had carried out its first attack, but even before it had changed from the order of march to the order of battle. The deployment took place under the protection of these 108 guns. After observing the manner in which the

artillery of the 5th corps was thus used, we involuntarily think of their gradual employment at Nachod.
The official account speaks strongly of the enormous
effect produced by this artillery.

In the 11th corps also, the 21st Division, which
led the march, sent all its artillery (24 guns) to the
front to Gunstadt, to join the leading battalion, and
thus made it possible for it to assist that of the 5th
corps. At a little after 1 P.M. this line of artillery
was reinforced by 3 batteries of the 1st Bavarian
corps, at Gorsdorf, batteries which the 1st Division of
that corps had also sent forward ; at this moment
nearly 200 guns—including the remainder of the
artillery of the 11th corps—were ready to reinforce
the front of the 5th corps. And this took place
immediately after the preparatory phase of the action,
for up to this time the only infantry of the 2d
Bavarian corps engaged was the 4th Division (which
was in wooded ground, and could not bring all its
artillery into action), the 20th brigade with part of
the 19th of the 5th corps, and the brigade of the
advanced guard of the 11th corps. But as soon as
the 5th corps had pushed forward its celebrated
frontal attacks, against the vineyards on the other
side of Wörth, sufficiently far to render a space available for artillery, we find that batteries hurried up from
our side to reinforce the line of skirmishers. The
11th corps also, while its advanced-guard brigade
(the 41st) was engaged with the enemy, had begun
by bringing 12 batteries into action before employing the infantry of the main body, who during
this time changed from order of march to order of
battle. Only two of its batteries were not engaged

D

from the beginning, and these were retained in rear, not because it was desired to form a reserve, but simply because there was not enough room to place them also in position.

Then the infantry of this corps seized the Nieder-wald.   When the infantry found itself prevented by the enemy's fire from continuing its advance from the northern edge of this forest, the artillery was pushed out to the front.   Eight batteries came into action in the very thickest of the infantry fire and supported the attack which was directed against Elsasshausen, just as later on they assisted the infantry to repulse the counter-attacks of the enemy ; on this occasion they many times fired case in place of shell.   Between 3 and 4 P.M., 13 batteries had already been hauled up the scarped heights on the other side of the Sauerbach, and prepared the way for the attack on Fröschwiller with the fire of nearly 80 guns at a very short range.   At this point single batteries advanced in front of the line of skirmishers attacking the village.   The 1st Bavarian corps, which had this day to fight principally in woods, could employ very little artillery except the first 4 batteries, which advanced beyond Gorsdorf.   During the pursuit, in the evening, the artillery still supported the other arms at all points.   It is impossible to avoid noticing the contrast between the manner in which the artillery was used at Wörth, and that in which it was employed at the battle of Skalitz.

On the same day on which the battle of Wörth was fought took place also that of Spich-eren.   This battle again was not designed beforehand, and might be described as the

Spicheren, 6th August 1870.

result of an accidental encounter. Nevertheless the artillery, in superior number, opened the action. A little before noon the battery of the advanced guard of the 4th Division was engaged, and shortly afterwards, at noon, 4 batteries (24 guns) opened fire. They took up their position fairly near the enemy's artillery and in a half-circle, and thus compelled the French battery, which stood on the northern extremity of the Rothe-berg, to retire to a position in rear, and so prevented it from firing on the low ground by which the infantry was to advance.

An hour later the Prussian batteries advanced to within reach of infantry fire from the enemy on the Galgenberg, in order to facilitate the advance of their own infantry on the Rothe-berg. They obliged the enemy's artillery, which had established itself there, to continue its retrograde movement, while at a later hour the advanced-guard battery compelled the artillery of the enemy, which was firing on the foot of the Rothe-berg, to fall back in rear of Stiring-Wendel. The divisions which arrived after General von Francois had taken the Rothe-berg also sent their artillery to the front. Thus the 16th Division, after 3 P.M., pushed forward 2 batteries under the escort of a regiment of cavalry, while before this, a little after 2 P.M., the 5th Division had sent 1 battery forward. At this time 6 batteries of the 1st army and 1 of the 2d were keeping up a fire superior to that of the enemy; they drove back his artillery and shook his infantry. While, from 4 to 6 P.M., the two infantries fought fiercely with alternate success, the batteries were in full play, and over and over again aided our infantry to repulse the very energetic counter-attacks which that of the French made, with the object of regaining from the Prussians the advantages which they had won. Eventually two other batteries of the 5th Division even climbed the Rothe-berg by a very steep mountain road, which had been considered as absolutely impracticable for artillery ; they came into action in the midst of the very hot fire of the enemy's infantry, and forced those of the enemy's troops who still held the height to continue their retreat ; and this although they themselves lost one half of their men. Though the result obtained by them cannot be considered as absolutely decisive, nevertheless the possession of the Rothe-berg was assured to us from that moment.

The final decision of the action could only be brought about by the capture of the hill of Forbach and the taking of Stiring-Wendel. This was commenced by sending the artillery to the front to prepare the attack. At 6.30 P.M. as many guns as could find place there (36) were brought into action on the hill of Folst ; 2 batteries had to remain in rear as there was not sufficient room for them. From the top of this hill the 36 guns fired vigorously not only on the above-named points, but also in part, during the last moments of the action, even farther in advance up to the hill of the Golden-Bremm, until darkness put an end to the contest. Eleven batteries in all (66 guns) had been employed in this battle. Not one battery, of all those which were able to reach the field of battle, remained inactive, and though the troops arrived for the most part by small fractions, as the railway brought them, it was yet found possible to obtain the action, one, complete and entire, which is produced by a mass of artillery. Thus the 4th light battery of the 1st corps, which arrived by rail on the field of battle, directly from Königsberg in Prussia, at once took part in the fight.

And now, my dear friend, compare all this with the use which was made of the artillery in the action at Trautenau, the 27th June 1866, which fight also was the consequence of an accidental meeting.

Like the battle of Wörth, that of Colombey-Nouilly had not been contemplated before-hand. It was the consequence, as was the former, of a reconnaissance made by an advanced guard, to whose assistance the nearest troops afterwards hurried. This advanced guard commenced its reconnaissance, as that of the 5th corps at Wörth had done, by the fire of artillery, and very soon engaged its 2 batteries. The advanced guards of the 1st and of the 2d Divisions of infantry hastened up to its aid, and sent forward at a trot, far in advance of the infantry, all the available guns under an escort of cavalry.

Colombey-
Nouilly,
14th August
1870.

Shortly after General von der Goltz had exchanged his first shots with the enemy, that is, a little after 4.30 P.M., 30 pieces had already opened fire, though no engagement had been expected. At 6 P.M. the number of batteries in the artillery line was increased to 10 by those of the main body of the 13th and 1st Divisions, which also had advanced at a trot in front of their infantry. A short time afterwards, also at the trot, the whole of the batteries of the 1st corps arrived in one group on the field of battle ; they had been in bivouac, and were pushed rapidly to the front, some with an escort of cavalry, others with none.   Shortly after 7 P.M. they formed a formidable line of 90 guns, of which 24 (of the 1st brigade) crossed the Colombey stream, and even un- limbered in the line of skirmishers.   Including the 7 batteries of the 7th corps, from that moment 132 guns took part in the action, and continued their fire until darkness came on.   They assisted powerfully to repulse the energetic attacks which the enemy directed against the front and right flank. Like the batteries of the 7th, 1st, and 2d Divisions, the artillery of the 18th Division and that of Luderitz's cavalry brigade, coming from the south, preceded their own troops to the field of battle, in order to prepare the attack, while the infantry followed and deployed.

The battle of Vionville-Mars-la-Tour was also

Vionville-
Mars-la-Tour,
16th August
1870.
rather an improvised than a premeditated battle, though, on the 16th of August, a collision with the enemy was expected.

The battle again began by a reconnais- sance, and this reconnaissance was prepared by the fire of a mass of Horse Artillery of no less than 30 guns ; for the effect produced by the artillery of the 5th cavalry Division, which had 4 batteries, was soon increased by that which, to the south, was caused by the battery of the 6th cavalry Division. After the fire of this artillery had thrown the enemy's bivouacs, particularly those of the cavalry, into the desired confusion, the French infantry, thanks to its immensely superior numbers, drove back the cavalry on the advancing infantry (10 A.M.)   The head of the 5th and 6th Divisions appeared on the field of battle advancing from Gorze and Tronville. While they were preparing to make head against the enemy, who were gaining ground, and while in part they found themselves committed to a most serious struggle with him (as was the case with the troops of the 5th Division), all the batteries of which the corps could dispose advanced at the trot in two lines of march; at 10 A.M. the 4 batteries of the 6th Division arrived, at 10.30 the 2 batteries of Horse Artillery of the corps artillery; about an hour later the brigade of Field Artillery of the corps artillery came up; while the 5th Division sent all its batteries, to the number of four, to which in addition the battery of Lyncker's detachment of the 10th corps joined itself. Between 11 and 12 o'clock a most powerful line of artillery crowned the heights from Tronville as far as the wood of Vionville. It included then 21 batteries or 126 guns, namely, 4 batteries of the 5th cavalry Division, 1 of the 6th cavalry Division, 4 batteries of the 5th, and 4 of the 6th Divisions of infantry, 1 battery of Lyncker's detachment, Major Lenz's 2 Horse Artillery batteries, and 4 batteries of the 2d brigade of the Field Artillery of the corps artillery, and finally, since 9.30 A.M., the battery of Lehmann's detachment. Some of these batteries had, up to the moment of the arrival of their own infantry, to defend themselves against the masses of the enemy's infantry without the assistance of any other arm. Before all this mass of artillery had as yet commenced to fire, the 6th Division of infantry had taken Vionville (at 11.30 A.M.) It then (at noon) captured Flavigny, being on this occasion supported by a fraction of the

5th Division.   The line of artillery of which we have
spoken above was, about 3 o'clock, reinforced by
4 batteries of the 20th Division, which brought its
strength up to 150 guns ; from that moment until
the end of the battle it did not cease firing.

I need not, doubtless, enter with you into the
details, nor tell you how the centre of this line gained
ground by advancing and holding its position along
the road which runs from Gorze to Flavigny, nor
how its left wing, posted at the high road, stopped
short a very dangerous turning movement which the
enemy attempted, nor how at length, in the evening,
the right wing advanced with the two other arms,
when they all assumed the offensive, and occupied
the plateau marked [1] 989, the possession of which
had been disputed with so much obstinacy.   It will
be sufficient for my purpose to show that this fact
proves decidedly that complete darkness alone imposed silence on this mass of artillery.

When, about 2.30 P.M., the 20th Division of the
10th corps arrived at Chambley, in proximity to the
field of battle, the first thing that it did was to send
the whole of the artillery which was present with it,
that is to say, 8 batteries, to the assistance of the
3d corps ; of these, 4, as I have already said,
supported the centre, while 4 prolonged the left
wing to the north of Tronville, in order to oppose
the turning movement by which they were threatened
in that direction.   A part of this artillery had left
its infantry at Saint-Julien and advanced at a trot.
It arrived just in time to support the left wing, which
suffered seriously until the moment (3.30 P.M.) when

_____
[1] On the plan of the battle.— *N.L.W.*

the head of the 20th Division came up. Thus the
10th corps brought all its available artillery into
action before the infantry took part in the struggle
(except such detachments as had been already placed
at the disposition of the 3d corps); for half of the
19th Division, with the two last batteries, were not
yet present. It was with the half of this division
that these last batteries also took part in the unsuc-
cessful attack directed against the plateau of Bruville.
They afterwards prolonged the line of artillery at
the high road. As regards the artillery of the
Guard, the 1st battery of Horse Artillery, which
came up with the brigade of dragoons, was on the
spot, and neglected no opportunity of participating
in the struggle. It was this battery which in some
degree prepared the way for the great cavalry fight
which took place on the left flank. Finally three
batteries of the 8th corps took part in the action
between 3 and 4 P.M. Every gun therefore, to the
number of 210, which could possibly reach the field
of battle, assisted in the contest, and during several
hours in the course of the afternoon they all fired
simultaneously.

In the decisive battle of Gravelotte-Saint-Privat
the artillery came upon the scene at every Gravelotte-St.-
point in still larger masses. This gigan- Privat, 18th
August 1870.
tic contest was begun by the fire of the
artillery of the 9th corps. That corps commenced
by bringing into action the artillery of the 18th
Division and the corps artillery. By noon 54 guns
were present at this point in advance of their
infantry, and allowed themselves to be carried by
their zeal so far to the front under a most effective

fire of the enemy's artillery and infantry, that one
battery was destroyed by the hostile missiles, while
the others, after having fired for two hours, were
no longer in a condition to continue the struggle.
About an hour after these 54 guns, the five Hessian
batteries of the other division came into line on the
left of the Bois de la Cusse, and on their arrival this
line of artillery amounted to 84 guns. This total
was increased to 90 by the arrival of the Horse
Artillery battery of the Hessian cavalry brigade,
which posted itself to the east of Verneville. Almost
at the same time the 4 batteries of the 1st Division
of the Guard and the Guard corps artillery took up
their position on the left of the Hessian batteries
and prolonged the line up to Saint-Ail. From after
1 P.M. there were therefore at this point 138 guns
which had opened fire before the infantry masses
had been engaged. During this time the 7th corps
supported the 9th in its struggle by bringing up its
artillery, which after 1 P.M. opened fire with 7
batteries. At the same time 11 batteries of the 8th
corps posted themselves on their left and commenced
firing, so that the battle was begun by the fire of 108
guns which stood before the front of the 1st army at
Gravelotte.

A very instructive episode, and one very interesting as regards the part played by the artillery, was
the capture by assault, during the cannonade which
then followed, of Sainte-Marie-aux-Chênes ; this
took place at 3 P.M. Thirteen Saxon batteries and 10
guns of the Guard corps artillery, a total of 88 guns,
were drawn up in a half circle around this village
and opened fire on it, and our brave infantry, attack-

ing with the greatest dash, passed without a check through the whole village, and seized at once the opposite edge. The artillery of the 12th corps came up also to prolong the mass of artillery in the direction of Saint-Privat, while the artillery of the 2d Guard Division did the same, by pushing three batteries into the line of battle at Saint-Ail and a fourth at the centre in front of Amanvillers. If we study the plan in the official account, which gives the state of the battle at 5 P.M., we find the German artillery acting in three great groups : the mass on the right wing at Gravelotte, directed against the position of Point-du-Jour, was composed of 27 batteries ; that of the centre, in action against Amanvillers, had 13, and that of the left wing, firing on Saint-Privat, 30 batteries. But 5 of these batteries had been already brought to the front at Gravelotte, and were engaged in the middle of the infantry fight. Only such batteries had been left in reserve as could find no room in the Gravelotte position. In the centre, on the other hand, the line of artillery had been reinforced by borrowing guns from the 3d corps, which formed a reserve. Seventy batteries, or 420 guns, had thus commenced firing before the masses of infantry were sent forward to the decisive attack. The available masses of artillery might have been employed as powerfully and successfully against the village of Saint-Privat as they had already been against Sainte-Marie-aux-Chênes, if they had been informed that the attack was intended. When suddenly the masses of infantry, as they advanced to the assault, masked the fire of their own batteries, and attacked the as yet uninjured village but were unable to continue their advance, the batteries hastened forward into the infantry fire, and so overwhelmed the place with shells that its capture became possible.

Wherever the infantry passed to the decisive assault, the artillery, as at Gravelotte, advanced absolutely into the line of skirmishers and supported the sister arm, fighting with it shoulder to shoulder ; it did this at the farm of Champenois and on the ground which lies immediately in front of Aman-villers, and again on the right of Saint-Privat on the hill which had just been captured. At this point it repulsed the numerous counter-attacks of the enemy's reserves, and assisted the effect produced by the fire of the infantry on the village, which stood like a fortress on its hill. When at length this village had been carried, which was towards the evening, all the artillery which was within reach crowned the chain of heights of which we had taken possession. On the left of Saint-Privat the whole of the batteries of the 12th corps (96 guns) took up a position. On the right of Saint-Privat I collected 14 batteries of the Guard, besides which all those who could reach the heights came up at once. Colonel Stumpff reported himself to me and announced that he had brought up 6 batteries, and as night fell Colonel von der Becke led up to me also 4 batteries of the corps artillery of the 10th corps, which was held in reserve. By these successive arrivals the total of my force was so increased that at last I had 24 batteries under my command. This total implied nearly 140 guns ; for some batteries were not at their full strength, since in the previous artillery fight some guns had been put out of action, and it had not yet been possible to refit them. On this height, as night fell, there was thus a continuous line of artillery, divided only by the village of Saint-Privat, which comprised 230 guns ; these swept the ground in the direction of the Bois de Jaumont and the Bois de Fêves so completely that the enemy renounced any attempt to recapture the height from us. The deafening noise of this cannonade lasted until it was altogether dark, and the battle was brought to a close.

Does not the recapitulation which we have just made of the employment of masses of artillery at Gravelotte-Saint-Privat, superficial as it is, recall to remembrance the small number of guns which we brought into action at any one spot at the battle of Königgrätz ? Does it not render it unnecessary for us to continue our comparison between the two ?

In no offensive battle could the difficulties which the direction of the lines of march always entails upon the deployment of large masses of artillery, on the part of the assailant, be of a more embarrassing character than in the battle of Beaumont. The columns of the 4th corps were painfully dragging themselves through the forest on two very narrow and very bad roads. Only seven battalions and a half had reached that edge of the forest which it was desired to occupy, the rest were still in the woods. And yet 48 guns were on the spot to commence the action. Shortly after, when the regiment of Saxon light infantry had driven the enemy's advanced guard, who were defending the defile, from the little wood which stands near the farm of Beaulieu, the 12th corps opened its cannonade with 6 batteries, or 30 guns. But very soon both corps hastened to push to the front all the remainder of their artillery, and between 1 and 2 P.M. the 14 batteries of the 4th corps, in one line, had opened fire, while almost at the same moment the whole of the artillery of the 12th corps did the same. The latter, deducting the battery of Horse Artillery which was attached to the cavalry division, had 15 batteries. But this Horse Artillery battery also took part in the action from the opposite bank of the Meuse. Thus the fight had hardly continued for an hour before 180 guns were actively employed. Towards the end of the battle the 4th corps, which was ordered to pursue the enemy, had 12 batteries or 72 guns still in action, their fire being directed towards Mouzon; this can be seen by looking at the plan of the battle.

The catastrophe of Sedan commenced very early

Sedan, 1st September 1870. in the morning, at 4 A.M., when the Bavarians made their way into Bazeilles. So long as a thick fog, during twilight, rendered it impossible to see even the ground in close proximity, there could naturally be no question of the employment of artillery. This state of things lasted until 6 A.M. In spite of this some effort was made to use the artillery. General von der Tann ordered his reserve artillery to open a very slow fire from the left bank of the Meuse; this produced absolutely no effect. At 6 A.M. a Saxon battery came into line to the east of La Moncelle; a little later Hutten's Bavarian battery drew up beside it, and the 6th battery of the 3d brigade took up its position to the left of it. Two guns in addition

made their way with the infantry into the interior of
the village of Bazeilles ; they took their share of the
street fighting, in the immediate neighbourhood of
the enemy, until almost all their men were killed or
wounded.

But it was not until 7 A.M. that the morning fog
dispersed altogether, so that it was possible to use
artillery. The first disposition that the General
commanding the 12th corps made, on receiving the
news of the struggle at Bazeilles, was to order the
corps artillery to advance at a trot. This artillery
was still on the march to the south of Douzy. One
hour and a half after the order had been given, it
opened fire from the east of the Givonne valley,
which is nearly one German (4.5 English) mile from
Douzy. During the interval all the batteries of the
24th Division had commenced firing, and at 8.30
A.M. a line of 12 batteries (72 guns) had been
deployed at this point ; this line, from the moment
that it was formed, suffered considerable loss from
the enemy's infantry fire, but nevertheless maintained
its position. Half an hour later this line of artillery
was increased to 16 batteries or 96 guns.

At that moment also the artillery of the Guard
prolonged the line of artillery towards the north.
The heart of every gunner throbbed with joy when
he found that all our leaders had but one desire, to
bring up their artillery. General von Pape had
accompanied the light infantry and Fusiliers of the
Guard when they drove the few skirmishers of the
enemy whom they found there from Villers-Cernay
and the adjoining forest. From the other side of
the wood he saw the French grand artillery line,

which was firing on the 12th corps from the opposite side of the low ground of Givonne. "Bring me two guns," he cried to me when I met him, "so that I may take that line in flank!"—"You shall have not only two, but ninety," I could proudly answer, for already the batteries were coming up at a trot, by the order of the General commanding the Guard corps. At 8.45 A.M. the artillery of the 1st Division of the Guard opened fire in front of the wood through a clearing we found there, and a quarter of an hour later it was reinforced on its right (to the north of the wood) by the Field Brigade of the corps artillery, and on its left by the brigade of the 2d Division of the Guard. At the commencement there was not sufficient room for the 3 Horse Artillery batteries ; but eventually the artillery of the 2d Division of the Guard took ground to the left, so that these batteries also were able to come up into line and take part in the action. Thus the artillery of the Guard commenced the struggle at this point (before the infantry were seriously engaged) with 72 guns, which were very soon increased to 90.

While the German artillery saw their superiority over the enemy, in this part of the field of battle, increasing every moment, while the brave Bavarians were little by little possessing themselves of Bazeilles, while Givonne was being taken by the advanced guard of the Guard corps, and the infantry of the 12th corps were carrying the posts which stood on the stream between Givonne and the village of Bazeilles, the advanced guards of the 5th and 11th corps showed themselves, shortly after 10 A.M., in rear of the French army. But these two corps had to pass the narrow defile of Saint-Albert before they could act against the enemy. They at once brought their artillery into action.

As soon as the first battalions of the advanced guard of the 11th corps had occupied Saint-Menges and the hill situated to the east of it, 3 batteries took up their position there and opened fire. General von Gersdorff at once pushed forward the corps artillery. By 10 A.M. 7 other batteries were in position beside the 3 former on the crest of this hill, and at 11 A.M. the 4 remaining batteries of the 11th corps came up to reinforce this line of artillery. Thus all the 84 guns of the 11th corps had been pushed to the front, and formed an enormous single battery, at a time when so small a fraction of the infantry had passed the defile that it would have been difficult for it to protect this line of artillery.

During this time the General commanding the 5th corps had been studying the situation from the hill where stands the farm of Champ de la Grange. He gave the order that all the available artillery should advance, without any regard to their organisation by commands, to the support of the artillery line of the 11th corps. After having occupied some intermediate positions, a mass of 10 batteries advanced, part by way of Fleigneux, and part round the north of that place, and at 11 A.M. came into position fronting Illy; its left wing was to be covered by the cavalry. The left wing of this mass of artillery, which numbered 24 batteries or 144 guns, already combined its fire with that of the artillery of the Guard, and from that time the circle of guns which was forming around the French army continued to

E

close in, to be shortly after still more contracted, for at this moment the corps artillery of the 4th corps and that of the 2d Bavarian corps forbade all issue to the enemy by the south of Sedan. The manner in which the artillery of the 5th and 11th corps was used gives most clear practical proof that it is quite possible, even when on the offensive, to open the action with the fire of masses of artillery, even though only one line is available by which to approach the enemy.

I fear I should try your patience too hardly if I entered into too many details, and showed how the masses of artillery of which we have just spoken were still more augmented, and how those batteries only for which there was absolutely no space available were left in reserve. It must be sufficient for me to say that all the generals, and particularly those who commanded the artillery, were filled with the idea that as much artillery as was available should be employed as soon as possible, and that none should be kept in reserve. I need not either insist upon this point, that, everywhere, the artillery pushed to the front quite close to the enemy, even into the line of skirmishers, and that it dared to advance beyond defiles, as soon as the infantry found itself sufficiently strong to make decisive assaults, in order to assist them in their close attack. I need not either speak here of the heroic struggles which the infantry sustained, on the one hand against the enemy's cavalry and infantry, who fought fiercely to disengage themselves, on the other in the attack of the various posts which had to be carried, for we have now to occupy ourselves only with the use made of the artillery.

It will be sufficient to study, with reference to
their effective strength, the different masses of artillery
which prepared the way for the decisive attack. We
find on the south of Sedan, at Frenois, a battery of
114 guns, belonging to the Wurtemberg division
and the 2d Bavarian corps; this was bombarding
Sedan. Next came a group of 6 batteries or 36
guns, belonging to the corps artillery of the 4th
corps; this was posted near Pont-Maugy, and had
fired, but at very long range, on the ground to the
north of Bazeilles. To the east 24 batteries or 144
guns, belonging to the 1st Bavarian corps, the 4th
corps, and the 12th corps, had crossed the Givonne
valley and had fired on Balan, Fond de Givonne, and
the old entrenched camp of Sedan. Eighteen batteries belonging to these three corps could not find
room to come into action, and impatiently awaited the
time when they might be of service. (I remember
very well how I annoyed the leader of a brigade of
the 12th corps. He arrived to reinforce the position
which I had taken up farther to the north, and I was
obliged to tell him that I had no more room even
for one gun. He received it almost as a personal
insult.) Farther to the north 90 guns of the Guard
corps had opened fire on the Bois de la Garenne.
To the north-west the formidable line of artillery of
the 5th and 11th corps amounted to 26 batteries
or 156 guns; these swept with their fire the Bois
de la Garenne and the ground to the north-east
in front of that wood. There were thus five principal groups which, with their 540 guns, fired at
the same time at the same target; and these constituted four-fifths of the artillery present with the

different corps which were able to take part in the battle of Sedan.

I will not speak of the use which was made of the artillery in the battle of Noisseville, since this was a defensive battle, and since the employment of masses of artillery is very much more easy in a defensive action than in an offensive operation. This battle, again, cannot furnish us with any materials for our comparison of the actions of 1866 with those of 1870, since in the former year we fought only on the offensive. It seems to me also that we have collected a sufficient number of data for our subject.

Let us summarise the observations which we have made on the comparative manner of employing the artillery in the two campaigns :—

1. In 1866 great unwillingness was shown to employ much artillery to prepare the action. In 1870, intentionally and from the first, as much artillery as possible was brought into action.

2. In 1866 it was assumed as a principle that, even at the moment when the fight was at its height, either a reserve of artillery should be kept, as well as one of infantry and cavalry, or a fresh reserve of artillery should be formed.[1] Thus half of the great mass of artillery of the army reserve of the 1st army did not fire a single shot at Königgrätz ; it remained near Dub in absolute inaction. In 1870 a totally opposite principle obtained, namely, that a reserve of artillery was useless. Even the name " Reserve Artillery " was abolished and replaced (except in the Bavarian corps) by that of " Corps Artillery."

---

[1] In the case, we may presume, where the original reserve artillery had been perforce engaged.—*N. L. W.*

3. In 1866, as was natural when it was determined to keep a reserve, the artillery marched as
near as possible to the tail of the column; there
were some occasions when it was some days' march
in rear of the corps (for example, the artillery of
the Guard at the time of the entrance into Bohemia).
In 1870, it was held as a principle that the artillery
should be as far to the front in the column of march
as was compatible with its due escort by the other
arms. We even find corps sending all their artillery
far ahead into the middle of the battle (for example,
the Guard and the 3d corps at Saint-Privat, the
5th, 11th, and 12th corps at Sedan).

4. Finally we find, in 1866, that masses of artillery moved during their marches for the most part
at a very slow pace, but finished by galloping at the
moment when they moved into position and were
about to unlimber. On the other hand, in 1870
great masses of artillery marched distances of many
German miles without ceasing to trot, and thus arrived
at their position with a gain of several hours. This
was the case with the corps artillery of the 3d
corps at Vionville, with that of the Guard at Saint-
Privat, with that of the 4th corps, the Guard, the
11th and the 12th corps at Sedan.

LETTER III

THE FIRE EFFECT OF THE ARTILLERY DURING THE WAR OF 1866

"CEASE to quote historical examples," you say, "and tell me the cause of all this." I will answer you, but not yet. I shall do that later. I must first obtain more materials for my answer, and prove by facts the statement with which I ended my last letter. Have therefore a little patience while I do this.

I said there that in 1866 our artillery did not hit its mark so often as we had a right to expect, judging from the results obtained on the practice-ground, and the success gained at the redoubts of Düppel. In order to prove this statement I must go back a little into history.

In the sixth decade of our present century our artillery tried to realise an idea which had hitherto been condemned as unpractical and ludicrous by all authorities of the arm ; this was to construct rifled guns. The trials which were made succeeded, and gave truly astonishing results as regards accuracy and the effect of fire, which with the fact that shells could be made to burst on impact and with the results of the experiments in breaching which took place at Schweidnitz in the autumn of 1857, decided our Government to introduce rifled guns of six, twelve, and twenty-four pounds for siege and fortress artillery. During the year 1858 the construction of a really practical rifled field gun was studied with German thoroughness, and a great deal of time was thus lost. Again every novelty has many opponents. Justifiable doubts as to whether so complicated a machine as was our rifled gun of those days could ever be of practical use, considering the rough treatment to which guns are exposed during a campaign, strengthened that opposition which the force of habit always presents to anything which is new.

Our committee of artillery experiments endeavoured to conquer all doubts, whether justifiable or unjustifiable, by means of inventions, proposals, and trials. In the meantime the French artillery heard something of the results of the breaching trials which took place at Schweidnitz. Napoleon during the year 1858 saw that contest approaching, which in 1859 brought on the war with Austria, and ordered his artillery to be armed with rifled guns without delay. But nothing new can be worked out in a day, nor can the artillery matériel for a large army be suddenly improvised. Time pressed. So the French artillery rifled their S.B. bronze guns, and thus arose the bastard system which continued to 1870, and which was called the " Lahitte system." Though this transformation was hardly completed when the war of 1859 broke out, though the French gunners were unskilled in the management of their guns, the French artillery obtained with them so considerable an advantage over the Austrians as regarded range, that all artilleries and all Govern-

ments took an immense interest in it. Our own
Government demanded that its artillery should not
be inferior to that of France. At this moment our
committee of artillery experiments had completed
their trials with reference to a 6-pr. field gun ; the
new gun satisfied the high military authorities who
were present, and consequently before the war
between France and Austria had come to an end,
orders had been given to construct, as a beginning,
300 rifled 6-pr. field guns.

The results obtained from these guns were indeed
astonishing to any one who had until then seen only
S.B. guns fired. Up to that time when firing at
1000 paces the result had been so doubtful that our
gunners acted on the proverb which says : " The first
shot is for the devil, the second for God, and only
the third for the King," that is to say, that at the
range of 1000 paces only one-third of the shot hit
the target then in use, which was 6 feet high and
50 paces wide. Moreover the greatest range was
only from 1800 to 2000 paces. At greater distances
there was no danger from S.B. field guns. Now
suddenly a gun was seen, which could hit the target
at a still greater range, and of which the shell burst
on striking the mark with such destructive effect,
that it seemed doubtful whether any enemy could
stand against such a missile.

There was, however, some hesitation in replacing
all the old S.B. guns by the new rifled pieces. We
had not yet succeeded in making a good shrapnel
with a time fuse for rifled guns, while the case-shot
of the rifled guns was not so effective as that of the
S.B. pieces. Great importance was attached to the

fire of shrapnel and case with regard to close fighting, in which it was not considered that there would be sufficient time to lay so carefully as is necessary in order to get the full effect of the rifled gun. It was considered ample then for the moment to give three rifled batteries, or one-quarter of the Field Artillery, to each army-corps, whilst for siege and fortress artillery as many guns were provided as the funds allowed. A lighter field gun, the 4-pr., was invented, and one battery was armed with it on trial.

The change in the armament was at this point when the war with Denmark broke out at the beginning of 1864. No conclusive experience was obtained with Field Artillery in this campaign. Such engagements as we fought in the open field were of a secondary importance. On some rare occasions only did I see our guns fire a few shots in the open. The enemy immediately abandoned his position. This was the case at Satrup on the 10th of February and at Fredericia on the 8th of March.

Our experience with our siege guns was more instructive. The effect of our rifled siege guns surprised not only the enemy but also ourselves. At ranges at which the enemy considered themselves absolutely safe from our shell, our 24-pr. guns threw their shell beyond the great Wenning-Bund, destroying block-houses by their explosion, dismounting the guns on the ramparts which they enfiladed, and causing, on the first day of the bombardment, such annoyance and such a panic, that had we considered such a result as possible, we should have held our troops in readiness to take advantage at once of this first terror. We should perhaps have met with less

resistance on this first day than we eventually did at
the time of the assault.   At least the prisoners told
us that on the opening day of the bombardment the
redoubts 1 to 6 were deserted by the whole of their
garrisons.   We could not see this on account of the
heavy snowstorm which was raging.   Later on the
defenders became accustomed to our shell, and learnt
how to shelter themselves in some degree by throwing
up epaulments of earth.   When the guns which were
captured in the Düppel redoubts had been brought
back in triumph to Berlin, the state of complete ruin
to which they had been reduced by our shell excited
general admiration for the effect of our new invention.   It was naturally believed that in the open also,
everything must give way to it under penalty of annihilation.   These sanguine hopes imposed silence
on some doubts, which might otherwise have been
excited by certain experiences, particularly with
regard to the difficulty of hitting with a rifled gun a
target which was in rapid motion.   This was especially
the case when firing on ships.   When in the month
of February at Fennö we tried to prevent a vessel
from passing the Little Belt, it went back, it is true,
but we did not hit it.   At the time of the assault
on Düppel an enormous quantity of iron and lead
was lavished on the celebrated ironclad *Rolf Krake*
before we succeeded in getting the few hits on the
monster in consequence of which she abandoned
the action.

Shortly after the storming of Düppel the greatest
zeal was displayed in the construction of more rifled
field guns, especially of 4-prs., and when the war of
1866 broke out we had four 6-pr. and six 4-pr. rifled

batteries in each army-corps, while only 6 batteries remained armed with the old S.B. guns. Many men of experience still believed that we could not altogether do without S.B. guns for close fighting, on account of their superior fire with case and shrapnel, and were confirmed in this opinion by the action of the only Power which had renewed its matériel during a great war.

For the Federal Government of the United States of America had found itself obliged to three times renew almost the whole of its artillery matériel, and on the last occasion had considered it necessary to have at least a quarter of short S.B. 12-pr. guns, against three-quarters of rifled pieces. This was the same proportion as that in which our artillery was armed in 1866.

In 1866 then we entered upon the campaign absolutely certain that nothing could resist our artillery. We knew, indeed, that the Austrian muzzle-loading gun, though it was rifled and was constructed with a little more care and exactness than the French gun on the Lahitte system, shot very much worse than our B.L. guns. We expected therefore to see the other arms, infantry as well as cavalry, scatter asunder and disperse like chaff as soon as our shell fell and burst in the midst of them.

I had not the good fortune to participate in the first engagements fought by the 2d army, at Nachod, Skalitz, Schweinschädel, Trautenau, and Soor. The reports of those batteries of my regiment which were attached to troops, and which took part in three of these actions, spoke only of one thing—the triple or even quadruple numerical superiority of the enemy's

artillery.   At Schweinschädel the 3d Horse Artillery
battery, armed with 6 S.B. guns, approached to within
1000 paces of 16 Austrian guns; it fired shrapnel
at them and did not seem to have a very high opinion
of the fire of the enemy, who was at last driven back.
At Königinhof I was present at the extreme end of
the action, and I was witness of a cannonade opened
at so long a range that I regretted to see such a
waste of costly ammunition; indeed the firing was
very soon stopped.

I likewise cared very little for a rapid fire which
four of the enemy's batteries opened upon me and
the officers who were with me when, towards evening,
I rode to Königinhof to make a reconnaissance with
a view to forcing the passage of the Elbe, an operation which was spoken of for the morrow, but which
did not take place.   I had consequently no personal
experience as to the value of our new field guns
during the period which preceded the battle of
Königgrätz.   But I was still full of the confidence
with which our experiences in time of peace had in-
spired us.   Nothing at least had as yet happened to
diminish it.

Confidence in one's self and a feeling of the certainty
of victory are the essential conditions of great successes.   But they must be based on realities, and
unless this is the case there is a considerable danger
that a check, at the decisive moment, may transform
this confidence into an opposite feeling.   Though I
met with no such bitter experience as this, yet the
results in the battle of Königgrätz did not altogether
come up to the expectations which I had cherished,
with regard to the effect of the guns under my com-

mand.   At that period the colonel of a regiment of
Field Artillery very often found a considerable number
of his 96 guns detached, by superior orders, from his
command ; thus I had only one brigade (the 2d) still
left to me ; this consisted of 4 batteries, that is of
24 guns, all rifled.   Very soon the order arrived for
me to advance ; we went off gaily at a quick trot
over hill and valley, from Rettendorf by Königinhof,
Chotieborek, and Jericek, up to the front line of the
advanced guard of our corps.   I ordered the batteries
to take up a position to the south of Jericek, against
the enemy's artillery, which was posted on the hill of
Horenowes ; this was crowned with a clump of trees
which has now a name in history.   The enemy's guns
had already fired shell at me as I was passing the
Trotinka at Jericek, but these shell, falling at a high
angle, buried themselves deeply in the ground, and
burst here and there, throwing the earth about, but
far from doing us any harm, they only put us into a
good humour.   The first trial shots gave the range
as 4000 paces ; we were then much too far from the
enemy, and I advanced my guns nearer to him, up
to the undulation which lies near to Horenowes, to
the north of that place.   The range was then 1900
paces ; we therefore engaged the enemy.   In my
first letter I have already said that his line of artillery
consisted of 40 guns ; I added that on my right and
left other batteries also fired on it, and that altogether
90 guns were firing on the target.   During this
artillery fight we saw coming out of Horenowes by
the road which leads to the hill where the trees stand
(therefore at a shorter range than that on which the
Austrian artillery stood), a battery of the enemy

which trotted up the hill from right to left, in column of route. It would be impossible to find a better target. All my batteries began to fire at this column. The shell fell in front or in rear, but not one hit the enemy. . The battery escaped without losing a single man or horse, and disappeared behind the hill. I felt as angry as a hunter who has missed a royal stag. Shortly afterwards I was a little consoled, for my shells broke up a hostile battalion which, coming from Horenowes, was slowly climbing the slope. A squadron of dragoons charged the enemy and carried off a crowd of prisoners. The Austrian artillery, after having kept up the fight for a short time, ceased firing and disappeared behind the hill. We gladly flattered ourselves that we had driven them off. During this time the main body of the 1st Division of the infantry of the Guard had formed line after passing the Trotinka, and advanced in this order against the hill with the clump of trees, while the advanced guard was engaged in the village with the rearmost troops of the enemy. As soon as the advancing infantry masked my batteries, I ceased firing, and stood ready with loaded guns to repulse any possible counter-attack ; I myself accompanied the infantry, as they advanced, in order to be able to select, as soon as the hill was captured, a new position for my artillery. While I was thus moving forward with the infantry, a battery of the enemy gave me most evident proof that the Austrian artillery had been by no means annihilated. It surprised us by firing from our left front eight shells, one quickly after the other, which all fell in the same spot, exactly where the battalion with which I was riding happened to be marching at the moment. Three shells burst in front of the battalion, three in the midst of the ranks and two in rear, immediately in the middle of the dead and wounded who were writhing one on the other. But the battalion was not broken up. I heard the word of command : " Leading file, advance from the right! March! Right, left, right, left," and the battalion continued its march as if nothing could stop it. (I think it was a battalion of the 3d regiment of the Guard, for I remember that I rode a little way with Captain von Lobenthal.) It was evident then that the shells of rifled guns, when they burst, did not produce so demoralising an effect as I had believed ; at least, they did not produce that effect on good infantry. After having opened for a very short time a rapid fire from the crest of the hill on the last remnants of the enemy's infantry, our own seized the hill with the clump of trees ; I then sent, by the adjutant of the regiment, an order to my batteries to come up to me at once, in order to secure to us the possession of the height. While awaiting their arrival I looked about me. I saw the enemy disappearing in the direction of Nedelist, and wished to convince myself how far the wreck of the enemy's artillery would bear witness to the annihilating effect of our guns. I found—nothing. Not one gun with broken wheels, not an atom of any limber-box torn to pieces by its explosion, not a horse with shattered limbs, absolutely nothing marked the place where the enemy's artillery had stood.

This was certainly rather discouraging. But when at a later date I read the Austrian official account, and saw there that the hill of Horenowes had been evacuated solely because Benedek had several times given the order to do so—for he had had no intention of extending his right wing so far—when at last I was really obliged to own that the enemy's artillery had by no means retired on account of the effect produced by our fire, then I was sad indeed. But on the 3d of July I had not much time, on that hill, to give way to any feelings. The infantry of the 1st Division of the Guard pressed back the yielding enemy. Some of the enemy's shells whistling through the air fell among us from the outskirts of Chlum, and my batteries unlimbered on the hill with the clump of trees and replied. The range was enormous. I therefore ordered them to economise their ammunition, and to fire only just enough to draw off the enemy's fire from our advancing infantry. After this I galloped along the steep crest of the hill of Maslowed in order to find for my batteries a position nearer to the enemy, so that their fire might be more effective than it had been up to the present. I met General von Colomier in the most advanced line of the infantry skirmishers, who were pressing on, and he agreed with me that it was useless to fire at so long a range. As the northern slope of the hill near Maslowed was very steep, I was afraid that our guns would run down it when they recoiled; I therefore chose a position half way between Maslowed and Nedelist, on the ridge which runs from one to the other. I ordered the adjutant of the regiment to bring the batteries there, while I went directly to the spot to select their posts. During the interval the enemy's artillery, whose strength I had previously judged at one or two

batteries, had increased so much that the crest of
the height which runs from Chlum to Nedelist, and
which bounded our view, appeared as if crowned
with a continuous row of guns.   There was at this
spot a road which was planted with small trees ; I
went towards it ; I saw behind me the leading
battery (the 4-pr.) descending the hill of Horenowes,
where stood the famous clump of trees ; the slope
was so steep that it was obliged to come down at a
walk.   I looked at the enemy.   He fired a shot.
The projectile fell in the cornfield about 100 paces
short of me.   A second shell followed, which went
about as far over me.   A third shell struck the
ground quite close to me and buried itself in the
earth, which was softened by the rain.   Then followed
a mournful silence, like that which, before a heavy
storm, precedes the first flashes of lightning.   I
thought that I could guess the design of the enemy.
He had recognised me as the officer who was seeking for the best position for the coming artillery ; he
then found his range on me, and was only waiting,
before commencing to fire, for the arrival of the
battery which had disappeared from his view behind
the hill on which I stood.   I then went back to the
battery, in the low ground, and gave the captain the
following order :—As soon as he came to the top of
the hill and the enemy opened fire on him, he was to
advance as quickly as possible, without taking any
notice of the fire, and was to unlimber at the spot
where I should halt.   I went back to my former
post, and watched the enemy with the greatest
attention.   Hardly had the leaders of the battery
appeared over the crest than the whole horizon in

F

my front was covered with blue clouds, and a rapid fire kept up by more than 100 guns commenced with such a noise and such whistlings of shell that it seemed as if hell was let loose. But at the same moment I spurred my horse and advanced at a gallop about 300 paces towards the enemy. The battery followed me as fast as the greasy and broken ground would permit. The enemy's projectiles all passed together whistling over our heads, and fell in rear of us in the road.

The enemy could not have been able to see, on account of the thick smoke produced by his fire, that we had passed under his shells, for he went on firing without changing his elevation; a thick hail of projectiles continued to fall on the road while we, very quietly, fired our trial shots, and found the range to be 1350 paces. The battery had only one casualty while passing under the hostile missiles: one man was wounded. When once it had taken up its position it suffered no loss at all.

I had at least the consolation of knowing that the enemy, with his new pattern guns, had also not yet learnt how to make good practice.[1] The other

---

[1] The trick which had just succeeded, and which consisted in passing rapidly under the enemy's fire, had been already practised by Strotha at the battle of Leipzig, when he was called upon to relieve a Russian battery which had been put out of action. Having arrived at the spot where the ruins of this battery lay, he gave the command to gallop, and advanced 300 paces nearer to the enemy. When I noticed at Königgrätz the silence of the enormous battery of the enemy, the recollection of Strotha's manœuvre passed like a flash of lightning through my mind, and I imitated it. He had many years before related the story to my comrades and myself, when we were quite young officers, at a discussion on technical matters at which we were present. I mention this fact merely to show how much good may result if the elder officers will take the trouble to relate to their juniors such events as have been of importance in their lives.

batteries of the brigade also passed to the right and left of the first (Mutius's battery), with very small loss, over the crest of the height which was bombarded by the enemy, and they, with some batteries of the 1st Division of the Guard, posted themselves on the same line with it.

I have already told you, in my first letter, that we had hardly fired one or two rounds after having picked up the range when we saw that some limber-boxes were exploding in the enemy's line and that it was falling into disorder. We attributed this, as I told you, to the effect of our fire, but, to our great disappointment, we afterwards learnt that our skirmishers, advancing in very high corn, had approached to within 200 or 300 paces of the enemy's artillery, who could not see them on account of the thick smoke caused by his fire. They had cartridges with explosive bullets, of which at that time the use had not been forbidden, and these bullets produced a most destructive effect on the limber-boxes and the waggons.

I afterwards heard that on this occasion one of the officers commanding the skirmishers (it was, I think, Lieutenant Chorus) had set quietly to work to fire a couple of trial shots at a white horse; when he saw the animal fall he gave the order to take the elevation at 250 paces, to open a rapid fire in order to knock over as many gunners and horses as possible, and then to rush in on the battery with a cheer. As a matter of fact the projectiles from our line of artillery may very probably have hit some gunners and horses, but it is very difficult to make sure of this after the event, or to judge how many

men and animals fell.   But the reports furnished by
the infantry establish as an assured fact that the
whole of the enemy's line of artillery continued to
fire without a moment's interruption until the infantry
opened their rapid fire.   Consequently, we gunners,
in this position also, obtained a very small number
of hits, and our fire had only one effect, which was
certainly essential, that of drawing upon ourselves
the attention and the fire of the formidable line
of the enemy's artillery, and of thus averting it
altogether from the infantry.   In this manner the
latter was placed in a position, while suffering only
relatively small loss, to reduce all this mass of
artillery to silence, and to take half the guns.

After having been many times stopped by the
enemy's infantry and cavalry, who threw themselves
from the right on my rear, front, and flank, I reached
the last position which I was to occupy during this
battle.   It was to the south of Chlum on a hill,
whence I could support the battalions of the 1st
Division of the Guard, which had pushed to the
front.   I certainly had before me there a target
which it would have been impossible to miss, whether
my guns had been rifled or not.   Two Austrian
corps were drawn up on the plain, at the very foot
of the hill ; their lines were admirably dressed, and
their white uniforms showed up plainly against the
green of the cornfields waving in the wind.   They
were massed with their front towards Sadowa, and
consequently showed me their right flank.   These
battalions, squadrons, and masses of artillery, concentrated in good order in their formation on parade,
looked from above like the squares on a chess-board.

Their masses filled the vast breadth of the valley as far as the heights of Problus, and their right flank was about 900 paces from the place where I stood with my guns. Their fire at once struck the enemy with surprise, terror, and confusion. An infantry officer (Major Erckert), who is a friend of mine, was at that moment stretched on the ground in front of Rosberitz. He was wounded, absolutely motionless, and believed to be dead. He has told me that the Austrian battalions, who were passing over his body as they advanced to the attack of Rosberitz, stopped short in their rush at the first shot fired from the hill of Chlum ; they were seized with fear, and seemed held fast to the spot by a magic force. I myself can also certify to the slaughter which our shells caused in the crowded ranks of the enemy. Each projectile which fell among them burst and mowed large gaps in these compact masses of men, who tried to escape to the right and left. But in vain I encouraged the zeal of my gunners, in vain I cried to them to hurl their projectiles into these masses of troops with redoubled rapidity, in order to cause yet more disaster ; the enemy did not take to flight, as in my heart I had expected. It is true that the ranks opened out, and that the men sought for cover everywhere where the ditches along the roads or the undulations of the ground offered them any protection, but at the last the mass formed front towards us and commenced the attack. The first attack, executed by the cavalry, came to grief in a hollow road which lay at the foot of the hill, from which some companies of our infantry received the Austrian squadrons with a destructive fire from their needle-guns. At this very moment I have my doubts whether the fire of our artillery, so little trained as it was then, would alone have sufficed, without the aid of the infantry, to compel the cavalry which charged us to wheel about. Upon this we saw in the low ground, at every point, hostile batteries unlimber, as soon as they could find space to deploy ; they opened fire on us with the greatest possible rapidity and violence. They once more formed a line of more than 100 guns. But this time they were drawn up in a half-circle around us, and the fire of their left wing was particularly severe ; splinters of shell bounded throughout the length of the line of our batteries. We now suffered very much more serious losses. Whole teams went down at a blow ; some guns lost the whole of their detachments.

It was once more a stroke of luck for us that the enemy's gunners had not very much skill in the use of their new weapons. Most of the Austrian batteries, as far as we could make out, seemed to choose the church tower of Chlum as their target, for shell after shell fell into it ; it began to totter, and the tiles and splinters of masonry flew all around. But we were drawn up about 200 paces in front of the tower, and the projectiles which hit it did us no harm at all. All the same, the hell which the enemy made for us was hot enough. We had, as they say, put our hands into a wasp's nest. This state of things may have lasted about an hour when the attacks of the enemy's masses ended by driving back our infantry. Our seven companies which were posted at Rosberitz had to give up that village. They were disordered and most of their leaders had fallen. They drew back therefore before the 17 battalions of the 6th corps which threw themselves upon them. These masses, it is true, yet hesitated for a few moments before the fire of the guns and that of the needle-guns. But with the fire of my artillery alone I could not stop them; the results which I had obtained up to that time showed me this clearly, and I therefore followed the general movement and drew my guns back to the nearest height, that which runs with the gentle slope from the northern part of Chlum towards Nedelist. The enemy followed us, but found themselves taken in flank, both to the right and left, by our 6th and 1st corps, who annihilated them.

This was the last action in which I took part during the war. At the battle of Königgrätz, when I had refitted my batteries and filled up with ammunition, at the moment when 1 was about to advance on to the heights at Rosnitz in order to take part in the pursuit of the enemy, I received orders to join the reserve in rear of the infantry of the Guard.

During the battle I had every possible reason to feel satisfied with the manner in which my batteries had behaved. They had shown very great courage, and everything had been carried out exactly as it was ordered. Not a man had flinched. But we had not, by very much, succeeded in shooting as well as we had a right to expect. This was because my men had not sufficiently learnt how to shoot, and I was obliged to acknowledge to myself that I also was not sufficiently instructed. From this came the feeling of constraint and trouble which I found in me, and I was curious to know how the other

regiments of our army stood in this respect. This
was what I found.   On every occasion when an
officer has told me frankly and confidentially what
he thought, he has owned to this same feeling of
constraint, and has confessed that he was not pleased
with himself.   My friend Scherbening, who was
under my orders at Sedan, and fell there also before
my eyes, acknowledged to me privately that this
was the case with himself, and yet he had at Königgrätz fought his four batteries with the greatest
hardihood in the position in front of the defile at
Sadowa, and at Blumenau, the last engagement of
the war, had particularly distinguished himself.   I
could further name to you some large bodies of
artillery, whose 4-prs., in the course of the long
cannonade, gradually threw shorter and shorter
distances, and at last were 300 or 400 paces short
of the target.   This fact was attributed to the
fouling caused by the powder in the bore, whilst in
reality it arose from the tangent scales of the 4-pr.
slipping down a little each time the gun was fired,
and from no one taking care to set them again.
The 4-prs. indeed had tangent scales of a different
pattern to that of the 6-prs.; with the latter the
tangent scale was taken out before the gun was fired,
and the recoil could not therefore make it slip down.
I could also name to you some large bodies of
artillery whose shells were blind, simply because, in
the projectiles furnished at the renewal of their
ammunition from the columns, they had forgotten,
as was afterwards discovered, to insert any percussion
arrangement; it is difficult to see how the shells
could have been expected to burst.   But I will not

name them to you, as I should not like to set in the
pillory, as it were, so long after the event, men of
recognised merit, and this for a really very pardonable fault. I say that this fault is pardonable,
because we had not then acquired the necessary
familiarity with the handling of the new armament,
or, to put it better, we had not yet learnt how to
shoot.

I have not a shadow of a doubt, for my own
part, but that all the regiments were exactly in the
same condition as ourselves; where indeed, during
the whole of the war of 1866, have we succeeded in
hitting a target which was worth the trouble of
hitting?

At the commencement of the battle of Nachod a
Prussian battery obliged the Austrian battery of
Hertwek's brigade to retire; during the battle of
Soor an Austrian battery left one disabled gun
behind it when it retired; during the fight at
Schweinschädel the 3d Horse Artillery battery of the
Guard had obliged, as it says in its report, two
Austrian batteries to abandon their position. But
this was all, absolutely all. In the great battle of
Königgrätz we captured nearly 200 guns; not one
in the whole number, as far as I know, had been
injured by fire. At Nachod and at Skalitz the
enemy, it is true, retired when our reserve artillery
made its appearance at the end of the engagement.
But even now it is by no means certain whether, at
Nachod, it was this advance of the reserve artillery
which decided the enemy to retire, or whether he
had not already resolved to abandon the field of
battle, owing to the failure of all his attacks. As

regards the fight at Skalitz, it is actually proved in history that the Austrian corps had orders to hold on till two o'clock only, and that its retreat was carried out without any reference to the appearance of the reserve artillery of the 5th corps.

Nowhere, during the whole course of the campaign of 1866, did our artillery play a decisive part with regard to the other arms of the enemy's army. No considerable mass of infantry, no grand corps of cavalry, was destroyed by it; against no object of attack, neither village nor position, did it open its fire in the preparation for the attack in such a manner as to render certain the success of the assault. And the reason that it did not do this was that, as I have shown in my former letter, it advanced in strength too far inferior to that of the enemy. Besides, six of every sixteen batteries were armed with S.B. guns, and a large proportion of the S.B. batteries did not fire a shot, owing to the long ranges at which the two artilleries engaged. As far as I know, that half of the grand reserve artillery of the 1st army which was armed with S.B. guns did not succeed in firing a single shot, and only a very few S.B. batteries had the good fortune to gain imperishable glory by pushing on to within short range of an enemy whose fire was more effective, as did Buddenbrock's battery at Schweinschädel, and Schmelzer's and Theiler's batteries at Königgrätz.

After the campaign of 1866 we all, as I have already said, felt that we had not shot sufficiently well. Nevertheless our consciences were easy, and we could say that we had done our duty, for we had fought wherever we had been ordered to fight, had

held strictly to the drill-books, and had shot as we
had been taught to shoot at the practice grounds.

If, in spite of all this, the results which we had
obtained were not such as the army had the right to
expect from the assistance of its artillery, then the
fault must have been in the orders which we had
received, in the recognised system of drill, or in the
instruction in shooting which had been imparted to
us. But when later on some things were written,
between the lines of which we could read that there
was an idea that the artillery had not done its duty,
we were filled with a feeling of most just indignation. But this indignation was considerably diminished when, still later, we learnt from historical
works on the campaign how much the other arms
had suffered from the superiority of the enemy's
artillery. From that moment every officer of the
Prussian artillery sought, as the object of his constant meditation, to discover by what means our
artillery might be placed in a position to furnish a
more effective fire. Even some meddling persons
occupied themselves with this question, and the best
proof that public opinion was excited against our
artillery is given by the fact that a book, such as
that which appeared under the pseudonym Arkolay,
was able to attract public attention, even though it
proposed, as the only means of saving the honour of
the artillery, to give up rifled guns and to return to
smooth-bores.

The effect produced by the Austrian artillery in
the war of 1866 has been frequently compared with
that obtained by the Prussian artillery in the same
war. For my part I have never been able to see

that they shot better than we.   But they used their
artillery in very much larger masses ; and when the
projectiles of masses of artillery, which often numbered more than 100 guns in one line, sweep all the
ground in front of that line the troops which are
exposed to the fire must suffer from it, thanks perhaps to some good shots, but also perhaps to some
bad ones.   But when I, as I mentioned above, could
come into action with at first only 6 guns against
more than 100 guns, at a range of from 1300 to
1400 paces, and that with the loss of only one man
wounded, the enemy cannot have shot well.   Our
infantry, in most of its reports, has spoken of the
violent shell fire through which during this war it
had to advance.   But did this infantry find that a
single one of its attacks was repulsed by the fire of
the enemy's artillery alone ?   No !   Then the enemy's
artillery also did not get a sufficient number of hits,
for it ought to be possible to demand from an artillery which shoots sufficiently well that the enemy
shall not be able to approach it by a frontal attack
when once it has opened its fire.   I venture to declare here that, as a general rule, during the campaign
of 1866 the artillery of both sides shot badly.   I
do not mean to say but that some batteries were
exceptions to this rule.   For example, I know from
information which is beyond doubt that Heydenreich's Saxon battery which, at the battle of Königgrätz, held its position, with such stubbornness and
so gloriously, on the hill to the south-east of
Tresowitz, hit with shell after shell.   It fired very
slowly, and never at long ranges, but every one of
its shells hit the mark and caused us some loss

This was the case with Leonhardi's battery also. At Blumenau, the Austrian artillery knocked a Prussian battery to pieces ; on the other hand, Scherbening's four batteries produced an excellent effect in the same engagement.

A great noise has also been made about the heroism with which the Austrian artillery sacrificed itself during the war to save the other arms. With respect to all the many guns which were lost, the reports of the victorious infantry declare that they in general captured only such guns as had lost their teams by fire ; the others succeeded in escaping. Most of them tried to escape, and those which were surprised had simply missed the right moment for retiring, either because they had not estimated the range and the effect of our needle-gun at its true value, or because they had not seen our infantry at all, attacking them as it did, according to the situation, either by advancing against the front through very high corn, or by turning their flank. Thus then the Austrian guns which, during the campaign of 1866, fell into the hands of the enemy did not all intentionally sacrifice themselves with a full knowledge of what they were doing, as was the case with Gröben's Austrian battery in front of the southern outlet of Chlum, and with the valiant gunners in the positions of Lipa, who continued their fire until they fell dead beneath their guns. Most of them tried to escape, and if many did not succeed, they did not, owing to their desire to fly, exhaust the full effect of their guns, by waiting until the enemy had come up to their very muzzles.

I maintain then what I have said : " We gunners,

on one side and the other, did not make a sufficient number of hits in the war of 1866." What, on the other hand, were the results of the fire during the war of 1870? Allow me to enter into that with you in another letter. To-day I am tired of writing, and you are probably equally tired of reading.

LETTER IV

IF I should wish to show, in comparison with the
very unsatisfactory results of the fire of our artillery
during the campaign of 1866, that it obtained far
better in 1870, and were to give reasons for this
improvement, I should be obliged to go through the
official account battle by battle.   But even this would
not suffice, since I could not exactly show from it
what portion of the effect was on each occasion to
be ascribed to the artillery.   I will not weary you
by taking you again over all the fields of battle, but
will only bring forward certain facts, and will relate
some personal observations of my own together with
some communications which I have received from
friends.   This will be sufficient to establish all data.
It is not astonishing that at Weissenburg the German artillery should have exercised a decisive
influence on the course of the action, since it was
possessed of a considerable numerical superiority.   I
have related in my second letter how this artillery,
posted in the foremost line of skirmishers, compelled
the defenders of the Château of Geissberg to capitu-
late, and also how at Wörth it prepared the assault

on Elsasshausen. At Spicheren it began by making the enemy's artillery abandon their post on the Rothe-berg; it next repulsed the frequent counter-attacks of the enemy on its position on the heights of Folst; and finally secured the possession of the Rothe-berg, for we did not consider that point as having been definitely occupied by us until Stumpff's and Voss's batteries had established themselves on it, and had repulsed several of the enemy's efforts to retake it. At Vionville our artillery commenced by harassing all the enemy's camps; it then maintained the fight in the centre until the infantry of the two divisions of the 3d corps had arrived in sufficient number; on this occasion, unassisted by the other arms, it had to defend itself against the enemy's infantry; later on it contributed, in conjunction with the infantry, to repulse the repeated counter-attacks of the enemy. Finally it pushed forward with the infantry when it was already dark, and assisted the latter to make certain of the victory, which had been so hard to win. At Beaumont it is less easy to distinguish the effect produced by the very numerous German artillery from that caused by the infantry. Need I speak again of Saint-Privat-Gravelotte and of Sedan, those two battles which, during a great part of the time that they lasted, were battles of artillery? It will be sufficient for me to recall that the assault on Sainte-Marie-aux-Chênes was prepared by the fire of 88 guns, in such a manner that our infantry was able, with one rush and without a stop, to push its way to the opposite edge of the village to that at which it had entered; at Saint-Privat the attack made no progress until the artillery advanced in a mass to the line of skirmishers, and bombarded the place. As for the battle of Sedan it will suffice to throw a glance on the two plans which are attached to the official account, in order to see that the French army was enclosed in a circle of artillery. If the question be asked, "What did the projectiles of the artillery hit?" a sufficient answer may be found in the information given by General Douay, that in the 7th corps alone 40 wagons blew up during the battle. For in this war the international convention had resulted in the disappearance of explosive bullets from the infantry ammunition, and thus the explosion of the wagons, mentioned above, can only have been caused by missiles thrown by the artillery.

But these data are too general for me to consider them as sufficient ground for a proposition, which I intend to take as my point of departure for further deductions. I shall therefore beg your permission to relate some facts of which my friends and I have been eye-witnesses.

At the battle of Saint-Privat, when the Guard corps advanced in line of battalion columns from Doncourt towards the village of Saint-Privat, it was received by the shells of those of the batteries of the enemy which had been pushed forward to meet us, from the crest of the heights which run from Saint-Privat to Amanvillers. The four batteries of the 1st Division of the Guard opened their fire against them in succession, that is to say, one after the other, with intervals as short as the deployment of the batteries from column would permit. Immediately afterwards they were reinforced by the corps artillery, and as each of these batteries, according to the orders

G

given to them, posted itself 200 paces nearer to the enemy than the battery on its flank which had already begun to fire, our fire becoming more and more intense and accurate (since its efficacy increased in proportion as the batteries approached nearer to those of the enemy) very soon obliged the latter to retire to their principal position on the heights. We continued the artillery fight against this position at the very long range of 2500 to 2800 paces, since the General commanding the Guard corps did not wish us to go in to a distance at which we might have produced a decisive effect ; for he had received orders to wait at first until the turning movement and the flank attack, which were to be carried out by our left wing, should have produced their full result. Thus from a little after 2 P.M. until a little after 5 P.M. we continued the artillery fight in a position of which the left flank, as a whole (for there were some modifications in detail), stood a few hundred paces in front of Saint-Ail, while the right flank touched that of the Hessian artillery, which was posted at the Bois de la Cusse. The result of this artillery fight was that the enemy, at the end of only an hour, ceased to fire, and disappeared behind the hill of Saint-Privat, which bounded the view in our front. On this occasion the fire of our infantry did not annoy the enemy's artillery, nor did the latter break off the action on account of orders from superior authority, dictated by the general tactical situation. If the enemy's guns were reduced to silence, we have the right to attribute this result to the effect of our fire, and this result was obtained by us, though the enemy was equal to us in number,

and superior with respect to the very favourable
position which he occupied. After this first hour
had passed, I kept up an extremely slow fire; I
obeyed the orders which I had received from the
General commanding the Guard corps, to lengthen
out the action and economise my ammunition. In
the interval the attack on Sainte-Marie-aux-Chênes
was prepared; ten guns of my left wing, as I have
several times mentioned, took part in this action, by
changing front to the left in front of Saint-Ail; so
that, as they opened fire on Sainte-Marie, they presented their right flank to the enemy's main position
at Saint-Privat; but his fire was so kept down that
he gained no advantage by this circumstance. When
one knows one's self superior, one can attempt the
incredible.

We could not dare to nurse the illusion that we
had annihilated the great line of artillery of the
enemy, of which I estimated the strength at 60 guns,
by our fire, which was delivered up a slope, at a
range of from 2000 to 3000 paces. But his complete silence and the retrograde movements which
he could be seen making from Roncourt to Saint-
Privat proved that he felt the superiority of our fire.
When, however, between 5 and 6 P.M., the infantry
of the Guard came out from under cover, and moved
against Saint-Privat, the enemy's infantry and artillery recovered their activity all along the height,
which proves that they had only sheltered themselves
from our superior fire in order to reopen the fight
at the decisive moment. Our infantry, rushing
boldly to the attack, very soon masked our batteries,
which had again opened a violent fire on the enemy

who were now visible, and I ordered the corps artillery (under Scherbening) and that of the 1st Division (under Rychelberg) to accompany the infantry. The right wing of this line of artillery (4 batteries of the 1st Division, and 2 batteries of the corps artillery of the Guard) galloped straight forward and reached at the same time as the skirmishers the nearest edge of the heights between Saint-Privat and Amanvillers, at the very moment when the enemy's skirmishers were giving way before our own. The left wing of the line (3 batteries of the corps artillery, and the batteries of the 2d Division of the Guard, to which, later, two other Horse Artillery batteries joined themselves) reinforced the firing line of the infantry, which was now firing from the open ground against the walls of the village. Farther to the left the batteries did the same, but I shall make no further mention of them, as they were not under my command. I did not myself see the effect produced by the batteries of my left wing, as I was with the right, and had ordered Colonel Scherbening to lead the other. But some French officers, who were taken prisoners, told us afterwards that this effect was so murderous that, if the infantry attack had taken place half an hour later, we should have found no defenders in the village.

I was then with the right wing, and I advanced with the 2d heavy battery, commanded by Prittwitz. It was the first which was ready to start after having limbered up ; this operation, by the way, takes much longer in a real engagement than at peace manœuvres : there are shells to pack away, horses which have been shot to unharness, or some little repair to be done to the gun. On this occasion the captain commanding the battery had made up his mind to advance before he received my order, and was thus ready sooner than the others. The battery galloped up the slope of the hill and joined the skirmishers as they moved to the assault ; only three guns at first reached the top, the three others having lost horses as they advanced. At the spot where the battery came up, the crest of the hill is so wide that it almost amounts to a plateau. The enemy's skirmishers were flying before ours. But at a distance of from 300 to 500 paces in front of us masses of the enemy, in quarter-columns, were advancing to dispute the crest of the height with our skirmishers. You can scarcely imagine the effect which the first shot of Prittwitz's produced on these masses. In an instant they became motionless as if they had received a violent electric shock. But when shell after shell began to burst in the middle of them, when our line of artillery was reinforced by my other batteries as they arrived in turn at a gallop, and by the three guns of the first battery, which succeeded in rejoining us, the columns at once took to flight. Then my 30 guns set to work to find the range by firing trial shots at different points, while on our left the fight was raging around Saint-Privat. The possession of our height was of the greatest importance. From it, to our right we could enfilade Amanvillers, for we could see its steeple above a slight undulation of the ground. To our front we were sending shell as far as the quarries of Amanvillers, near the Bois de Fèves, and it was possible for us to reach, at a point near the Inn of Marengo, the end of the main road from Metz to Saint-Privat, by which the reinforcements which the enemy might send from the former to the latter place must pass. But at the moment there were very few of our infantry on this height. The principal masses were engaged in the fight and the attacks directed against the village. Only the six companies which the General commanding the Guard corps had sent me during the cannonade to serve as our escort, were available for the attack on the height to the right of the village. But these companies had been cruelly decimated ; the battalion commander who led them lay on the ground severely wounded. The captain who had succeeded him, though his head was bleeding from a wound, managed to rally 20 or 30 men round the colours. Other small detachments were collected at different points, and were divided between the batteries, so that they might be ready to open a rapid fire at point-blank range should the enemy push towards us. When all these arrangements had been made, I placed myself behind the captain of the 4th heavy battery (Seeger), because this officer was the quickest at finding the range by his trial shots. As he gave me the ranges, I sent them to the other batteries by my orderly officers.

We had not long to wait for the first movement which the enemy's infantry was to make in our direction. It advanced in quarter-column from Amanvillers, and attacked us energetically. When the head of the column became visible over the hill, our trial shots reached it at a range of 1900 paces, and my 30 guns opened a rapid fire. The enemy's infantry was enveloped in the thick smoke which the shells made as they burst. But after a very short time we saw the red trousers of the masses which were approaching us appear through the cloud. I stopped the fire. A trial shot was fired at 1700 paces range; this was to show us the point up to which we should let them advance before reopening the rapid fire; we did the same for the ranges of 1500, 1300, 1100, and 900 paces. In spite of the horrible devastation which the shells caused in their ranks, these brave troops continued to advance. But at 900 paces the effect of our fire was too deadly for them; they turned short round and fled; we hurled shells after them as long as we could see them. Here was an infantry attack which was repulsed purely and simply by the fire of artillery. A few years later I had the opportunity of talking with an aide-de-camp of General de Ladmirault, the very man who had carried the order to make this counter-attack, and who had been present during its execution. Two regiments of infantry had been despatched on this duty. The French officer said to me, " It was impossible to succeed. You have no idea what it is to have to advance under the fire of your artillery."

These infantry attacks were repeated. They continued to come from the same direction. Altogether three were made, but the two last were not carried out with the same energy as the first. They were stopped at about 1500 paces in front of our line. A mass of cavalry also appeared, before the infantry attacks, with the object of trying to disengage the defenders of Saint-Privat from their position. The head of the mass showed itself near the farm of Marengo on the high road from Metz to Saint-Privat;

it halted while the column deployed.   As soon as we
had found the range with the help of a few trial shots,
we opened a rapid fire, and our shells, falling among
the crowded ranks of the cavalry, broke up the mass,
and it disappeared in the same direction from which
it had come.   At length our infantry made their way
into Saint-Privat, and the remainder of the batteries
of the artillery of the Guard hastened up also, and
posted themselves on the height to the right of the
village.   The enemy, on his part, deployed a grand
line of artillery in front of us, in the low ground
along the edge of the forest near the quarries of
Amanvillers.   We found no difficulty in silencing
this artillery (it was that of the Imperial Guard), for
we knew our range ; we were superior in number (the
batteries of the 10th corps and of the Hessian Division had reinforced our line), and we had the better
position.   When night came the enemy's artillery
had disappeared.

Allow me to tell you also what was the result of
our fire at the battle of Sedan.   I have already
related in my second letter, how the artillery of the
1st Division of the infantry of the Guard had, at the
moment when the Guard corps began to appear,
passed through the Bois de Villers-Cernay by a
forest road, in order to open fire from the other side
of the wood.   When we had reached the edge a
powerful line of artillery (field guns and mitrailleuses)
presented itself to our view at a range from which its
fire was very effective.   Most of these guns were
covered by earthen parapets, and they were hurling
death and destruction on the Saxons, who were
already engaged from a position which lay close to

the right edge of the Givonne valley, and of which the left wing was extended in a nearly northerly direction beyond the farm of Haybes; we had thus the opportunity of attacking this line energetically in flank. This was specially carried out by the three batteries which stood at the end of the wood-road, close to the edge of the forest. Three batteries only had found room at this spot, the fourth was posted on their left rear. They obtained the most brilliant result; proof of this was furnished by the considerable number of disabled guns and mitrailleuses which our infantry, when they advanced, found in the emplacements. It is impossible to decide how much was due to our fire, and how much to that of the artillery of the 12th corps, which stood in front of us (it is well known that when shooting, every one says that he hit the hare), but this much is certain, that the guns were disabled by artillery fire. At first, it is true, the three batteries of the 1st Division of the Guard had no easy work, for when they appeared the enemy fired at them; he tried, on his part, to take them in flank, by firing obliquely from the northern end of the Bois de la Garenne, near where the Calvary of Illy stands. I suppose that this was the artillery of the French cavalry, which was held in reserve at that point. On our side we at once placed the Field Brigade of the corps artillery in position against the French batteries; this was posted to the north of the Bois de Villers-Cernay. Although at this point also the batteries pushed on as far as possible to the front, the edge of the hill, which is very steep at this place, obliged them to come into action at a considerable distance from their target.

The great distance and many other circumstances rendered it difficult to observe the effect of the fire, so that it was some little time before we could be sure of its efficacy.   But when once we were sure of it the enemy's artillery disappeared, and our shells very much annoyed the masses of cavalry, which at last retired towards the north.   During this time the enemy had endeavoured to bring his artillery into action at a closer range against the batteries of the 1st Division of the Guard, whose position had become particularly troublesome to him.   A battery horsed entirely with grays trotted up from the Fond de Givonne to Givonne itself, and tried to take up its position between that village and the Bois de la Garenne.   As soon as it appeared on the hill the three batteries mentioned above opened fire on it.   It fell to pieces, as it were, and its ruins remained where they fell.   It did not fire a single shot.   A second and a third battery met with the same fate.

In a French pamphlet which appeared shortly after the war, I read the following :—

" The Emperor himself tried to post three batteries at the exit from the low ground of the Givonne. They were demolished without having fired a shot."

It is possible that the episodes mentioned in the book entitled *Sedan*, by General de Wimpffen, Paris 1871 (page 193, 13th line from the top, and page 341, 7th line), have reference to the same phase of the action.   At any rate, the hour mentioned was that at which the batteries appeared which were crushed by our fire ; consequently I may have had the honour of having the Emperor in person in front of me.   During this time the 2d Division of the Guard attacked the flank of those of the enemy's troops whose counter-attack seriously annoyed the 12th corps. (It may now have been about 10 A.M.) In this operation they were assisted by the whole of the four batteries of the Division. It is impossible to decide how much of the result obtained was due to the infantry and how much to the artillery. But the losses which the latter suffered by the fire of the chassepots proved that it advanced well into the middle of the fight. Captain von Roon and Ensign Tesdorpf were killed, and Lieutenant Baron von Tauchnitz had both legs hit by a chassepot bullet, which passed through them. On the right wing, to the north of the Bois de Villers-Cernay, the corps artillery directed its fire during the morning (after the enemy's artillery and cavalry had been driven from the ground near the " Calvary of Illy "), sometimes on one point, sometimes on another, against such of the enemy as still showed themselves. At one time a battery appeared here, at another a body of troops showed itself there, and on these it opened fire. The longer the target remained in one position, the more certain and the more effective was the fire. At one moment something was seen moving to the right, in the forest of the Ardennes. By the help of field-glasses, this was made out to be some cavalry marching in two ranks towards the north, and passing through a clearing in the forest on the hill. The batteries endeavoured to find the range. With elevation for a little more than 4000 paces we appeared to hit. I considered that the range was too great for the fire to have any effect, and I was about to order it to cease, when an evident disturbance in the ranks of the enemy proved that our projectiles had reached him. We continued then to fire slowly at this moving target as long as it remained visible. I suppose that this was the same French cavalry which was at first posted at Illy, and which must have turned to the west towards Corbion, moving on an arc of a circle by forest paths, in order to take part in the charges which were directed against the 5th and the 11th corps. On the following day Lieutenant von Kaas, while doing duty as aide-de-camp, passed by this point, and found on a narrow crest which ran between very steep ravines, an entire French battery which had been abandoned there. The team of the leading gun had been blown to pieces by our shells, and the other guns could not pass it; thus the whole battery fell into our hands, a trophy of the accuracy of our fire.

These visible results increased the confidence of our men in their guns and in the regulation of the fire. They became more and more careful to obey all words of command, and to make the corrections ordered, while the tangent-scale was set with yet greater accuracy and the guns laid with greater exactness, so that their effect became more and more irresistible.

The Guard corps had up to this time been ordered to remain on the defensive, with its right flank on the Belgian frontier, and thus to prevent the enemy from breaking out towards the east. When the successes obtained by the left wing of the army of the Meuse permitted it at length to assume the offensive, in order to extend a hand to the left wing of the 3d army, which was making visible progress, so that the enemy might be completely surrounded, I received permission to take my batteries in to a range at which their fire would produce a decisive effect. From that time the 1st and 2d Brigades of Field and the Brigade of Horse Artillery were posted as near the valley of Givonne and the village of that name as the steep side of the valley would permit. The four batteries of the 2d Division of the Guard remained to the south of Haybes, and altered their front and their position very little. There was thus a total of 90 guns which, in their new position, very quickly found their ranges to the various important points on which they were to fire. The effect of their combined fire at such a short range was truly terrible. On a former occasion, when I spoke of the questions relating to the infantry,[1] I mentioned to you the devastation which our shells caused in the crowded ranks of the left wing of the troops (Grandchamp's Division) with which General de Wimpffen tried to pierce the circle which we had formed round him. Some troops of the enemy appeared also at other points, but almost all our batteries overwhelmed them with such a hail of missiles that they broke up and fled into the forest, where they hoped to find shelter. The spectacle of the carnage worked on these masses of men was horrible : the fearful cries of the victims of our shells reached as far as where we stood.

It was perfectly clear that by taking the Bois de la Garenne we should complete the entire defeat of the army of the enemy ; it was therefore determined

[1] In *Letters on Infantry*, a companion work to the present.— *N.L.W.*

to carry this wood.   The 1st Division of the infantry
of the Guard formed up for the assault.   But since
masses of infantry, which had composed two of the
enemy's beaten corps, were crowded together in this
wood, it was necessary to begin by preparing the
attack.   With this object I divided the long edge of
the forest which extended before us into sections,
and I assigned one section to each of my batteries.
The first gun of each of these units was to fire at
the very edge of the wood, and each of the following
guns was to fire in the same direction, but was to
give 100 paces more elevation than the gun on its
right.   In this manner the edge of the forest and
the forest itself, to a depth of 500 paces, would be
covered with a hail of shells.   The splinters would
carry yet farther.   But as soon as any portion of
the enemy's troops should appear outside of the forest,
then immediately all our guns were to direct their
fire on it and destroy it.   At this phase of the battle,
and at the point where we were, our superiority over
the enemy was so overwhelming that we suffered no
loss at all.   The batteries fired as if at practice.   We
had spectators, as we have on the practice ranges.
Ours were officers of the troops which were held in
reserve, military surgeons, and even a chaplain.

All at once a line of Prussian cavalry coming
from the direction of Illy, approached the northern
point of the wood at the spot where the Calvary
stands.   A thick mass of infantry with red trousers
rushed out of the forest against them, and fired on
them from the quarry by the Calvary.   It was an
exciting moment.   Will our guns, which are laid
exactly on this point, be able to throw back the

enemy's infantry, and prevent it from destroying
our cavalry, upon which they have opened fire?
This was the question which interested each of us.
The chaplain himself said, very justly, to a gunner
who was by his side near one of the limbers, "Now
you ought to make plenty of Prussian shells burst
in the middle of that French infantry!"—"Make your
mind easy, sir," replied the gunner, who had heard
the order given to lay the guns on the enemy's
infantry, "we will look after that; you have only got
to watch." At the same instant the greater part of
the guns opened their rapid fire; a cloud of shells
which burst as they touched the ground enveloped
the enemy in a thick smoke, and they very soon fell
back into the forest. The chaplain shouted with
delight, which made us all laugh. I will not tell
you what he said, but if you desire the evidence of
one of the Lord's anointed to assure you of the
efficacy of our fire, I will give you his name, and
you can ask him for information.

The batteries were once more pointed at the
forest and continued to bombard it. At length the
moment to attack was come; orders had been given
that a salvo fired by all our guns should serve as the
signal to carry it out. We fired the salvo at 2.30
P.M. precisely, as had been arranged, and our infantry,
starting from Givonne, began to climb the hill. We
were in a state of feverish expectation; every eye
was fixed on the forest; we asked ourselves if the
capture of the edge of the wood would cost as many
lives as had that of Saint-Privat. But this time the
resistance met with was almost *nil*. At most points
the French, utterly discouraged, advanced to meet

our troops crying—"Mercy! mercy! we can do
nothing; we are crushed by the fire of your artillery."
Only in the interior of the forest did they try to fight
at certain points, and even there the resistance was
not stubborn.   Unless I am mistaken, the Guard
corps at this place captured from 11,000 to 14,000
unwounded prisoners.   The whole of the infantry of
the corps lost, in this battle, only 120 officers and
320 men killed or wounded.

   I have thus given you a summary of the results
of our fire in the two principal battles of the war, so
far at least as I could judge of it myself.   I will
pass in silence over the lesser engagements in which
I took part; and will content myself with relating
some special observations which were made by others.
I have here before me a private letter from one of
my comrades, Herr von Dresky, who was at that
time a Colonel, but is now a Lieutenant-General.
He then commanded the corps artillery of the 3d
corps, and wrote this letter shortly after the great
battles which were fought round Metz; he completed
it later on with notes.   I copy the following passages
(he begins with the battle of the 16th of August):—

   "I received no orders at Tronville, and therefore
moved on Vionville.   I had just commanded two
Horse Artillery batteries to unlimber, when General
von Bülow told me to go and occupy, with the corps
artillery, the hill which runs east and west to the south
of Flavigny, and to hold my ground there.   General
von Alvensleben warned me that the corps artillery
was intended to form the centre of his position, and
that he counted fully on me to hold my ground.

   "I gave orders to limber-up again and, while the

Horse Artillery Brigade were doing so, pushed on quickly to the front to search for a point where we might cross the deep and marshy ditch which extends to the west from Flavigny. I found a bridge at Tantelainville, on the other side of which the hill on which I was to take up my position rises immediately from the stream in a steep slope. Before leaving the bridge I attentively examined its situation in order to make sure that it could not be commanded by the enemy's fire. The nearest place occupied by the enemy was Flavigny. I could see only infantry there, the distance between us being, as I judged, about 1600 paces ; for this reason I did not consider that there was any danger to be anticipated in passing the bridge. But at the moment when the head of the brigade was about to cross it, we suddenly received from Flavigny such a hail of chassepot bullets that one officer, the trumpet-major, three men, and six horses were hit. I sounded the 'Gallop!' upon which the guns and waggons which had not been hit quickly crossed the bridge, and found an immediate shelter behind the hill, which here has a very steep slope. The troops re-formed, and we gained our first position without any further loss. The gun which we had been obliged to leave behind was quickly repaired ; it rejoined the battery after a short time, without suffering any other damage, though the ·infantry fire continued from Flavigny.

" After the Horse Artillery Brigade had taken up its position on the hill near the bridge, I opened fire against Flavigny. Our shells soon set the farm in flames. When the French abandoned it I advanced

H

in echelon and pursued the enemy with a fairly effective fire.

"At this moment the Field batteries arrived, and when the enemy had evacuated Vionville and Flavigny and had retired to Rezonville, I advanced the whole of the corps artillery in echelons, and arranged my troops in such a manner that two batteries under Captain Stumpff stood together to the north of Flavigny, while the whole of the remainder were on the south of that place. The Horse Artillery was on the right, and its flank rested on the slope of the hill marked 311.[1]

"The left wing of the 5th Division was at this point ; and here, on account of the excellent view to be obtained from it, I remained with Generals von Stülpnagel and von Schwerin during the greater part of the battle. I occupied this position at 2 P.M., and I remained there until 7 P.M. During this time the 2d Horse Artillery battery (which had been attached to Rheinbaben's Division) and the 1st 6-pr. battery of the 5th Division came into line with the other batteries. Between 2 and 4.30 P.M., one Horse and four Field batteries of the 10th brigade also arrived in turn ; they placed themselves under my command. As at first I had placed my guns with very wide intervals, owing to the great extent of ground which I had to occupy, I had plenty of room for the batteries which joined me afterwards.

"There were therefore in position at Flavigny, at about 5 P.M., 4 Horse Artillery and 7 Field batteries;

[1] Herr von Dresky refers to the map of the French Staff, which gives the height in metres ; on the plan attached to the Prussian official account this hill is marked 998, in feet.

at this hour the Imperial Guard made an extremely violent attack upon us. We had 6 French batteries in front of us (I counted them several times), which for the most part fired salvoes at us. When the artillery fight had lasted about half an hour, the French infantry advanced to the attack. We could only see a very thick line of skirmishers ; as for the troops in column in rear we could see nothing of them. Our fire was directed against this line of skirmishers as it advanced, and since we had been in position from 2 P.M., and knew all the ranges, our shells made such gaps in the enemy's line that it, after having very bravely approached to a distance of about 1000 paces, and having been received with a rapid fire, answered with a hurried and ineffective discharge, and then turned to the right-about and retired.

"On this occasion I acquired the certain knowledge that a line of artillery cannot be beaten or broken by a frontal attack. At that time we had common shells only, and what an overwhelming effect did we not obtain with them. At the present day the artillery have shrapnel, and a frontal attack would be repulsed with even more terrible loss. . . .

"The fight at Vionville has also made me sure that the only way to close open ground efficiently is to employ artillery for that purpose, for the very reason that it cannot be driven back by a frontal attack. But such a line of artillery has a yet further use ; it serves as a substitute for a reserve to receive troops which have been driven back. During the alternate successes and failures of the infantry fight around the hill marked 308, near Vionville, I often saw detachments, which the enemy had just repulsed, form up again immediately in rear of the line of artillery, for there they knew themselves to be in safety ; and thence they were led forward once more to the attack. We had no longer any infantry reserves. . . .

" But to return to Vionville. About 7 P.M. some batteries of the 8th brigade arrived on the field of battle ; they filled up the interval between my guns and those of the 5th Division. We had then from 20 to 24 batteries in one line. There was no fear that the French would ever force this. Consequently we had done exactly what General von Alvensleben desired. It was fortunate also that we had so much artillery there, for the infantry was wasting slowly away in these terrible struggles. At nightfall our fire and that of the French little by little died away.

" I was riding round my batteries in order to learn what losses they had suffered, when I received an order from Prince Frederic Charles to advance quickly with the corps artillery on Rezonville, taking great care not to expose myself to the fire of the enemy's infantry. When I had sent the order to advance to the different brigades, I myself rode on to Rezonville, which was about 1500 paces distant, but I could not see a single Frenchman in any direction. The first batteries which advanced were those of the 10th brigade, under Commandant Krause. As they unlimbered they suddenly received, on their front and left flank, a very heavy fire delivered almost at point-blank range by some infantry which had escaped being seen. Though they lost many men and horses, they nevertheless came gaily into position and opened fire. The other batteries arrived one after the other and took their places in the line, and a cannonade followed, in which there could be no question of aiming or laying with any exactness. It was impossible to follow the regulations, for it was already night, and the smoke helped to make the darkness deeper still. The fight lasted about 20 minutes, at the end of which the enemy's infantry ceased firing.

"On page 637 of the official account we read: 'The Prussian artillery replied during a certain time with a rapid fire, after which it returned, battery by battery, to the position which it occupied before.' This passage does not mean (and according to trustworthy communications which I have received on the subject, this sense cannot be attributed to it) that this return to our original positions was the consequence of the fire of the enemy, for we had caused that fire to cease. The battle was finished. I received from General von Alvensleben the order to return to my former position. The night had fully come; from that moment there was no longer any object in maintaining the artillery in the most advanced line. I therefore ordered it to fall back by batteries. We afterwards bivouacked at Flavigny.

"The total losses suffered on the 16th of August were very great, greater than the whole of those which the artillery had undergone in all the battles which had been fought up to that time." (According to the official account, this corps artillery lost 10 officers, 119 men, and 219 horses; the 2 Horse Artillery batteries, which formed a part of it, alone lost 139 horses, which makes 70 horses per battery.)

"On the 18th of August, at 1 P.M., the corps artillery, which was bivouacking to the south of Flavigny, was called to arms. We had already heard the noise of a violent action to the north of our bivouac, and we expected every moment to be sent to the front. But only the corps artillery of the 3d corps took part in the great decisive battle of the 18th of August. The remainder of the troops of this corps were held that day in reserve.

"I was assigned a position to the south of the cemetery of Verneville, with orders not to advance on any account, even if I seemed to see a favourable opportunity, since a forward movement was to be executed by the wings of the army. As my position was large enough for only 4 batteries, I posted the Field batteries there, and held back the 2 Horse Artillery batteries, which had suffered so much on the 16th in rear of Verneville, very much to their detriment, as I found later. . . .

"In my position at Verneville I had in front of me 4 French gun batteries at Montigny-la-Grange and 1 battery of mitrailleuses on the height of La Folie. I was not exposed on that day to infantry fire. At the commencement, I fired on the gun batteries and, after a fight which lasted nearly an hour, reduced them to silence. Then I went on to the mitrailleuses ; after I had thrown a dozen shells at them they too disappeared. I suffered small loss that day, and this was all caused by the French gun batteries. The bullets of the mitrailleuses all fell at the foot of the gentle slope on the crest of which my batteries were posted. Soon after the mitrailleuses had gone, when my batteries were idle, since they had no longer any object at which to fire, the officer who commanded the troops which were posted in the Chantrenne farm (in front of my position) begged me to fire on a wood situated in front of the farm, and strongly occupied by the French, in order that our men might attack and capture it. I agreed to this request against my own wish, for I had comparatively very little ammunition left, and besides I did not expect much effect from my fire. Apparently the result entirely confirmed my opinion. Although I bombarded the forest several times, our men, in spite of their repeated attacks, did not succeed in carrying it. Regularly as soon as I commenced my fire that of the French ceased, but as soon as our skirmishers attempted to pass the meadow which extended in front of the wood, and thus masked my batteries, the French returned to their posts, and received our men with such a formidable fire that before it even the best troops must have failed. Thus we did not capture this wood; during the night the French evacuated it of their own accord. The fight had cost me 200 shell. Two days afterwards I visited the field of battle with General von Bülow, and gave particular attention to the points on which I had fired. What was my astonishment when I found that the effect produced on the 18th of August by our batteries on the wood was very considerable and really extraordinary. We were filled with a profound esteem for its brave defenders, who, notwithstanding their enormous losses, had not retired. . . ."

In another place General von Dresky says :—

" On the 3d of December 1870, an engagement

was fought near Santeau and Chilleurs-aux-Bois, which is of great interest with respect to the action of the artillery. On that day the forest of Orleans was to be attacked by the 2d army. The 3d corps had orders to advance by the road from Pithiviers to Orleans. We met the enemy at the outskirts of Mareau-aux-Bois, and after a short fight drove in his outposts on Santeau. At that place the enemy held his ground against us. We reconnoitred with care and discovered that we were in front of a strong position defended by several batteries, which were covered by entrenchments.

"General von Alvensleben ordered the 6th Division to advance on the right of the road, and the 5th Division on the left of it ; the corps artillery was to follow the 6th Division, and to take up a position on the right of the high road.

"As the artillery of the 6th Division was also to be posted between the road and the embankment of the railway, there was no room for the corps artillery. A reconnaissance which was made from the top of a windmill informed us that on the south-west of the village of La Brosse there was a more excellent position, whence that which the enemy occupied at Santeau could be taken in flank, and from which it was also possible to sweep all the ground which extended to the forest of Orleans.

"In order to get to this position it was necessary to cross the embankment of the railway (which was not yet completed) from Pithiviers to Orleans. This could be attempted by artillery at one place only, namely, in the neighbourhood of the bridge over the stream of the Oeuf. It had frozen during the night and a little snow had fallen ; this passage had already served for a great part of the 6th Division, and for all the divisional artillery, so that a sort of frozen slime lay all over the unfinished slopes. Many horses slipped and fell, and one wagon turned over, which especially caused a long delay. During the time that the corps artillery took to pass this place, I watched the enemy's artillery at Santeau with great anxiety. We could clearly see the French officers standing on the parapets, their telescopes in their hands, watching us, and might fully expect that they would at any moment open fire on us. The range was 3500 paces, but nothing happened. The corps artillery had fortunately already crossed the railway embankment, when that of the 6th Division opened fire ; then at last the French answered. I had to pass round to the north of the village of La Brosse, in order to get to the position which I had already chosen. The batteries could move but very slowly. The soil of the meadows, being only slightly frozen, had no consistency, and the horses kept going through the crust, while the wheels sank half way up the spokes. During this long flank march in column of route I was fired on incessantly, but suffered no loss at all.

"A little to the south-west of La Brosse there is a small wood. I had ordered the Horse Brigade to take up its position between the wood and La Brosse, while the Field Brigade was to stand to the south of them. By this arrangement I covered the front of my batteries with an excellent protection, the embankment of the railway. The 2d regiment of dragoons formed up to protect our left flank, while

the railway embankment and the small wood were
occupied by some detachments of infantry belonging
to the 6th Division.   The latter was in a sheltered
position in rear of La Brosse.   All the open ground
which extends from Santeau to Neuville-aux-Bois
was commanded from the position occupied by the
Field Brigade. . . . After having given the necessary
orders to the officer who commanded the Horse
Artillery Brigade, which was leading, I went back to
the position of the Field Brigade.   The Horse
Brigade formed line and advanced and at once made
a mistake,[1] for it unlimbered at a salient point of the
wood which I have just mentioned.   At any rate
the French knew the exact range, for the first of the
enemy's shells burst in the middle of the horse-
holders of one of the guns, and another took off the
foot of First-Lieutenant Frank, who commanded the
battery.

"As soon as the Field Brigade opened fire the
enemy's artillery, which was posted at Santeau,
abandoned the fight and retired, under an ample
escort, to a position situated between Moulin de
l'Epine and Chilleurs, whence it renewed the action
against the corps artillery with three batteries of guns
and one of mitrailleuses ; this did not continue long,
for it soon retired farther yet.

" I took advantage of the opportunity, and pushed
my artillery across the railway embankment by successive batteries ; we approached Chilleurs-aux-Bois
to within a range of 2000 paces, and set to work to
bombard the village.   The enemy did not wait for

---

[1] In choosing their position near such a conspicuous point, of which
the French were sure to have found the range.—*N.L.W.*

our infantry to deliver a decisive attack upon them, but very soon commenced to abandon the village, and to retire towards the forest of Orleans. During this retreat one of the enemy's columns was fired on with so much success that it broke up and disbanded itself.

"The fact which I am going to tell you has nothing really to do with the subject of which I am speaking, but it has some interest, for it shows how well the gunners knew their worth.

"When I saw the French infantry leave Chilleurs, I rode, after having given a general order that the fire was to be directed on them, up to the 4th light battery, whose leader, Captain Müller, had been through a course of instruction at the School of Gunnery, and had learnt to shoot on a good principle. I turned to his men and said, 'For every shot which you throw directly into the enemy's infantry, I will give you three thalers.' A gunner replied, 'That will cost you a lot of money, Colonel; we shoot pretty well in this battery.' The first shot went over, the second was short, then seven hit directly, which was, without doubt, the principal reason that the column broke up. I paid my 21 thalers in the midst of the cheers of the battery."

Farther on we read :—

"As for the effect of our fire on that day, we found afterwards, on passing by the abandoned positions of the French, near Moulin de l'Epine, a certain number of gunners and horses killed and wounded. Not a gun was put out of action. At the place where the French infantry had been fired on by the 4th light battery, we found, in addition to a score of dead, three men stretched side by side, whose bodies had been entirely or partly cut in half. It was a horrible sight. The effect produced by the enemy's artillery on us was as follows :—infantry and cavalry, 2 officers, 57 men, 14 horses ; artillery, 4 officers, 39 men, 54 horses.

" The comparative severe loss suffered by the artillery is easily explained, for at Santeau and at Chilleurs it was the artillery principally who sustained the action."

But I have quoted enough examples from history in support of my theory. I can hear you, my dear friend, say wearily—" *Sapienti sat !* I believe you; you shot very well in 1870, the whole world knows it." However, do not be angry with me if I have wearied you with my examples. We find in a very well-known work, indispensable to every officer of the Staff, and the production of the pen of an officer of the first rank (*The Duties of the General Staff*, by Bronsart von Schellendorf), these words : " It is well known that military history, when superficially studied, will furnish arguments in support of any theory or opinion. But, in order to obtain a clear insight into the principles of war, it is necessary to examine a considerable number of examples of the same character, and also to be sure that these examples are really of the same character, with respect to their cause and their effect." And this is why I have been obliged to quote to you so many examples of the same description.

LETTER V

THE LOSSES OF THE ARTILLERY IN GUNS IN THE CAMPAIGN OF 1866, AND IN THAT OF 1870

IT remains for me to examine a few other conditions which in the war of 1866 hampered the action of the artillery, while in the war of 1870 they exercised no deleterious effect. I am of opinion, as I have already implied at the end of my first letter, that in 1866 the artillery frequently failed to produce the desired effect on account of the supply of ammunition running short; that here and there it fell back to "refit"; and that as a rule it avoided exposing itself to the fire of infantry, either by not advancing, or by retiring as soon as it was exposed to that fire. Nothing of this sort happened in 1870. You will excuse me, will you not, if I do not enumerate one by one all the individual cases where, in 1866, a battery ceased firing because it had expended all its ammunition. As a rule the waggons had not followed the battery, through being either separated from it by other troops, which delayed their advance, or through not having found points of passage over rivers, etc. The batteries when under fire found themselves, when they could not shoot, absolutely useless in their positions, while their horses and men afforded a target to the enemy, and the guns were exposed to the danger of serving as his trophies of victory. So they limbered up and fell back to look for fresh ammunition.

It is true that there were, even in 1866, some batteries which, after expending their ammunition, remained silent at their post in the line of battle, waiting until their ammunition was brought to them. Such was Von der Goltz's battery, which stood to the right of the forest of Sadowa between Unter-Dohalitz and Ober-Dohalitz, during the battle of Königgrätz. But this heroic action was but an exception in that war. The batteries ordinarily fell back as soon as they had no more ammunition, and looking at the matter impartially, this seems natural. What can guns do when it is impossible for them to fire? The answer seems easy enough. Had not the infantry also fallen back when it had no cartridges left, and no one had ever blamed them for it? And yet the infantry had at any rate its bayonet with which to fight, while the artillery, when it has no more ammunition, is absolutely defenceless. Nevertheless the artillery, even more than the other arms, must take care never to fall back, for when it retires a very great effect is produced on the other troops by its retirement. The cavalry may charge and afterwards retire towards the other arms, and this will happen even if the charge has succeeded, for it will often find itself obliged to rally in the main position beyond the zone where the enemy's fire has a decisive efficacy: for example, when a victorious charge has been thrown back, owing to the pursuit being continued up to the bayonets of fresh troops.

Lines of infantry, particularly lines of skirmishers, need not blush to have yielded with elasticity to the overpowering pressure of the enemy, only to recover the lost ground as soon as they are reinforced.

But both these arms have a habit of regarding the artillery as the stable element, and when they hear the rolling thunder of its guns, it is for them a guarantee that the position is firmly held. Therefore as soon as infantry or cavalry see the artillery retire, they conclude that the struggle is abandoned, and that the battle is regarded as lost. When the minds of troops are possessed by an idea of this kind, it may, even though it have no foundation at the moment, nevertheless bring about the loss of the action. This is why it is desirable that the artillery should hold its ground with the very greatest stubbornness, and why, even when it has expended its ammunition, it should not abandon its position in order to retire, so long as the General commanding the troops engaged has not given up all idea of continuing the action.

As regards the war of 1870, I know of only a very small number of cases where the artillery retired for want of ammunition. The duty of replacing the ammunition was. as a rule regularly and punctually carried out ; it was consequently very rarely that a battery completely expended its cartridges. What should be done in this case was shown by that battery at Châteaudun which, when it had no more ammunition, mounted the gunners on the guns and limbers and made them sing the " Wacht am Rhein," in order that they might pass the time agreeably while waiting for fresh cartridges. Many others stood their ground in a similar manner in other engagements. As for myself personally, I have never during the course of the war seen the artillery retire when before the enemy ; I except the fights against the troops which made sorties during the siege of Paris. When we had repulsed them within the line of their forts, we, when the action was over, received orders to retire to our position of investment and to our cantonments. In the course of the war we fought a certain number, very few it is true, of battles of which the result was unfavourable to us. In that case our artillery fell back, seldom, as far as I know, for want of ammunition, but as a rule by order of the General who had supreme command of the troops engaged, when he judged it advisable to discontinue the action. The fact that it has always been found possible to obviate the want of ammunition is the more remarkable, since we expended a far greater quantity of it in the battles and engagements of the Franco-German war than we did in those of the war with Austria.

In the battle of Vionville-Mars-la-Tour the corps artillery of the 3d corps alone, with 6 batteries, fired 5699 rounds. At Saint-Privat the artillery of the Guard fired more than 8000 ; at Sedan more than 5000 rounds. The latter expended altogether more than 25,000 shells, a greater quantity of ammunition than was issued as the total supply for the Field army. If, nevertheless, there was never a lack of ammunition during the course of an action, there must have been a very good reason for the fact. This reason I propose to speak of later on. It must be sufficient, for the present, to say how important it is that the artillery should never, during an action, suffer from want of ammunition. It is indeed asking very much of a battery to stand still without firing a shot, to wait quietly for the renewal of its ammunition, and to remain defenceless in position instead of leaving the line without orders. Only men gifted with extraordinary energy can at these moments, of their own accord, decide to remain in action when their ammunition has been expended, unless this be formally laid down in the regulations as their duty.

The same may be said of the movement to the rear made by batteries out of the fire of the enemy's artillery in order to "refit." In the official account we shall find several cases of this kind mentioned during the war of 1866, among the Austrians as well as among the Prussians. At the first meeting, in the battle of Nachod, an Austrian battery fell back and took up a less advanced position because it could not compete with the fire of the Prussian artillery. A little later, in the same fight, the two Prussian batteries which came first on the scene, and which consequently had held out the longest against the fire of the superior number of guns of the enemy, were withdrawn to the rear to refit ; they did not come into action again until towards the end of the battle. A 4-pr. battery, which was in action at the beginning of the battle of Soor, was "relieved" by another battery, on account of the great loss it had sustained, in order that it might "refit," and after this it took no further part in the conflict. We find that cases of the same description present themselves in all the engagements of the war of 1866, and are most frequent in the battle of Königgrätz.

I

It appeared justifiable not to leave in the line of battle those guns which had been put out of action, and which were consequently incapable of doing any work, but to withdraw them in order to leave them in safety so that if the battle at any time turned against us, they might not fall into the hands of the enemy and serve him as trophies; and this seemed the more right as the regulations of that date contained instructions according to which guns which were so injured that they could not be made serviceable under fire, were to be taken to the rear.

But by doing this, and by also taking to the rear all batteries incapable of holding their ground, and who needed to refit, the line of fire was considerably weakened. If on the other hand it be made a rule to absolutely forbid that disabled guns shall be withdrawn, or entire batteries retired in order that they may refit out of fire, the detachments will be compelled to repair the injured guns quickly, and to continue to fire, so that at the end of a short time most of the guns will be again in action. If batteries cannot hold their ground, they should be reinforced by others, and not retired and relieved, and when there are a sufficient number in the position they will end by holding their ground very well. But if you replace a battery by another because the first could not hold its ground, the other in its turn will not do so, for it will find itself exposed to the same fire as its predecessor. There is a danger that in this way an enemy superior in number may wear you out, may drain your forces as it were drop by drop, whilst by making all the batteries act together you might have been able to dispute this superiority with him.[1]

Picture to yourself what it means when a gun or a battery is disabled. No. 1 gun has had all its horses killed—one effective round of shrapnel has sufficed to do this damage; No. 2 gun is on the ground with both of the wheels of its carriage broken; No. 3 gun has been hit on the muzzle by an enemy's shell, and is so dented that no projectile can be fired from it; No. 4 gun has had its limber blown up; No. 5 has had its tangent-scale shot away, and cannot be laid; No. 6 gun has had its breech-block demolished. Certainly this battery has been put thoroughly out of action. It must retire, they said in 1866. But if it be ordered to remain in position, what will it do? It gives No. 1 gun four of the horses of No. 3. As for No. 2, you can send for the spare wheel from the wagon (obviously the latter must be near at hand), or you may give it the wheels of No. 3. No. 3 will give its limber to No. 4 gun, and its wheelers also, to replace those killed by the explosion; it will give its tangent-scale to No. 5, and its breech-block to No. 6 gun. In less than ten minutes the battery will be able to open fire with five of its guns. If another comes up on its flank to reinforce it, instead of relieving it, there will be eleven

---

[1] We have no intention, in saying this, to blame the principle of withdrawing guns when on the defensive; it is very judicious to do so when there is no intention of continuing the artillery fight against an enemy who is too superior in number. In that case the artillery is withdrawn from their position in order to put them under cover. It will come into action again at the moment when the enemy's infantry executes its attack. But before this is done, *and in every case of the retirement of artillery, the orders to this effect of the General commanding the troops must first be received.*

guns in action, which will hold their ground far more easily than would the six of the second battery alone. Only No. 3 gun will remain permanently disabled. What shall we do with it? To my idea the best thing to be done is to throw it away, for it is impossible to make any use of it ; that is to say, if it is of cast steel or iron, but not if it is of bronze, for then it can be re-cast. A gun which has been put entirely out of shape by a projectile of the enemy may be considered as permanently out of action, and then the uninjured parts of it should be used to replace those which are damaged in the other guns.

But it is very rarely that a gun is so injured. Given the long range at which two artilleries engage, the actual gun is such a very small mark that the chance that it has of being hit approaches the differential of the calculation of probabilities in high mathematics. Again it is not every projectile which strikes a gun that will knock it so out of shape that it cannot be used any more. There are certainly such exceptional hits. Did not the first shot fired, in 1866, at an absolutely incredible range, by a 4-pr. Field gun, hit a bronze 24-pr. in the fortress of Mayence straight on the muzzle, and so deform the gun that it could no longer be used? But this was such a chance that all the guns of the German artillery might fire for years without such a thing occurring again. What happens far more often is that shells hit a gun without injuring it so much as to put it out of action. I was a witness of one of these cases when, on the 5th of September, I was obliged to bombard Montmédy with Field Artillery. A heavy projectile, fired from a garrison gun, struck a 6-pr Field gun and burst. The man who laid the gun was killed, but the explosion caused no other damage. The gun continued to fire, bearing on its side a glorious scar.

Our artillery, in the course of the war of 1870-1871, conformed to the principle which I have mentioned above ; guns which were out of action did not leave the line of battle so long as the fight was going on ; on the contrary we tried, whenever it was in any way possible, to repair them during the struggle itself, and never during the whole length of the war were batteries seen to relieve others, in order that they might fall to the rear to refit. You may perhaps open the official account at page 1195, and Leo's *The German Artillery* at page 59 of the 8th volume, and say to me, book in hand : " At the battle of Sedan, under your own command, the 4th light battery was relieved by the 3d heavy." This is perfectly true, but that battery was not relieved in order that it might fall to the rear to refit, but entirely because the range at which we were firing was too great for the efficient power of light guns, and because in that position there was no other place in which to put the 3d heavy battery ; for at that time we could not yet dream of occupying that closer position on which later on all the batteries of the Guard could be deployed ; at that time the Bavarian and the 12th corps were engaged in a struggle of which the issue was so doubtful, that it was not at all impossible but that the whole of the Guard might have to go to their assistance and come into action at that point.

But I can quote another example to you which shows what was done to allow batteries which could not hold their ground to remain nevertheless in line. It was in the attack on Le Bourget, on the 21st December 1870. In the belief that the sortie directed against Le Bourget would not assume the gigantic proportions which it developed later, it was thought sufficient at the beginning to send two batteries only (the 4th light and the 4th heavy), under the orders of Captain Seeger, beyond the inundated ground, that they might take up a position on the left of Le Bourget to support those troops of ours which were defending the village.

But when Colonel von Helden, who had accompanied these two batteries, sent to say that the enemy's artillery were too numerous, and that Captain Seeger could not hold his ground against them, we simply sent forward more artillery. First the Horse Artillery Brigade went off at a gallop, and posted itself near Captain Seeger's batteries. Then the batteries which the 1st Division of the Guard sent to his aid also took their place in the position ; lastly the batteries of the 2d Division of the Guard also entered on the scene, and these 11 batteries, or 66 guns, were easily able to hold their own, which the enemy could not do, so retired into the fortress. Captain Seeger was thus placed in a position to refuse to retire, though he had sustained considerable loss.

On the following day he inspected his horses, and found that not one of those which had been engaged had escaped without at least a slight wound. He might, therefore, if he had wished, have returned them all under the heading " Losses."

Perhaps you will also show me on page 59 of the

8th volume of Leo's *German Artillery* the passage
where it is stated that at the battle of Sedan the 5th
and 6th light batteries of the Guard corps were
withdrawn, and you will attribute this withdrawal to
the fact that they could not hold their ground in
their advanced positions. But this retirement was
not on that account, but was necessary in order to
correct the alignment, since these batteries in their
advanced position obscured the field of fire of the
others, which on their part on account of the shape
of the height could not advance farther to the front.
In the whole of the war 1870-71 no battery under
my command ever retired for the reason that it was
compelled to do so by the fire of the enemy. It
very seldom happened that any other battery allowed
itself to be driven back by the enemy's fire. It cannot be said that a battery is forced to retire when it
is drawn back by the permission or the orders of
superior officers, whether they may judge that such
a movement is demanded by circumstances, or do
not consider that there is any necessity that the battery should run the risk of being put out of action.
When batteries have received orders to hold their
ground they would have allowed themselves to be
annihilated rather than have given way (for example, before Vionville, and at Beaune-la-Rolande).

Perhaps you will think that we were, in the war
of 1870, so superior to the enemy, comparing our
system of guns to the defective construction of theirs,
that the relief of batteries was never necessary for us.
Our guns always shot better than those of the French,
until the latter after the loss of their old Field guns
(on Lahitte's system), made their 7 prs. on a new

pattern.   But the French understood very well from
the beginning how to use their masses of artillery,
and the number of projectiles they fired often supplied the place of accuracy of fire, so that they did
not fail in efficiency.

During our advance on Saint-Privat, and during
the artillery fight which followed, against the enemy's
guns on the hill of Saint-Privat, my batteries suffered
considerable loss from the enemy's shells, though by
far the greater part of their heavy losses on this day
must be ascribed to the chassepot fire.   I saw some
limbers blow up and many guns during the cannonade
lying miserably on the ground "winged," as we say,
that is, with a broken wheel.   But not one was withdrawn ; the injured guns were always soon repaired
by the aid of the wagons, which stood very near to
them, so that after the battle I could not exactly tell
how many guns had been put temporarily out of
action.   But when towards the evening it was
necessary to support the infantry in their attack,
everything had been so entirely repaired during the
unceasing cannonade that three guns only could not
immediately be brought up and had to be left in
rear.   These guns would have been undoubtedly lost
if we had retired instead of advancing.   But if we
had sent every gun which was put out of action back
from the line of battle in order that it might refit, in
that case perhaps a moment might have arisen
during the battle when we should have had no guns
in this position, in which case the battle would have
been lost at this point.   By keeping the guns which
were out of action in the line of battle we ran the
risk of losing three guns if we had been obliged to

retire, but perhaps this was the very reason why we were able to hold our ground.

At the battle of Sedan the first six batteries of the artillery of the Guard which advanced into the line of battle were met by a very heavy fire of shell. Splinters of wood and iron flew in all directions, and the wagons of the batteries were freely called upon to remedy defects. I remember to have seen one of these wagons, in rear of the wood at Villers-Cernay, which had not only lost its spare wheel, but also its own wheels, while its horses had been taken to supply the place of a gun team which had been shot. The wagon looked very wretched as it lay there, and reminded one of a torso dug up from the Roman Forum. But, in spite of these losses, our batteries never slackened their fire.

Such details as this cannot be found in the official account, or it would have grown even larger than it is. We have no detailed history of each of the batteries. But I am certain that the experience of all the German artillery during the last war was similar.

The same result is obtained if we compare the manner in which our artillery behaved under infantry fire during the war of 1866 with its conduct under the same circumstances in 1870. In the former of these campaigns it was assumed as a rule that artillery must not be exposed to infantry fire. It was to carefully avoid exposing itself to it, and if the enemy's infantry approached so near that the fire of the skirmishers became effective, then the artillery was to retire out of the reach of this fire, which was considered to be irresistible. We read of only a few

exceptions to this rule, such for example as the case
where Rüstow's brigade remained under fire at
Gitschin, and that of Schmelzer's and Theiler's
batteries which advanced into it at Königgrätz.   But
the cases are much more numerous where the batteries have withdrawn from under infantry fire by
retiring from their position, which was then held to
be a ruling principle.

The behaviour of the German artillery towards
infantry during the last war was entirely different.
The advance of the two batteries (Stumpff's and
Voss's), in the battle of Spicheren, up the lately captured Rothe-berg under the very hottest infantry fire ;
the advance of the guns up to the very counterscarp
of Weissenburg, in order to blow in the gates ; the
pushing forward of guns into Bazeilles in flames, for
the purpose of firing at the very shortest range at
houses which were still in the possession of the
enemy : these facts may all be considered as individual deeds of heroism, and as exceptions to the rule.
But it was the rule in 1870 for the artillery to advance to within infantry ranges, and to hold their
ground there ; this is proved by the presence of artillery masses within that zone in all the battles of the
war.   So early as in the battle of Spicheren the
principal mass of artillery engaged in the action was
posted on the Folster Hill under infantry fire ; at
Wörth, as soon as the opposite side of the valley
had been occupied by infantry, the artillery hurried
over ; in the attack on Elsasshausen 8 batteries took
up their position in the very thick of infantry fire ;
80 guns did the same to prepare the storming of
Fröschwiller.   At Colombey-Nouilly the whole of

the line of artillery which passed the low ground held their own under most effective infantry fire. At Vionville and Mars-la-Tour the whole mass of artillery, 210 guns, was almost constantly within range of a very energetic fire from the enemy's infantry ; it fought under it and held its ground. I have no means of knowing how large a part of the enormous losses of this artillery, in that battle, was due to artillery and how much to infantry fire. But I do not doubt that this artillery, which had alone to repulse many counter-attacks of the enemy's infantry, sustained the greater part of its loss from the chassepot fire. And yet it maintained its position. (The two Horse Artillery batteries of the 3d regiment lost 75 per cent of the horses which they took into action.)

I think also that I can make a guess at the probable loss of the artillery in this battle by the light of my own experience at the battle of Saint-Privat. The batteries of the artillery of the Guard, which lost there 25 per cent of the horses and 20 per cent of the men present in the battle, attributed 75 per cent of this loss to chassepot bullets. Whilst these batteries were, from 2 P.M. until nearly 6 P.M., standing in position under fire in front of Saint-Privat, three French battalions all extended in skirmishing order lay in their front at a range of from 900 to 1000 paces, all their men being covered by the fences between the fields. A similar line lay 100 yards in rear, and a third farther back still. The foremost of these three lines fired without ceasing at the batteries.

I have already mentioned that the General commanding the Guard corps had sent six companies of infantry as an escort to my extended line of artillery; they could not injure the enemy's infantry on account of the short range of the needle-gun, but were kept in little groups in the intervals of the batteries, in order to prevent small bodies of the enemy from rushing in on the guns. When the fire of the enemy's rifles became too troublesome I ordered, at one time, when we had the better of the French artillery, that two batteries should fire on this line of skirmishers. This kept them quiet, and they lay flat in the furrows and left off firing. But at once a superior officer advanced from the hill, bringing reinforcements from the second line to the first; he ordered the fire to begin again, with which object he rode along the whole line and spoke to the men. This was three times repeated. But the enemy's infantry fire could not drive us back.

Later on the batteries advanced to the attack under the very heaviest infantry fire, some of them, as I have before mentioned, to within 300 or 500 paces, where at first they could open fire with half their guns only, the others having been put out of action as they advanced; but they held their ground. It was the same in other battles and with the batteries in the other corps of the German army. German batteries were seldom known to allow themselves to be driven off by infantry fire during the war of 1870-71. But it did happen that batteries, having gone in too close to the enemy, were in a moment almost annihilated; this was the case with many batteries of the 9th corps between Verneville and Amanvillers, and with the batteries at the farm of St. Hubert, for they lost nearly all their horses and men, and became the object of a struggle for their possession. Having been filled up with fresh detachments, they again set to work ; but they did not suffer themselves to be driven back. I could find other examples no doubt in the battles of Noisseville and Beaune-la-Rolande.

There was at one time a strange expression, thus turned "To drive back artillery by the fire of skirmishers." This expression was formerly considered one of great power in instruction in Tactics, and for umpires in manœuvres. For this reason it was received as an axiom in the war of 1866, when we for the first time fought battles in the open field. But in the war of 1870 the artillery scouted it, and refused to be driven back ; for this reason it could not be driven back.

You will observe that in the war of 1866 it was held as a tactical rule that artillery must retire when it had no more ammunition, when it needed to refit, or when it came under fire from the enemy's infantry; it was the exception to remain in position. But in 1870-71 it was the rule to stand fast, and the exception to retire.

This arose from the fact that in 1866 the artillery tried with all their power to avoid losing guns, while in 1870-71 they let them take their chance. ·

In the former war it would have been considered as a disgrace to the artillery if they had lost their guns, in the latter the principle had been established that under certain circumstances it was an honour to have sacrificed them. The loss of a gun in the battle of Beaune-la-Rolande forms a bright episode

in the history of the artillery of the 10th corps.
This is the case also with regard to the guns which
the 9th corps lost at Amanvillers.   I could name to
you two artillery officers of high rank, who emulated
each other's actions in the last war.   One of them
said to the other, " I have an advantage over you in
one point ; I have lost guns and you have not !"

LETTER VI

I WILL no longer try your patience, but will now begin to answer your question as to the causes of the astonishing difference between the effect of the artillery in the two wars, taking as my text the historical facts and such of my own recollections as I have quoted. With regard to the employment of artillery in masses, we certainly adopted it long before the war of 1866. It was a principle, at least in theory, that artillery must be employed in masses, in order to prepare for decisive action at the point where it was desired to produce the crisis. We had learnt from the Napoleonic wars at the beginning of the century that such artillery masses decided the result of the battle. At Friedland General Senarmont advanced his great line of artillery to within 300 or 400 paces of the Russian infantry, and bowed their proud heads with a storm of case-shot. Who had not read of the great French batteries at Austerlitz and Wagram, and who did not know that at Gross-Görschen Napoleon, solely by means of his great mass of artillery, succeeded in stopping the advance of the enemy, until he had assembled sufficient force to change the condition of affairs.

His enemies were compelled to imitate him before they could master him. Old Blücher knew this. When the Duke Eugene of Wurtemberg, in the beginning of the war of 1813, first made his acquaintance and said some flattering words with regard to his cavalry attacks during the Rhine campaigns, Blücher answered, "What is the use of hussars; they are no good against Buonaparte. We must have plenty of guns to do his business."

And on these lines they worked. It is true that in the first battles (Gross-Görschen) we were not always successful, for it is a long way from "what shall we do?" to "how shall we do it?" It is not so easy to overcome the enormous friction which must take place in war as it is to start new theories. Also a novelty does not readily make its way, and we find still, in the battle of Bautzen and the fight at Goldberg, some captains of batteries who did not advance into action with the whole of their guns, but kept back at first a part of their 8 pieces in reserve. But when Napoleon saw at Leipzig the great artillery masses of the allies open fire against him, he cried angrily, "At last they have learnt something."

Our artillery was organised with respect to mobilisation on the basis afforded by the experience of the war of 1813-15. This organisation was continued in its entirety up to 1866, except some few alterations which were the natural consequences of changes introduced in the general organisation of the army (such, for example, as the temporary allotment of four small divisions of infantry to a corps).

This organisation of the artillery with a view to mobilisation should have opened the way for the use of artillery in masses, for it gave little more than half of the artillery in the corps to the divisions, and told off the remainder as reserve artillery. Of this reserve artillery many corps attached a part to the reserve cavalry, but as this reserve cavalry was also intended to be used at decisive moments, so the artillery was expected to be able, when the moment arrived, to prepare the decisive action. The disposable mass of artillery held in reserve was further increased by the batteries which were, by the organisation, attached to the infantry reserve (for example, two with the 7th corps in 1866), and thus the mass of artillery held in reserve amounted to more than a half of the total. When this force had been brought to the point where it was proposed to take decisive action, it was intended that the batteries which by the organisation were attached to the infantry should unite with them, and that thus more than three-quarters of the total available strength should be present for use at the decisive point on the field of battle. In Austria they went even farther, and formed an army reserve artillery in addition to the corps reserve artillery (in the Northern army, in 1866, there were 4 divisions of 4 batteries of 8 guns, that is, 128 guns), which was intended to prepare the attack on the principal tactical point on the field. All these arrangements were most excellent, so long as the experiences of the war of 1812-15 were taken as a guide.

But I beg you to observe that these great artillery reserves were not intended to be used until the time

K

when the moment for decisive action was believed to
have arrived, that is to say, at the time when the
decisive point had been selected, and it was desired
either to deliver or to ward off an attack on it ; and
that they ought logically to be kept back out of
action until a decision had been arrived at as to
which was the decisive point.   Napoleon I., our great
teacher in tactics and strategy, never did otherwise,
and kept his great artillery masses always in hand,
using them as trumps, when he proposed to strike
the decisive blow.   What was the reason for this
mode of proceeding ?   Because he would not allow
his artillery to get out of hand until, from the
development of the course of the fight, he had
decided where he must use it.

But with the introduction of rifled guns this
reason for holding back the great masses of artillery
lost its force.   The artillery of the Napoleonic wars,
which was of but little use at a range exceeding 1000
paces, and which, in order to produce a decisive
effect, was obliged to approach to within 300 or
400 paces of the enemy (for example, Senarmont at
Friedland), was undoubtedly let out of hand when
once it had been sent into action, and it was then
impossible to count with any certainty upon the
power of employing it anywhere else during the
same battle.   But an artillery which can produce
good effect at a range of from 2000 to 4000 yards,
and which in the ordinary course of the artillery
fight need not act at a shorter range, is not let go,
but is held fast in the hand of the leader of artillery,
even when it has opened fire.   He is still in a
position to move this artillery to another point, and

the artillery is in a condition to carry out his order, so long as the fight has not yet assumed a decisive character.

Therefore the General takes his artillery into use, even though he intends to prepare the decision with it, and no longer holds it back inactive in reserve until the arrival of the decisive moment.

The extraordinary increase of range afforded to the artillery by the introduction of rifled guns has another effect, namely, that it will more rarely be necessary to change the position of batteries when it is desired to fire on the decisive point, and that it will, as a rule, be sufficient to change the direction of their fire. Remember that the fighting front of an army-corps extends for the great distance of four miles (English). A gun which can make good practice at 4000 yards has the power, if it be posted in the centre of the line, of firing on any point along the whole front, granted always that the ground in front is exceptionally open and free from cover for the enemy. But a gun which was of little use over 1000 paces, and which in order to produce a decisive effect was obliged to go in to the short range of 500 paces, can command only 1000 paces of the front of battle, that is to say, about one-seventh. It was impossible to reckon on the assistance of such a gun in preparing the decision, when this was to take place at a greater distance than 1000 paces from it.

So long as we were armed with S.B. guns it was therefore an absolute necessity to hold back a considerable mass of artillery in reserve. This necessity diminishes with every increase of the range of guns, and at the present ranges of rifled guns ceases to exist.

But if the necessity of holding back artillery in reserve no longer exists, the contrary becomes at once the rule, namely, to bring forward as much artillery as possible into action at the beginning ot the fight. Picture to yourself two strong and well-trained bodies of artillery, who find themselves face to face, of which one comes into action as a whole, and the other by successive fractions ; will not the latter be destroyed piecemeal, before it can fire a shot ? This is so clear and distinct that I can hear you ask, why were not our organisation, and the tactical principles of the use of artillery, corrected at the time of the introduction of rifled guns ? To this I must answer : " We always leave the Council-house wiser than when we entered it." The new invention ot rifled guns found very energetic enemies among our highest authorities in artillery. It was considered too scientific by the men who had gained their experience of war in the years 1813 to 1815. One of them broke out into this jest : " We want trained (gezogene) Generals, but not rifled (gezogene) guns." His dislike to the new invention went so far that, as he lay on his death-bed, he begged that at his funeral the salute over his grave might be fired with S.B. and not with rifled guns.

Our entire experience in large wars dated from the struggles of 1813 to 1815, for we cannot count the campaigns of 1848 and 1849 as great wars. It was no wonder then that much weight was attributed to the doubts of the heroes of that period, and that the leaders of the artillery hesitated to predict all the consequences of the invention, until they had practical proof of its efficiency, that is to say, until it had done good work in the field during a great war. The war of 1864 afforded us no experience as to the tactics of Field Artillery on a large scale, since the fights in the field which took place during that war were of only a minor importance as regarded masses of troops, especially of artillery, while wider experience had been gained only in matters affecting a siege.

It was very different in Austria. The war of 1859 in Italy, and especially the battle of Solferino, had made the Austrian army fully sensible of the predominating influence of a mass of rifled guns which is brought into action at the right moment. The same day which, on account of the splendid and victorious bayonet-charge on the right, by which Benedek saved the whole army, saw the birth of the prevailing idea that the bayonet was the only efficient rival to arms of precision, that same day of battle begot in the Austrian army the determination both to supply the artillery with guns of precision and to use the latter in masses earlier than had been the custom. In 1864 the Austrian troops in Schleswig were armed altogether with rifled guns, though in 1859 they had not one, and in the little fight of Veile they brought up early the batteries of the corps reserve artillery, and after they had prepared the attack, then followed their heroic charges with the bayonet.

As was natural, the Austrian army in 1866 used their corps reserve artillery far less as reserves than as great bodies of troops whose weight was to be thrown as soon as possible into the scale, often even at the beginning of the action. This was easier to them, in the defensive actions of Skalitz, Gitschin, Soor, and Königgrätz, than it was to the attacking army, who had with difficulty to deploy its long columns out of the mountain defiles ; but it is clear from the character of the battles which arose from an accidental meeting, such as Nachod and Trautenau, that at that time the Austrian army had recognised more distinctly than the Prussian the principle of engaging the reserve artillery early in the battle. Only the army reserve artillery was held back as a true reserve, and it thus was of less use than the others.

Would the battle of Königgrätz have degenerated into a defeat on so large a scale, if the Austrian army reserve artillery had been divided into two halves, of which one, in conjunction with the corps reserve artillery, might have hindered our 1st and Elbe armies in passing the Bistritz, while the other might have stoutly defended the heights of Horenowes against the advancing 2d army? I think not.

You will perhaps tell me that we might also, as well as the Austrians, have deduced these rules from the war of 1859, since some of our officers were present as spectators during that war. But as a rule every army holds to its own form of development, and we may congratulate ourselves that our highest authorities did not make the same deductions as did the Austrians from the results of the campaign of 1859, and thus did not adopt the Shock Tactics for infantry, but trusted to the carefully-trained fire of the breech-loader, which is acknowledged to have had the principal share in gaining for us the laurels of 1866.

Also you must not forget to take into consideration that the Prussian artillery of 1866 was not all armed with rifled guns. Six-sixteenths of the batteries had S.B., ten-sixteenths rifled, guns. Among the latter two-sixteenths, that is to say, two batteries per corps, had been armed with rifled guns in great haste at the moment of mobilisation, although they knew only how to work with smooth-bores. For nearly half the armament the old and tried principles of the War of Liberation were still in force, and there was no just ground for inventing new principles for the other half, for the army would have regarded them with mistrust, since they had been nowhere tried, had not as it were any standing, and had not been proved to be necessary by any experience in war.

We find in the Prussian artillery in 1866 only one item of organisation which, since it was absent up to that time, appears to have been borrowed from the Austrian artillery. This is the formation for the 1st army of a large army reserve artillery, which resembles the Austrian army reserve artillery. It amounted to 4 brigades of 4 batteries, therefore to 96 guns, of which half were rifled and half S.B.; the latter were for the Horse Artillery. But this organisation had as little direct effect upon us as upon the Austrians, as far as regards the making use of large masses at the beginning of the action. Any one who has ever had the opportunity of observing the movement of large masses of troops will see at once that so large a mass of artillery, which marches under one command, and also as a rule on one road, cannot be brought up early into the foremost line ot battle ; as indeed it should not be, but should be kept back in reserve. " Divide to march and concentrate to fight," is the secret of the great art of moving troops, but even with this secret it cannot be learnt at once any more than any other science or art ; it must be learnt by practice after it has been studied in theory. But it is sufficient as to the matter in question to state, that it was not desired to use great concentrated masses of artillery at the very beginning of the action.

Thus it happened that they were allowed to march in the extreme rear. The great masses of the ammunition-columns belonged also to the reserve artillery. They covered the roads for miles, and the foremost gun followed after the hindmost efficient man of the other arms. Thus it was that, even a detached army-corps marching alone, should it during the march come unexpectedly in contact with the enemy, found its great mass of artillery to be more than a day's march distant from the field of battle, and could only get them up, even with the greatest exertions, towards the end of the day. In the case where the whole army marched concentrated, it was impossible to get up the reserve artillery in time for any but a pitched battle. Thus it failed us at Münchengrätz and Gitschin ; while at Nachod, Trautenau, and Soor, it could not get into position until very late, until indeed night began to fall.

The sight of the long columns of guns and wagons, with which the reserve artillery covered the road for several miles, filled the officers of the Staff with a natural anxiety lest these clumsy masses might block up the defiles where the road was bad, and might thus cause considerable annoyance. This is why a part of the reserve artillery, when we crossed the Silesian mountains, did not follow at once in rear of the other troops, but was left one or two marches in rear, so that, when the corps at the end of its day's march came in contact with the enemy, the reserve artillery would have had to make three full marches in one day in order to take part in the action, an exertion which was beyond the power of the teams.

The almost simultaneous engagements which took place with the enemy at Nachod, Trautenau, München-chengrätz, Skalitz, Soor, and Gitschin, partial as they were, made our leaders sensible how great was the effect of the numerical superiority which the Austrian artillery showed at the beginning of the fight. On this account orders were given at various times, which all tended to the more timely arrival of the artillery in masses. But such orders, when they are given suddenly, and when the whole instruction of the troops in time of peace is opposed to them, as are also the organisation and all previous principles, must be partly rendered inoperative by that friction which has always to be struggled against in time of war. There is then no wonder if a case occurred where an artillery officer wished to trot through a defile, while the officer commanding an infantry division refused to allow him to push in front of his troops ; the division moved on in the position which it had originally occupied in the order of march, so that the artillery again arrived too late. Or what wonder if an artillery and a cavalry commander, on an occasion when both arms occupied the same camp, disputed with each other as to which should lead the march, and so effectually barred the road for each other that they both arrived too late.   In accordance with the above-mentioned orders a few brigades were, at Königgrätz, brought up in fairly good time into the action.   Both rifled brigades of the reserve artillery of the 1st army were available for use shortly after the passage of the Bistritz, and one brigade of the Elbe army also came up early into the fight.

As for the artillery of the Guard, I succeeded in bringing the reserve artillery under fire very soon after the arrival of the batteries of the advanced guard, but to do this I had to ask so much from the teams that some of the horses fell dead in their harness.   If you measure on the map the space from our bivouac at Rettendorf by Königinhof and Chotieborek to a point south of Jericek, which I got over without breaking the trot, and also consider that the country is very hilly, and that I was, for the greater part of the time, trotting across country through high corn, by the side of the roads on which the infantry were marching, you will be able to imagine the exertions which we had to make in order to answer the sudden call for artillery in the foremost line, while our place, according to regulation, was in the extreme rear.   But the other reserve artilleries must have suffered from even greater difficulties.   That of the 6th corps first came into action at Sweti late in the afternoon, while the following, to the best of my knowledge, did not fire a shot at Königgrätz: the reserve artillery of the 1st corps, the 8 batteries of Horse Artillery of the reserve artillery of the 1st army, and 2 batteries of the cavalry division of the 2d army.

It is not then sufficient to wish that masses of artillery shall be brought up in time ; it is necessary also to have learnt and practised the manner of doing it. There is, moreover, one circumstance which cannot be left unmentioned, since in the war of 1866 it frequently prevented our artillery from coming into action in time, and from remaining in action sufficiently long. I mean the reckless advance of our brave infantry, who, feeling the superiority of their breech-loader, and of their training, stopped at nothing, and went straight at any enemy without regard to his strength or weapons, and thus masked the fire of their own artillery, and did not even give the reserve artillery time to get up. The result has justified this behaviour of the infantry, which has also excited the wonder of our veterans of the War of Liberation. One of them replied to the statement that the men of 1813 had been our models and masters : " We were good enough men in the year '13, but we did not go ahead so foolhardily as you." The result, as I said, justified the behaviour of the infantry when they had to do with the muzzle-loader only. But against the breech-loader of 1870 it would have led to too terrible a loss.

It is a fact also that there were some among the infantry leaders who were of the opinion that they did not need artillery, and could carry out the business alone. This opinion was in accordance with the efforts which were made, about the middle of the century, to find some sort of invention for the infantry, such as battalion guns, etc., since artillery was too expensive. It was received with very comic dislike by the artillery, who complained of the infantry, that they were in too great a hurry to finish the fight, and wanted to keep all the glory for themselves. The war of 1866 lasted too short a time to allow of use being made during the war itself of the experiences which were gained in it. With the exception of the final fight at Blümenau, all the combats of the great war in Bohemia took place in the short space of seven or eight days. So much the more eagerly did we set to work, during the peace which followed, to remedy all the defects in the army which had been brought to notice during the war. The highest authorities of the army set the example with inimitable self-sacrifice. Instead of revelling in self-satisfaction and self-content at the successful results, and crowning themselves with the laurels which they had won, they sought out the causes of all the defects which they had observed, and considered them carefully, so that they might be avoided in a future war.

The artillery had to consider the manner in which the leaders of troops should use that arm. We had during the war attained to the knowledge that, since the introduction of rifled guns and the increase of range thus obtained, artillery which had been pushed into an action is no longer let out of hand, but still remains at the disposal of the General, and further, that the artillery has now a wider zone of efficiency, and thus, without changing its position, each battery can co-operate with the others in fire on a distant point of attack. In accordance with these decisions it was laid down that it is not necessary to hold back any artillery in reserve, but that as numerous an artillery as possible should be brought into an action at the earliest possible moment. This idea was given expression by a change of name. The name " reserve artillery " was abolished, and changed into " corps artillery." Many philosophers have said " What's in a name ? " But you think with me on this subject, that the army is not composed of philosophers. On the contrary, they are men, and thus human, and in the stress of battle pay little attention to abstract principles. Names, gaudy uniforms, orders, and an empty stomach, all things which a philosopher treats with contempt, play a decisive part in war. Thus the change of name by regulation was an act with far-reaching results. When the reserve artillery had been re-named " corps artillery," every leader of troops, and every Staff-officer, was at once compelled to recognise that they were no longer to be held in reserve, but had become a part of the line of battle.

Together with this change of name came also a change of the position in the order of march which had, as a rule, been occupied by the corps artillery, and on the same principle by the divisional artillery. It was to march far nearer to the front than in former wars, and thus all artillery would be able to arrive earlier on the field of battle than formerly. Thus we find that in the war of 1870 the battery of the advanced guard marched almost always, in the German army, in rear of the leading battalion ; the artillery brigade of a division marched in rear of the leading regiment ; while the mass of the corps artillery marched, when the corps was moving concentrated on one road, in rear of the leading brigade, or at latest in rear of the leading division.

But an effort was made, whenever it was in any way possible, to use several parallel roads for an army-corps. If two were available the corps artillery generally marched in rear of the foremost brigade of one of the divisions; when three roads could be used, the corps artillery marched in the centre near the head of the column. It was thus the rule (naturally not without an exception) that 11 batteries (viz. the 4 of one of the divisions and the 7 of the corps artillery) out of the 15 batteries of the corps marched well to the front, accompanied only by from 6 to 9 out of the 25 to 29 battalions which belonged to the corps. This order of march clearly prescribes that in an action two-thirds of the artillery should be available for use, while as yet only a quarter or a third of the infantry can be in position. This proportion betokens an intention of using as much artillery as possible at the beginning, and to allow only so many infantry to march in front of them as may be needed for the protection of the artillery on the march and as their escort in their first position, from which it is intended to occupy the enemy until a decision can be arrived at as to the decisive point to be attacked.

The difference in the strength of the two arms as they first advance to the battle will become yet greater, as soon as the artillery moves forward to their position at a more rapid pace, while the infantry can follow only at a walk. Thus it often happened that only a few battalions had reached the fighting line when the artillery was already under fire, and that, at the commencement, only one wing of an artillery position, from one to two miles in length, was covered by infantry, the other being at too great a distance from the line of march ; in this case the other wing was covered by cavalry (for example, the artillery line of the 5th and 11th corps at Sedan). It also sometimes happened that the great line of artillery pushed forward in front of the whole of their corps, though now and then not without great danger of a catastrophe : for example, the 9th corps at Saint-Privat.

In spite of the more advanced position which it held in the order of march, the artillery could not have come so quickly in masses into position as it did, as a rule, in 1870, unless in time of peace they had themselves contributed their part. They would have been little fitted by their earlier instruction for undertaking such long forced marches. The principles of this instruction, up to 1866, were drawn from the experiences of the war from 1813 to 1815, but were afterwards modified in accordance with the experience gained in the war of 1866, which now influenced the instruction.

At the time of smooth-bore guns and muskets it was possible to stand safely at a distance of one (English) mile from the enemy's guns. At this distance the lines of artillery could quietly deploy, and when they received orders to move into action, an advance of 1500 paces was quite sufficient, in order to fire on the enemy's position at the most favourable range of 1000 paces. Very little was thus demanded from the mobility of the artillery. Field Artillery required to trot only a few hundred paces.

Some inflexible gunners of the old school at one time declared that it was ruin to the existence of true artillery to allow the N.C. officers of Field Artillery to be mounted, and no longer to make them march, stiff and grim, with their packs on their backs, in front of the leaders of their guns. Horse Artillery was indeed called upon to move very fast, but when it had rapidly passed over a total space of 1500 paces, galloping over the last 500, in order to reach its position, it was then considered to have done its utmost, indeed all that was necessary or possible.

The introduction of rifled guns and the experience which was obtained in 1866 considerably altered the demands which must be made on the mobility of the artillery. The necessity of employing the great artillery masses early at the beginning of the fight demands quickness of movement, not over distances of 200 or at most of 1500 paces, but over distances measured by miles and days' marches. In order to come in time into action when moving from Rettendorf by Königinhof and Chotieborek to a point south of Jericek, I had to trot 14 (English) miles in a hilly country. And even this, as far as one can see, will not always be enough in the future. Even when the artillery had been given a position in the order of march nearer to the head of the column, the corps artillery was yet over 4 (English) miles from the front of the advanced guard; when therefore the latter encountered the enemy, and the General determined to bring his artillery into action, the corps artillery had to be brought forward with a good long trot, if it were desired to be certain that

they would be on the ground in less than an hour,
including the despatch of the order and the advance
of the guns. When the force is in bivouac the
artillery masses cannot be brought nearer to the
enemy in future than in times past, since in bivouac,
especially at night, artillery is defenceless and must
be left in rear. It was thus foreseen that forced
marches, such as that from Rettendorf to Jericek,
would become the rule, and indeed this was the case
in 1870 ; for example, the corps artillery of the 3d
and 9th corps at Vionville, and the Guard corps at
Sedan, etc. But even greater demands than these
must be made upon the artillery, when it is a
question of moving artillery from one flank of the
theatre of war to the other, or of sending them
quickly to bodies of troops which have been detached
to a distance ; for example, the 1st Horse Artillery
battery of the Guard marched, on the 13th of
August, 32 (English) miles from Bermering by Oron
to Dieulouard, where it encamped on the same
evening, and the 3d Horse Artillery battery of the
Guard marched in one day from Saint-Mihiel to
Saint-Privat, where it took part in the battle. This
will also be the case when the artillery of corps,
which have been held back in reserve, is pushed
forward quickly into the foremost line of battle, in
order to strengthen the masses of artillery ; for
example, the corps artillery of the 3d corps at
Verneville.

On the other hand, since the introduction of
rifled guns, it is considered less necessary that
artillery should gallop over short distances. For at
the great range at which fire can now be opened the

L

enemy will often first become aware of our guns when the latter open fire; as a rule he will first see them at the moment of unlimbering, when they show themselves over the crest which serves as their position. It is no longer, as it used to be, desirable to gain a few seconds, in order to fire the first shot quickly; on the contrary, a long time is now taken over the first shots, in order to lay and observe them quietly and accurately. It is now a matter of hours, which we must endeavour to gain in coming into position.[1]

With a full knowledge of this necessity the Prussian artillery, after the war of 1866, practised getting over extremely long distances at a steady unbroken pace, in preference to galloping with a rush over short spaces. They learnt how to keep their horses in wind, and to make quick forced marches, in preference to learning elegant peace-manœuvres. At the inspection by the Inspector-General the regiments of artillery were directed to await his orders in bivouac, at a distance of from 3 to 4 (English) miles from the practice-ground. They were then ordered, at the sound of the Alarm, to make their way to their position by a rapid

---

[1] At the battle of Sedan the corps artillery of the Guard marched 9 (English) miles on the road from Carignan to Villers-Cernay at a gentle trot, in one spell; after this I allowed them to dismount and to get their breath for a moment during the reconnaissance, for the horses were blown. After a halt of from five to ten minutes the batteries climbed up the steep hill out of the ravine, not, however, in a showy gallop, but laboriously, assisted by the gunners, some men of the Fusilier regiment of the Guard, and some dismounted Hussars, who pulled and shoved at the guns. The long-continued trot had enabled us to bring up our artillery mass several hours earlier into position, and thus we could employ the necessary minutes in selecting the best position and in occupying it quietly.

forced march. Thus the artillery were systematically practised in time of peace in quickly concentrating into large masses from a distance.

But another factor must not be forgotten, since it materially assisted the concentration of the artillery masses at the beginning of an action. I mentioned to you in an earlier letter the feeling of uneasiness which the leaders of the artillery in the war of 1866 endured, fearing that they had not done enough. In the knowledge that they could distinguish themselves more in this war (of 1870), every one of them burned with the desire to prove it, and their longing to get at the enemy was thus, if possible, greater even than that which every Prussian officer feels. Thence it came that they not only carried out every order willingly and readily, but also that such orders were more often carried into execution before they were received, on the responsibility of the officers themselves. It was often necessary to take care that this good was not overdone. Allow me to quote to you some examples from my personal experience. In the battle of Saint-Privat, as we were approaching the enemy's position, I received an order from the General in command, after his reconnaissance had been completed, to call up the corps artillery, which on the march followed the 1st Division of the Guard. I sent off an adjutant, and turned towards the General, to make some remark as to my view of the situation. But my first sentence was interrupted by a report from Colonel von Scherbening—" The corps artillery has come up, sir." I was immensely astonished, and said, " How have you got here so soon." He answered, " Lieutenant B. brought me

the order."—"But," said I, "you were marching in
rear of the 1st Guard Division."—"I was there,"
replied the brave Colonel, "but as soon as I heard
the first gun I gave the order to trot. There is
plenty of room near the Division, and I thought to
myself, if I am not wanted there, I can always be
ordered to halt and wait." Indeed the whole mass
of the corps artillery trotted up in column of batteries
on the left flank of the 1st Guard Division, and filled
the air with the thundering rattle of 100 carriages.
Thus it came into action by batteries at the same
time as the artillery of the 1st Division, and opened
the fight on the part of the Guard with 54 guns,
long before the foremost infantry soldier had come
within range of the enemy's shells.

But this is not all. When those batteries of the
enemy, which were at first pushed to the front on
the heights of Saint-Privat, had been withdrawn, our
line of artillery advanced nearer by batteries, in order
not to waste our ammunition by firing at too long a
range. I, fortunately, at this moment, received from
the General instructions which amounted to permission to move up in front of the artillery line, and to
direct the fire. I could see then from my position
on the hill that a strong advanced skirmisher line
of the enemy, concealed by the furrows which ran
through the apparently open ground, were hurrying
towards the advancing artillery, in order to prepare
an ambush for the latter, which the battery commanders, marching as they were in a valley, could
not see. I came up in time to be able to carry out
the orders of the General, to advance no farther to
the front. Troops which are so hot for the fight,

that one has nothing to do but to caution them against a too bold advance, can certainly be easily collected in masses against the enemy.

General von Dresky writes: On the 6th of August we had marched 13 (English) miles up and down hill, and were comfortably quartered in Ottweiler, when suddenly an order arrived, to call the troops to arms and to hasten to Saarbruck with all our force. I received the order at 3 o'clock; at 3.30 the corps artillery began to move, starting to hasten over the 15 miles which separated us from Saarbruck. The country was terribly hilly. But we never put on the drag-shoe; that would have delayed us too long. The brigade of Horse Artillery took only 3 hours to get over this 15 miles of hilly but excellent road. At 6.30 I was able to report their arrival on the battlefield to General von Alvensleben. The Field batteries arrived an hour and a half later.

He writes again: On the 16th, we marched early in the morning from our bivouac at Pagny and Arnaville to the north in the valley of the Moselle. At 10 o'clock I received an order to push on as quickly as possible with all my force. At Tronville I received further orders. We had now to cross the hills on the slant by narrow stony roads. The Horse Artillery Brigade did the 7 miles to the field of battle in three-quarters of an hour. The Field batteries could not come on so fast, and the head of their column first arrived three-quarters of an hour later.

Speaking of the fight at Beaune-la-Rolande, he writes: The Horse Artillery Brigade on this day marched 31 miles to the field of battle.

The war of 1870-71 is rich in such events. I should weary you if I were to relate to you those of which I have heard from the lips of my comrades, or if I borrowed from the number of analogous cases which the official account describes. It would always be the same song in another key. But this desire for the fight, this initiative on the part of the artillery, must exist, if it is to be possible to bring up large masses of artillery into the action at the right moment; it is only thus that the friction which opposes such an obstacle can be overcome. This longing for the fight, and this initiative, cannot and will not die out, for the artillery will always remain conscious that, in order to do its work well, the first necessity is to get well into position. How this is to be done it has shown in 1870, after that it had learnt it in 1866.

LETTER VII

THE SPIRIT OF CASTE

THE statements in my last letter with regard to the circumstances which made it possible to bring up the artillery in 1870 and 1871, at the right time, and in sufficient masses, will be incomplete unless I mention another factor, which formerly hindered the artillery from coming up at the right time, but has now been removed. I refer to the spirit of caste and the isolation of the artillery. It is true that this arm had already, in 1866, got rid of this feeling for separation, but its consequences were still at work here and there, and may be regarded as being first entirely abolished in 1870. In order to prove this, I must go far back, not quite so far as did a certain fire-worker in his report upon a fuse, for he began with Nimrod ; but I must commence at the beginning of the century.

You already know that the artillery took up a recognised position as an arm at a later date with us than with other armies—for example, with the French. Up to the time when, about the beginning of the century, the artillery was placed, as a special weapon, under the command of a Royal Prince as Inspector-General, gunners (with the exception of the Horse Artillery) were regarded among us more as a species

of skilled mechanics than as soldiers. This was in
part their own fault. The little that they had to
learn more than other soldiers, in order to discharge
the duties of their profession, was exaggerated by
them into a great science, which, being surrounded
with an impenetrable veil of mystery, kept soldiers
of the other arms so much the more at a distance, as
its substance appeared more wearisome by the diffuse-
ness of its treatment. I need only refer to the
chapter, "On the art of making paper and paste,"
with which, at that time, every manual of artillery
began, or to the handbooks of geography, history, and
the higher mathematics, which formerly formed part
of the equipment of the limber of every field gun.
The gunner of those days took pleasure in a mask
of learning under a veil of mystery, which, though it
estranged the other arms from the artillery, yet
caused them to entertain a certain respect for it on
account of its unknown erudition. But the young
gunner, when he had lifted the veil, and knew that
there was not so very much hidden behind it, after
he had recovered from his disillusion, was in the
position of the youth who unveiled the statue of Sais.
"What he saw and learnt there his tongue never told."
And he also soon found a pleasure in posing, among
his comrades of the other arms, as a member of the
scientific arm, and as something peculiar. There
were long ago, however, some among gunners who
knew that the reputation of wisdom could not alone
conquer for the arm that position which would secure
for it such co-operation in war as they desired, and
that a closer union, social as well as tactical, to the
other arms would assist their power of mutual aid in

war. You know well the influence which social relations have on tactical co-operation. Men are not
machines, and those who know each other well, and
live together on equal terms, work more harmoniously
together in action, than they would if they were
strangers to each other. The tendency of the arm to
draw nearer to the others in social matters became more
and more general, and we may truly say that some
time before 1866 it had already got rid of the spirit
of caste which was formerly inherent in it, and that it
had attained to a social equality with the other arms.

But there still continued to be a certain line of
division between them, which arose from various
regulations and their consequences. At the head of
these regulations stood the "promise of secrecy."
By it every officer of artillery was strictly forbidden
to betray anything whatever of the secrets of the
artillery beyond the regiment. But he learnt no
secrets at all, and as on the other hand he was not
told that what he learnt was not a secret, he never
knew whether he was not divulging secrets whenever
he spoke about his arm, and he gladly stopped all
conversation on the subject by saying that these
were technical things about which he was not at
liberty to speak. As for the expression "technical,"
it frightened every officer of the other arms, for he
thought that it was equivalent to "wearisome pedantry." It sometimes happened that an old field-
officer of one of the other arms would, on questions
connected with the tactical employment of artillery,
follow the opinion of a young lieutenant, who happened to be in command of the battery which was
attached to his command ; and this on "technical

grounds," which could not be more distinctly put into words. The gunner was very much afraid of betraying secrets ; but how could he betray them when he did not know any ? I can assure you of this at least, that I myself never learnt one. Ah ! I am afraid that, by saying this, I have betrayed to you the very greatest secret of all.

There was an earlier regulation respecting the artillery which still more interfered with the tactical employment of that arm, since by it every artillery officer was made personally responsible for its employment in action, and in manœuvres, even when he had to obey the orders of a superior officer. If an artillery officer received an order with regard to some tactical disposition which he did not consider to be right, he was compelled to protest, and was held guiltless only in the case when he was, in consequence of his protest, expressly relieved from responsibility. I remember well some manœuvres, during which I, as a lieutenant, was ordered to take up with my division a position, which in peace time was charming, but which in war would have had many disadvantages. I protested against the order to the General who commanded the advanced guard, who expressly relieved me from my responsibility, and laughing said that I was right, but that we were merely at manœuvres, and that he only wanted to get off a couple of rounds quickly. Soon after up came the Inspector of Artillery, who was in command of us, Lieutenant-General von Strotha, well known in the artillery. He disapproved of my position, and asked me if I had protested against the order ; when I answered that I had he said, " That is lucky for you ; if you had not I should have put you in arrest."

In consequence of this principle, indiscipline, in-subordination, the spirit of contradiction, and the art of making difficulties were officially and skilfully taught to the young artillery officer. It was indeed too tempting to a young lieutenant to be authorised by it to give tactical lessons to an old field-officer of the other arms. Many a field-officer of the infantry and cavalry, when at manœuvres he received from some beardless subaltern of artillery, whom he had ordered to go to the right, the answer that on technical grounds he preferred to go to the left, and that the Major must free him from responsibility, thought it better not to argue with him, and said politely to the young fellow, who would probably in an hour cease to be under his orders : "Do as you like ; you understand the technicalities of your own arm best," and so rode on, thinking within himself what the old Napoleon once said : "Let the gunners alone, they are an obstinate lot." But no one can blame these Majors if they preferred to have nothing to do with the arm, and in consequence never used it, or at least let it do as it liked, rather than meet with constant contradiction or expose themselves to be instructed by a junior officer. If then, in the war of 1866, it may have happened that the artillery in some battle received no orders, or was left behind and was entirely forgotten by the Generals, this fact may in great part be attributed to the condition of things brought about by the above-mentioned regu-lation. And if many infantry Generals, after they had won the victory in 1866, although they were not at all or not sufficiently assisted by the artillery, felt a certain triumphant joy at the fact that the scientific arm was not needed, I for one cannot wonder at it.

In peculiar opposition to the above-mentioned tendency of the artillery to amalgamate with the other arms tactically and socially, we find mentioned in many writings an outspoken desire to argue, and to prove practically, that artillery is an independent arm. For my part I can find nothing intelligible in these words. I should like very much to know how an army-corps would act independently if it were composed of artillery alone. Under the present system of conducting war there is only one arm that can be called independent, and that is the infantry ; there were formerly armies of cavalry, but that was long ago. The infantry is strictly the Army, the nation in arms. It needs the assistance of other arms, and these are, and will continue to be, auxiliary arms to the infantry, and can fulfil their object well and rise to their highest efficiency only when they are always conscious of their character as auxiliary arms, and have no other aim than to help the army, that is, the infantry. If, on the other hand, the artillery starts the pretension that it is an independent arm, it will desire that the battle shall be conducted solely in accordance with its tactics, that the other arms shall serve only to cover its positions, and that no attack shall be made until it has prepared the way. But this implies a mistake as to their relations, for the artillery should prepare and help where the army, that is, the infantry (or in cavalry actions the cavalry), wishes to attack.

If these relations be reversed the artillery will often be an impediment instead of an aid, and a burden in place of being an auxiliary. The infantry, that is, the army, will not and cannot be guided by the auxiliary arm ; in no case when the artillery arrives late will the infantry wait for it, for it will not allow itself to be shot down while it waits, and it will, in that case, prefer to carry the fight through without artillery. The first battles of the war of 1866 showed distinctly to those gunners who up to that time had raved about the independence of the arm, that it is in a position to be of use only when it always remembers its character as an auxiliary arm, and is always ready to *help*.

The war did not last sufficiently long to give practical expression to this sudden change of opinion. But immediately after the war it manifested itself in speech and in writing. In opposition to the tendency to treat the arm as independent, the wish was generally expressed among the artillery to give up their independent organisation, and like the cavalry to pass at once, in time of peace, under the Generals commanding corps. When the war of 1870 broke out, a zealous desire was shown, both during the mobilisation and on the march, to make the artillery useful to the other arms and to help them, and, on the other hand, not to be troublesome with self-pretence, or with a tendency to raise difficulties. If, on the one hand, in 1866, there were loud cries when a General once asked for a team from a battery to bring up bread for the infantry, that " the artillery was a combatant arm and not a transport train " ; on the other hand, in 1870, during the first days of the march, batteries offered of their own accord to do this sort of work, in order to help the heavily-loaded and wearied infantry. The artillery can easily do such duty, as it is not nearly so tried by the march itself as is the infantry, which has to carry a pack, or the cavalry, which must reconnoitre in addition to the actual march, an addition which considerably extends the distance passed over. I could tell you of many other occasions on which, before the battle, the artillery made itself useful to the other arms, but it will be sufficient, in order not to weary you, to tell you that I then heard some of our Generals say, before the first battles : " It is marvellous ; the artillery in this war helps every one, makes no difficulties, and thus is no trouble to us ; it even asks nothing for itself." In this manner the artillery during the first marches became honoured and useful to the other arms ; it was everywhere welcome, and all things were made easy to it when it wanted to get forward to the fight.

You can picture to yourself what this means in practice, if, for example, you imagine the Staff of a division on the march, when the officer commanding its artillery has, in the course of the first day's march, made all sorts of difficulties with the General. The consequences are friction, hard words, ill-humour, and estrangement on both sides. On the march, or in quarters, neither individual wishes to have much intercourse with the other. The General calls for the gunner only when it is absolutely necessary ; the latter waits for his orders. As a rule he rides with the divisional Staff. But it is no wonder if he gladly prolongs the time during which his presence is needed with his batteries. Some information about the enemy is received from the advanced patrols in

front of the head of the advanced guard. The
General talks over the situation with the Chief of his
Staff, and then issues his orders. These eventually
arrive at the officer commanding the artillery, but it
may well happen that he has spent some time in
seeking for them. On their receipt he will come to
the General, and must first ask to be informed as to
the enemy and the particular plan which has been
arranged. He thus becomes troublesome, for the
General is in a hurry ; either he has other orders to
issue, or he wants to ride forward to reconnoitre, or
perhaps he has already gone on, and can be found
only after some time. The officer commanding the
artillery will thus get very hasty directions or none,
and his orders will therefore be insufficient, or, in any
case, will not be issued until after a considerable lapse
of time.

Imagine next the Staff of a division on the march,
when the officer commanding the artillery is warmly
welcomed by it, since he has made no difficulties but
has always helped readily and willingly. Without
thinking of it the General is happy to see him at his
side and to spend the weary hours of march in conversation with him, while the officer commanding
the artillery gladly takes every opportunity which
arises of riding by the side of the General. The information which arrives about the enemy may be
first communicated non-officially to the officer commanding the artillery, and nothing is more natural
than that the General should allow him to speak as
to the plan to be carried out. As soon as the plan
is decided on, the officer commanding the artillery
hears of it at once and can immediately issue his

orders. There may be circumstances in which, in the last case, the artillery would come into action half an hour, or more, earlier than they would in the first.

You, who know war, can yourself realise how much the friendly relations and the difference of time, of which I speak, depend upon whether harmony or discord reigns in cantonments, and in the common daily life.

The artillery was very welcome in the year 1870, before the battles had taken place, and the goodwill of the other arms and of the Generals towards it naturally increased, after that in the first battles and fights it had come into position early, and in sufficient strength. From that time it was, one might almost say, spoilt. It was entirely owing to the modesty with which it considered itself only as an auxiliary arm, and thus seized every opportunity of serving and helping the army, that it was fully and entirely accepted by the other arms as their complete equal.

After the last war, also, a desire arose on many sides within the artillery, to do away with its isolated organisation in time of peace also, and to be placed, like the cavalry, under the Generals commanding army-corps. So much the more was I astonished when, at a later date, I heard some important and much - read authors of the artillery express the opinion that the arm is tactically independent, and should preserve and prove its tactical independence. I believe that they have themselves not thought out the full practical meaning of this remarkable expression. But how hurtful the consequences of it may be I have pointed out to you by what I have already said. It is true that a General now holding a command, who was an infantry man, once said to me, after he had expressed his wonder at the heroic perseverance of his artillery, that he had in the last war observed qualities in the artillery for which he had not formerly given it credit, since it was now able to carry through a fight independently. But he can have meant only a defensive fight against a frontal attack, carried on over open ground which is well swept by artillery fire. In any offensive battle the independence of the artillery comes to an end.

Let me tell you what General von Dresky says of this in the letter which I have already quoted to you : " With reference to firing on infantry which is under cover, I gained some experience at Vionville, which was confirmed in later battles. I have found that it is impossible with artillery fire alone to drive *good* infantry from a position. On the high road from Rezonville to Vionville, about 1000 paces to the west of the former, a field road leading to Flavigny branches off to the south. A bank of earth, about 300 paces long, and planted with a hedge, stands in this position. Behind this lay some French skirmishers, who inflicted much loss on the two batteries which stood to the north of Flavigny, the 4th light and the 4th heavy. Repeated firing on this hedge, from the two batteries named above, as well as from the batteries of the left wing to the south of Flavigny, could not drive out the enemy's infantry. It was from this point also, in all probability, that the fire came which towards evening delayed the advance of the 4th light and the 4th heavy, as also that which inflicted such great loss on the left wing of the advancing artillery."

M

General von Dresky had a similar experience on the 18th of August, when he fired from his position at Verneville on the wood in front of the farm of Chantrenne, as I have already mentioned (Letter IV.), and he finishes his account with the remark: "With artillery fire alone *good* infantry cannot be driven out from a position under cover."

The improvement of the infantry firearm contributed no less to do away with the spirit of caste in the artillery. This appears to be a paradox, and yet it is not far-fetched. So long as the infantry had a smooth-bore musket, and had thus no precision in action beyond 100 paces, it was little inclined to exact scientific researches. But the precision, and the long range of the rifled weapon, and in particular the improvement of it due to various breech-loading systems, compelled the infantry to occupy themselves seriously with the sciences which have to do with the trajectory, in order to see how far the precision and the range could be improved, and the best possible infantry arm be obtained. The effect of the composition of the powder, of the resistance and elasticity of the air, the proportion between the weight of the bullet and that of the charge, and the influence of the rotation on precision and on drift, all compelled infantry men to turn their attention to chemistry, physics, and mathematics, which had before been necessary to the artillery only; thus the latter was no longer superior to the infantry in knowledge. The glory of science which had separated them faded yet more, when the less learned infantry, by the introduction of breech-loaders, went so far beyond the artillery that the latter could re-

gain their earlier relative position only by means of
improvements, grounded on principles which had
been first used by the infantry, namely, breech-loading and the rifled barrel.

Since that time, the firearms of the infantry,
cavalry, and artillery are almost alike, and demand
similar knowledge for their proper employment. For
there is now, strictly speaking, no other difference
between the trajectory of the shot of a rifle or a
gun, whether it be a carbine, a Mauser rifle, a field
gun, or even an 8-in. mortar, than this, that that of
the one is flatter and not so long, by one-third or
one-half, while that of the other is more curved and
longer. The use of shrapnel shell causes a slight
complication for the artillery. But these do not
require any greater science. Moreover, the weapons
are, as to their breech-closing arrangements, etc., all
fairly complicated, and must all be studied. They
differ principally from each other in their size ; but
perhaps the duty of a gunner is a little more complicated than that of an infantryman, on account of
his having to look after wagons, harness, and horses.
This is, however, not a science, but a soldier's duty,
being less easily learnt by the study of books than
by continual practice.

If we compare the knowledge of their profession
which is necessary to the three arms (I prefer this
expression to that of "science"), I hardly think that
any arm is inferior in any way to the artillery ;
neither the infantry with its various firing exercises
against vertical and horizontal targets, its study of
the trajectory and the dangerous zone, its firing in
masses and class firing, its field exercise and outpost

duty, and its instruction in hasty entrenchments—nor the cavalry, with its riding-school, its carbine practice, and its duties in reconnaissance and scouting, for the due discharge of which we might ask that the youngest lieutenant should have mastered the whole range of strategy and tactics. I say nothing of the engineers, for they have always had to learn as much as the artillery. An officer, of whatever arm, must learn a great many solid things, in order that he may do his work thoroughly.

They must all be indefatigably active, from morning to evening, from January to December, active not only to do their duty, but also to continually improve themselves. The conviction of this equality has established itself in the minds of all, without, as far as I know, having ever been expressed in words ; the infantry and cavalry no longer wonder at the artillery as a peculiarly scientific arm, nor does the artillery consider itself as more learned or better than the others, now that the intervening clouds of "science" have been cleared away. But it is the artillery which has gained the most by this change of opinion. It has now first become one in every respect with the others, an arm of equal standing.

These changes were not fully made, as I said, at any one time between the years 1866 and 1870, but were in embryo long before the war of 1866. But the war of 1870 set the stamp of approval on them for the reason, that in it the artillery fully recognised its modest position as an auxiliary arm, strove to do great things in this capacity only, and won its way by their successful performance.

LETTER VIII

HOW THE ARTILLERY LEARNT TO SHOOT

IF I set to work to answer your second question, namely, why the artillery shot so badly in 1866, and how it was that after that war it so quickly learnt to shoot, I must first describe to you the manner in which in former times the practice of the artillery, by which they were supposed to learn to shoot, was carried on.

To begin with, I imagine that you, during your stay at the Academy of War, have had the opportunity at some time or other of being present at such practice. But if you have never seen it, it will be sufficient if you procure one of those lithographed books of regulations of the time of S.B. guns, which were called "Directions for Inspection," and compare them with the "Directions for Inspection" for the year 1869 or 1870. These Directions contained all the special regulations for the exercise of a brigade on its practice ground, and were, as a rule, intended for a space of time of five weeks and a day. Since all the batteries and garrison companies could not shoot at the same time, it was usual, while some of them practised, to work the others at various artillery exercises and drills.

If you follow, in the " Directions for Inspection " of which I have spoken, the distribution of time for the employment of a battery, you will find that some days were first devoted to the so-called " Practice of instruction," at different ranges with solid shot, common shell, case, and shrapnel.   After this followed an exercise called " Trial practice at known ranges " ; then another, " Trial practice at unknown ranges," and one day for " Practice for prizes."   Two other days at the end of the training were devoted to the so-called " Practice for study," while four days were taken for the inspection by the Inspector-General or his representative.   Of these four, one day was given up to practice.   Thus a battery in the five weeks practised eight or nine times, and had, in addition, the opportunity of watching the practice during the "Study practice."   For this last exercise consisted of the carrying out of different experiments, partly to bring to the notice of the troops proposals of the Artillery Experimental Committee, which they thought should be introduced into the service, or to try the practical utility of such proposals ; partly to exhibit anything out of the common which the Special Committee appointed for this practice had thought out.   All officers and N.C. officers were ordered to attend this practice as spectators.

Four kinds of target were in use for Field Artillery; one of wood, a vertical wall, for practice with solid shot, 50 paces long and 6 feet high.   The second was a target for shrapnel, representing a column ; it consisted of three of the above targets, placed behind each other with 20 paces interval.   The third was used for case, and was of the same length as the first, but 9 feet high, as it represented cavalry. The fourth was a redoubt, of which only a small part was thrown up, the remainder being merely traced. These targets always stood at the same place, not only during the whole course of practice, but in part from year to year, for a butt stood in rear of the shot target, in order that the shot might be more easily found after practice, while the redoubt was year by year a little advanced towards completion. Only the targets for case and shrapnel could be set up in any one year in another spot to that which they had occupied in the preceding. Even this was rarely done, since such movement was not considered necessary.

The ranges at which practice was carried on during the "Practice of instruction," and the "Trial practice at known ranges," were settled in advance, I think, by the Inspector-General, and were measured very accurately with the chain. Pickets marked with numbers were set at every hundred paces. These pickets were, it is true, taken up for the "Trial practice at unknown ranges," in order that a battery, which had to advance in accordance with some tactical idea, and which received the order to commence firing at any point, might begin by finding the range. But any one, even if he had been only a few times on the practice ground, knew so well the distances from the targets, since the latter always remained in the same place, that a mistake was seldom made, and a mistake, when it was made, excited general astonishment. It was, therefore, altogether a delusion to believe that the practice took place at unknown ranges, and the practice resulted in no better instruction than did the " Practice of instruction " and the " Trial practice at known ranges." In these last not only was the distance measured, but the elevation to be used was strictly laid down. Owing to the inaccuracy of the old S.B. guns there was seldom any question of correcting the elevation. As a matter of fact this inaccuracy could not be corrected unless several rounds in succession from the same gun had gone over or short of the target, while no one gun fired a sufficient number to give grounds for correction. It sometimes happened that a gun, though laid correctly, would, out of 4 rounds at 1200 paces, throw 2 short and 2 over, and never hit the huge target at all ; and in this there was nothing to be astonished at. It was thus quite natural that no particular value should be attributed to exact and careful laying, and that hardly any effort was made to correct it by observing the effect, except at most in the case of the fire of shrapnel or of common shell with a high trajectory. But even this correction by observation, when it was made, taught nothing, for each shot was marked with pre-arranged signals by a range-party (commonly called " markers "), who reported whether it was over, short, to the right, or to the left. Thus no one learnt how to judge by their own observation of the effect of their fire.

Consequently the importance attached to the effect of fire was very much less then than it is now. It is true that after each practice the men were taken up to the target, in order that they might see the general effect, but the manner of handling each individual gun and the corrections which had been made in its elevation, etc., could not thus be criticised, and no instruction as to the handling of the guns could be obtained by merely looking at the shot-holes in the target. A general idea only was obtained of the effect of the gun, namely, that at such and such a range so many per cent of hits would be made on a target so high and so long, and from this might be drawn the conclusion that against smaller targets, such as guns, skirmishers, or supports, the effect would be very small. At the same time, the conviction was arrived at that the manner of serving the guns had very little influence over their effect, and it is not surprising if it was the universal opinion that artillery, when in action, ought to keep on blazing away, and trust to luck for its effect.

On the other hand, this inspection of the targets taught every one that artillery which wished to advance to within case range of the enemy must make great haste to pass from movement into action ; since, if it halted 400 paces from its target, the latter would, if it were infantry, in less than a minute and a half run up so close that the artillery might expect to receive from them an overwhelming fire of musketry ; while, if they were cavalry and made a determined charge, they would be in the battery in less than half a minute. For this reason it was considered as of the very greatest importance that the artillery, when it pushed on, should be in a position to come quickly into action, if it wished, like that of Senarmont at Friedland, to play a decisive part. At that time, strictly speaking, a really overwhelming effect could only be obtained by the fire of case, for the effect of shrapnel was as yet very doubtful ; as compared with the certainty of that fire at the present day the effect was almost *nil.* For this reason a demand was urgently made upon the artillery that they should be in a condition, half a minute after the command to halt and unlimber, to open a strong and effective fire of case. It is scarcely necessary to mention that the first point observed by the inspecting officer on the practice ground, as he sat with his stop-watch in his hand, was to see how much time elapsed between the order to halt and unlimber and the first shot, and you will remember that this space of time was on an average not more, or very little more, than 20 seconds. At manœuvres this time was considerably less, and how often were those who were not gunners astonished at a battery of Horse Artillery, which fired its first shot almost before they were able to see that it had halted. If any one watched closely and had a quiet horse, which would allow him to make careful observations notwithstanding the pace of the gallop and the confusion in the battery caused by unlimbering, he might easily see that the battery had advanced with its guns loaded (which was totally against the regulations), and that the gun which gained the prize for firing the first shot (for the captain gave such a prize at important inspections) had not its trail on the ground when it was fired, but was still held in the arms of the detachment. You may imagine there could have been no question of laying or of hitting if the gun had been loaded with shell, and also that thus a wild manner of serving the gun was introduced, which was not conducive to a good effect of fire, and which sometimes caused accidents. For it might happen that the firing number fired in his haste while the trail was being thrown round, and when the muzzle of the gun was pointing at the other guns instead of at the enemy. Even when the guns were loaded with shot or shell the time between the command " Halt !" and the first shot formed the criterion of excellence of the battery. The greater the importance attached to this, the less was the notice taken of good shooting.

I have never, up to the time of the introduction of rifled guns, known an inspecting General use the effect produced by the fire of a battery as a standard by which to judge of the excellence of its instruction. This was judged by the correct execution of the drill, of marching, of the service of the guns, the turn-out of the men and horses, and the time which the battery took to come into action ; all things which are certainly very important. But when the effect of fire was inferior to the average percentage as established by experience, this was passed over with great indulgence and with the remark that all that was very much a matter of chance. Indeed this indulgence was compulsory, on account of the defective accuracy of the guns. Thus if a captain who had accidentally made good practice had plumed himself upon it, he would then have been simply laughed at, since it would have been the general opinion that he and the whole battery had nothing whatever to do with it.

At the time of the introduction of rifled guns, an officer, who was much interested in shooting and the effect of fire, complained bitterly at a meeting for discussion that it was most objectionable that the senior officers on the practice grounds occupied themselves with the inspection of shoes, bits, and harness, and considered the practice only as an opportunity of getting rid of so much heavy shot and shell ; the whole of his hearers were exceedingly indignant at this—most of all, perhaps, those who felt that the cap fitted.

At all events, it was considered right at that time to attach more value to showiness in drill than to good practice, and the paradox which owes its being to a Horse gunner : " The artillery would be a beautiful arm if it had no guns to drag after it," was the expression of a very general feeling, but one which was not usually put into words. This mis-understanding of the duty of artillery was the natural consequence of the inefficiency of our guns, and of a long period of peace, which had caused its purpose in war to be nearly forgotten. I only ask you to remember the many complicated evolutions which you have formerly seen on the drill-ground, —for example, deploying from mass of batteries, or forming column of sections on a named section, carried out by a whole brigade, or the change of front of a four-gun battery in action on the centre, where the pivot lay between Nos. 2 and 3 guns, an evolution which has tormented me a good many times when I was a subaltern.

You will perhaps answer me, that one day of practice was given up to shooting for prizes, a fact which proves by its very existence that some value was attached to the effect of fire. But if you look a little more closely into the management of this shooting for prizes, you will make no such answer. It was carried out at the large target, on a range exactly measured with a chain (if I remember aright, for the 6-pr. it was about 1000 yards), and the number of hits decided the competition. In full consciousness that the result was solely a matter of chance, the winners did not keep the prize for themselves, but the money was clubbed together, and, as was customary, was spent by the battery in common. It appears that they had at that time totally forgotten that the winners might choose a commemorative medal instead of the money. When I commanded a regiment, and, after the introduction of rifled guns, turned up the old regulation in question and made inquiry about it, no one in the whole regiment had any knowledge of it, nor could any one tell me where these medals were to be obtained.

I must now say a word or two about the " Study practice." As I have already told you, this practice took place at the close of the course. Thus no practical advantage was gained in that year by the troops from the practice which was then carried out ; and by the next year most of it was forgotten. Often also some not very fertile ideas of one or other of the members of the Committee were alone worked out. It was laid down that the troops should receive valuable instructions (in the form of regulations), with regard to anything of the sort, only when the introduction of some novelty was impending ; for example, in 1849 the use of reversed shell, or afterwards indirect fire with the 25-pr. S.B. howitzer, or later still the short 12-pr. We were seldom shown

how to fire at a moving target. This was very difficult to manage, and was also in consequence of the cost
of the large targets very expensive, and bore heavily
on the funds which were provided for the supply of
targets. It was difficult because, on account of the
inaccuracy of the guns, the moving target had to be
drawn along by a proportionally very long rope,
which constantly fouled the inequalities of the ground,
so that the target stopped moving; and because it
was in general very hard to make so large a target
as was required for S.B. guns in any way movable.
Thus we very seldom indeed even saw such practice
as is customary in war, namely, at a moving target
at an unknown range; much less did we ever gain
any experience of it. And when we did see it, we
were merely convinced that the target could not be
hit. Such practice did not tend to give confidence
of success against an attacking enemy, which feeling
could only be founded upon the effect of case. How
would it be now if the enemy's infantry, armed with
rifled breech-loaders, kept outside of the range of
case, and fired from longer ranges than case shot
could reach?

We were therefore content with general rules for
practice at a moving target, as well as for the purpose of judging distances. That for the first case
was pretty short: " Push on, and fire at the head of
the column." Judging distance was certainly made
a special object of instruction, in the course of which
the gunners had to learn by heart the optical rules
connected with the subject. But these rules, as is
well known, do not suit every one who learns them,
since each person's eye has its own peculiar impres-

sion of distance.   Practice is thus the only means to produce good results.   Such practice required more time than could then be allotted to it, for to pace a range, estimated at from 1000 to 2000 paces, takes from a quarter to half an hour.   Besides, there was no opportunity of turning to account, or of recording, dexterity in judging distances ; so much dexterity was altogether neglected.   The accurate rifled gun which, with its shell bursting on impact, shows in a moment what error has been made, first caused each shot to have its use for every man in the battery for training in judging distance, and induced every officer to accustom himself to judge distances, since if he judged them wrong he did not hit the target.

In the year 1860 the artillery received the first rifled guns, originally, as is well known, in the proportion of a quarter of the armament.   You may say, perhaps, that there was plenty of time between 1860 and 1866 to learn how to shoot with the new guns, and at first sight every one will agree with you. But who could teach, when no one had fired with the new invention under the conditions which obtain on service.   The only possible teacher was the inventor.   These inventors were the Artillery Experimental Committee, of which the President, Lieutenant-General Enke, had greatly benefited our matériel in that he, on the one hand, pushed on and encouraged, and on the other assisted and brought to notice, the actual maker, the meritorious Colonel (as he then was) Neumann.   The rifled gun seems to have been taken by Enke as the object of his life. He lived for it entirely, and as he took no interest in anything except the service of the artillery (it was he who said, "The day has 24 hours of duty, and it is possible to make use of the night also"), he took as great an interest in the practice of 1860, when the men shot for the first time with rifled guns, as a child in Christmas. But he was not permitted to see the practice. A few days before the beginning of the course he was found dead in his armchair. The new discovery was not sufficient reason for entirely changing the system of practice, the less so as we had lost the man who had been the mainspring of the movement (also as three-quarters of the guns, and thus by far the majority, were of the old pattern), and as the new gun had many opponents, who held that it was too complicated for war, and regarded with mistrust its defective fire of case.

The course of practice was still carried out on the old system, and this principle could not be condemned so long as the majority of our guns were not rifled. They were therefore fired on the same principles with which practice had been previously carried on, only here and there at somewhat longer ranges; we were immensely pleased with them, for every shot hit (we fired at ranges at which, in these days, the fire of guns is annihilating); this, on the other hand, was very unpleasant for the target-fund, for we knocked the targets all to pieces. Moreover, the artillery was not yet quite in a position to use the gun with its percussion shell as an infallible range-finder, since we principally fired with plugged shell, which were to be recovered and used again.

In the year 1864 the number of our rifled guns was not yet half of the total number of field guns. Great as was the superiority which our rifled siege guns, in the action against the Düppel redoubts, showed over the enemy's S.B. and rifled guns, we were still convinced that the troops had not exhausted all their advantages, since they had not been able to learn to shoot sufficiently well with them. Now also the opinion made its way, that it would next be necessary to teach the officers to shoot with these guns, in order that they might direct the laying, and properly control the executive functions of the detachments who worked under them. At the same time, it was seen that only by a different course and by frequent practice could any one learn to shoot. But for this the amount of ammunition which the Ministry of War was able to grant for the annual course of practice of the total number of artillery brigades and regiments was insufficient. For this reason a School of Gunnery, for officers, was at once instituted, at which, as a beginning, the officers themselves undertook the service of the guns. The zeal of the officers of artillery went so far that they, at first, gladly took upon themselves the expense which their presence at this school occasioned to them, and the Ministry of War had to grant only the ammunition for this first tentative course at the School of Gunnery. Every one who has paid the smallest attention to the machinery of a constitutional State, in which every increase of expenditure must be first sanctioned by the representatives of the country, knows how slowly any improvement can be brought about, if that improvement necessitates a greater outlay of money. The Ministry is unable to propose the demand until it has not only convinced itself practically of its expediency, but is also in a position

N

to prove that it is desirable. Thus it came about that the new School of Gunnery had as yet produced no general effect when the war of 1866 broke out, since the Ministry of War had not yet been able to increase the amount of the expenditure on ammunition.

Being convinced of the importance of such an institution, since it was the general opinion that the effect of the new guns must have been far greater in 1866 had the troops been properly instructed, the artillery urged the definite organisation of a School of Gunnery. They met with assistance on all sides, and such a School of Gunnery was established.

A singular fate was reserved for the scientific arm. It had to accept the principles of the unscientific infantry, the rifled firearm, and the breechloader, and also their method of theoretical instruction.

It will be evident to you that no immediate improvement was possible. A number of instructors had first to be perfectly taught ; these had next to settle definite rules as to the manner in which the troops should be taught to shoot, before they could be allowed to actually commence the instruction of the troops. On the other hand, it was wonderful how soon they succeeded. The School of Gunnery held two courses during the year, which worked in all weathers,—in the heat of summer as well as in snow or frost. The year 1867 was nearly over before a sufficient number of instructors had been provided to teach the troops a rational manner of shooting. At this time also it became possible to replace almost all the S.B. guns with rifled ordnance.

The time had now, in all respects, come for

changing the system of practice of the troops. The Inspector-General, in the beginning of the year 1868, forwarded propositions on this subject from the School of Gunnery, and from all the brigades. By this time every one had thought about the subject, and had formed opinions from his own point of view. The propositions put forward, being founded on each one's point of view, and on individual experiences in the war of 1866, differed so much from each other, that the Inspector-General of Artillery, with respect to the "Regulations for Inspection" for 1868, allowed the commanders of brigades the very greatest liberty, bounded only by the amount of the now more ample grant of money. It was ordered that an "Introductory Instructional Practice" should take place at each course of instruction; this was to be carried out by a Horse Artillery battery with one light and one heavy Field battery, the whole to be under the command of a captain who had been instructed at the School of Gunnery; it was intended to show the assembled officers what mode of proceeding had been approved by the School of Gunnery as the most suitable. Under these instructions the brigades collected their experiences during the course of practice of 1868, and made them the grounds for the new regulations. These in connection with fresh experiences of the School of Gunnery were issued as definite instructions, in accordance with which the "Regulations for Inspection" of the years 1869 and 1870 were to be carried out.

All this now belongs to history, and a young gunner of the present day would be astonished if he were told that the artillery, not 20 years ago, was able to exist without a School of Gunnery. But any one who has lived through the time when no School of Gunnery existed, and during the development which brought it into existence, still warms at the remembrance of these changes ; and if any one wishes to answer the question which is the motive of my letter of to-day, he must spend some little time in describing the foundation of the School of Gunnery.

Having gone rapidly through the history of these transitions, I will ask you to take in your hand a copy of the "Instructions for Inspection" for 1869 or 1870 (or for any one year after the whole of our field guns were rifled), and to compare it with one of an earlier date.

You will find there, first of all, that the targets represented troops, and were much smaller than formerly. The infantry and cavalry target was only 15 paces wide (the breadth of a section or a sub-division) ; the artillery target represented guns, horses, and men in action. Skirmisher targets were also used, sometimes standing (man-targets), and sometimes lying down (head-targets), after the pattern of the targets used by infantry. The smaller targets took more work, but cost less money. Thus funds became available to keep a moving target always in use, and to carry out practice at it. In the brigade which I commanded it was even found possible to build a small railway, upon which the target ran. The course of practice began with an "Introductory Instructional Practice," in which 3 batteries at war-strength (1 4-pr., 1 6-pr., and 1 Horse Artillery), commanded by captains who had passed through the School of Gunnery, took up different positions from which they had to fire. All the officers looked on. The principal subject of instruction was practice at a moving target, either advancing directly against the battery, or moving obliquely across its front, or passing from flank to flank. Plenty of ammunition was always provided for this practice. Then followed the "Elementary Practice" (unless it had already taken place); in this the recruits, after they had learnt to fire blank cartridge, gained some idea of the fire of shotted guns against a target.

After the officers, as well as the men, had been instructed in the elements of gunnery, the true "Instructional Practice" followed. This was always practice with shell under service conditions. The targets were moved daily, and the ranges were daily varied, and a battery was often stopped during its practice and ordered to fire at another target. Not only did the batteries fire one by one, but the divisions also came into action one by one, so that even the youngest subaltern had plenty of opportunity of showing whether he could judge distance, and whether he could pick up the range correctly. Plenty of ammunition was always supplied. Each battery fired also in "Practice for prizes," and, in addition, fired 182 rounds at the inspection by the Inspector-General. This was not sufficient to make each one of the 40 or 44 recruits belonging to each battery a good shot, but the amount sufficed to teach what was necessary to the battery, without insisting on every gunner being able to lay. This latter point was also considered as not essential, since, at

the ranges at which practice is now carried on, not
every man can see sufficiently well to be able to lay
with the needful accuracy. The eyesight of each
recruit was tested on joining, and only those who
had good sight were practised in laying. From
these again were selected such as showed most
accuracy in laying guns, and these always laid when
practice was carried on with shell. It was found to
be quite sufficient if 12 out of the 40 or 44 recruits
in the battery were well practised in laying, and
these were told off in turn to lay at shell-practice.
Everything was thus arranged to teach the arm how
to shoot and hit the target.

It may perhaps interest you if I go a little more
into the subject of practice at a moving target. As
an ardent sportsman you know well how difficult it
is to hit a running animal with a bullet. But the
difficulty is greater in the case of a gun, since you
cannot, as with a carbine, follow the moving target
with it, and fire at the moment when the back and
fore sights are on the object, for the number who
lays the gun does not fire, but must get out of the
way before he can give the order to fire. The case
is also complicated by the fact that he must receive
the order to fire, and thus the guns of a battery
must wait after they are loaded until it comes to the
turn of each, and a considerable time elapses from
the moment when the gun was laid to the time when
it is fired, during which time the moving target has
changed its position. From this fact, as the habit
of practising at moving targets gained ground, there
resulted a hot discussion among the captains of batteries as to how it was to be carried on, and in the

first year (1868) I allowed each of them to fire 20 rounds of filled and fused shell, during the "Elementary Practice," in any way he pleased, at a moving target. I laid down no regulations on the subject until from the experience thus gained I had found out the best manner of carrying out the practice. In 1869 and 1870 it was possible to lay down a system to be observed.

All, for instance, were agreed in one thing, namely, that it was necessary to choose some point on the ground over which the target would pass, and to lay the gun on that point. As soon as this had been done, the order should be given to cease firing until the target reached the point in question, and that then it should be fired on. The method of proceeding is very much simpler in the case where the target advances directly against the battery, that is to say, when the enemy directly attacks it. In this case the gun can be laid on the enemy, and it is only necessary to give a range which is less than that at which the enemy now stands; this range may be determined by the point of impact or burst of a shell. But in what manner should you fire when the target reaches this point? On this question the views of the captains of batteries varied very much. Some wanted to fire a salvo with all their guns, others to open a rapid fire, and others again thought that the greatest number of hits would be obtained by a very slow fire commencing from one flank.

You will perhaps think, and so did I at first, that a salvo at the moment when the enemy reaches the point on which all the six guns are laid must be the most rational proceeding. But, strange to say, those officers who used salvoes made the fewest hits. The simultaneous explosion caused among the detachments a nervous restlessness, which arose from the effect on their ears of so great a detonation. Again, the battery felt itself defenceless when once it had fired its salvo, and by this their quiet laying on a fresh point was decidedly prejudiced. Also clouds of smoke, which hung round the battery after a salvo, were found to be in the way of the captain's observation of the effect. And again, if the trial shot had not been well laid, and had given a false impression of the range, then the whole salvo was wasted.

The effect of those batteries which gave the order " Rapid fire," when the target came near to the point on which the guns were laid, was better. In these, the officers, after the order had been given from which flank the fire was to commence, fired the guns at much shorter intervals than had been up to that time permitted (the order was to count slowly up to 15 between each gun), but only at such a rate as allowed them to direct their attention from the gun last fired to the next gun, and thus to secure the proper service of the guns.

But the greatest percentage of hits was obtained by the regulation fire from a flank, since thus the guns were the most quietly and best served, and were also the most carefully laid. This was the result when the percentages of hits were compared with the expenditure of ammunition, since, with the slow fire, less ammunition was used ; but the rapid fire produced more effect in a given time, though at the cost of a greater expenditure of ammunition.

The conclusion arrived at was that, ordinarily (against infantry), a slow fire from a flank should be employed, and that only exceptionally, against a target moving quickly (such as cavalry), should a rapid fire from a flank be used. Salvoes were altogether forbidden. Thus the batteries under my command in the campaign of 1870-71 used salvoes only when, at the beginning of an action, it was not possible to observe a single shot, and a group of six explosions was needed, in order to judge of the effect, and also to measure the range. I shall probably have an opportunity later on to tell you more about this.

Thus, with regard to practice at a moving target, we had laid down a recognised principle and system, and had accustomed the troops to it, when the war of 1870 broke out. For this war gave us (at least, the brigade which I commanded, and most of the other brigades) time to finish what was most necessary of our "Instructional Practice," and of the "Shell-practice under service conditions," so that we went into the field with our artillery perfectly trained.

I could never have believed that the instruction given in time of peace would have borne such excellent fruit, in spite of the excitement of action. How much the more agreeable was my surprise when, standing behind the captain of a battery in action, as troops were advancing to attack him, I heard him quietly give the order: "Against infantry in front, 1900 paces, from the right flank, Ready! Fire one gun!" Then he waited, holding his field-glass to his eye, until the enemy approached the point on which the guns were laid, and gave the order:

"Rapid firing from the right flank!" Then there was a hellish sight, for the advancing enemy disappeared from view in the clouds of smoke which the shells threw up as they burst and tore their way through his ranks. After one or two minutes the attacking enemy came out on our side of the smoke. It had passed the point on which the guns were laid, and, in spite of terrible loss, approached with undeniable bravery. Then the captain gave the command: "Cease firing! 1600 paces—one gun!—cease firing!" and when the enemy drew near to the new point on which the guns were now laid, he cried: "At 1600 paces, from the right flank, rapid firing!" The effect was brilliant, horrible, and overwhelming. No attack could have resisted it.

When you think that the School of Gunnery in the year 1868 had not advanced sufficiently far in their organisation to draw up regulations for the new management of practice, and that these were first given out in 1869, you must be astonished at the fact that in the year 1870 the artillery, as a whole, had already learnt to shoot so well. This result was entirely due to the excellent orders of the Inspector-General of artillery, who directed that all officers who had returned to their batteries from the School of Gunnery should act as instructors during the practice. In these days, when every captain of a battery has been through the School of Gunnery, and the commanders of brigades have all passed twice through the course, the troops are in a still better position, and not only will, but must, shoot better still. You may imagine my astonishment when, after the last war, I asked a great authority on artillery, belonging to a neighbouring nation, whether they had a School of Gunnery in his country, and received the answer : " What is the use of a School of Gunnery ? Our men shoot well enough."

If you bear in mind that during these years the Inspector-General of Artillery, at his annual inspections, judged of the quality of the troops by two points, viz. the hits made at practice (for these are possible only when the gun is well served), and the quick movement according to regulations over long distances, with the object of arriving in position at the right time ; and that he considered elegant drill as quite secondary, and entirely forbade all artificial movements ; and remember, also, that even among those who were not gunners, great value was attached to the time which is necessary for laying and getting the range (the very highest authority has in his criticism blamed excessive hurry in firing the first shot);—you will then possess the key to the riddle how it was that we learnt so quickly to shoot properly.

The regulations were also altered. The new gun of itself called for other regulations. But even the principles of the new regulations were different. Whereas, formerly, marching past and correct drill were considered the highest expression of discipline, these were now entirely neglected wherever they interfered with the careful direction of the guns and of the ammunition and thus prejudiced the effect of fire. But when an alteration of the regulations had once been commenced, the whole of them were revised, and everything omitted which had no reference to the proper objects of the arm, namely, the timely arrival on the field of battle and good practice

when there.   From this time no more complicated
movements were to be seen on the drill-ground.
We strove to get the horses into good condition, and
thus to enable them to get over long distances, say
from two to five miles, even on the drill-ground, at a
good pace.   When the guns had arrived at the
position in which they intended to fight, there was
to be no hurry about the first round ; it was to be
fired only after very careful laying, even if some
minutes were required for this.

I am very much inclined to think that we did
not then go far enough in the simplification of our
drill movements, and might have laid more stress
upon the correct training of the battery, and have
reduced the movements of larger masses under one
command to a minimum.   Judging by my experiences in war—and you will own that in matters
connected with artillery they are fairly numerous—
the only movements which are of use in the field
are, the advance in column of route, deployments,
and the advance in line.   At the moment when he
first came on the ground at the battle of Königgrätz,
Major von Miesitschek, immediately after crossing
the Trotinka, by the bridge of Jericek, when they
were under the enemy's fire, made the 2d brigade
form line to the left by batteries, after which he
formed quarter-column of batteries, and then deployed
to the left.   I asked him why he spent so much time
in these movements, and did not rather lead the
heads of batteries at once into their position.   He
answered that this was the first time that his troops
had been under fire, and that, therefore, he wanted
everything to be done in a strictly correct manner,

in order that the men might remain calm, and
"might not feel that anything extraordinary was
taking place." I could not disapprove of this
principle, and so let the brave man do what he
chose. I will tell you on some other occasion why
I have bitterly regretted this inclination towards
brigade movements. Once again, in the battle of
Sedan, it happened, when I was in command, that
movements were made by the brigade, as a whole,
under the orders of the commander of the brigade.
This occurred as I was leading forward the whole of
my artillery near Givonne, with the object of opening
a decisive fire on the Bois de la Garenne. The 1st
brigade of Field Artillery was then standing in front
of the defile which runs through the forest of Villers-
Cernay, and blocked the way. The 2d brigade
stood on their right rear. It was therefore necessary
that the 1st brigade should move as soon as
possible, in order that the 2d might pass through
the defile. But we were too near to the enemy for
me to call upon the 1st brigade to make any movement to a flank ; it had, therefore, to push forward,
while, at the moment when it opened fire, the 2d
could be brought to the front. The 1st brigade thus
took up a position of which the right rested on
impassable ground (precipices), while on their left
flank there was room for the 2d brigade. The
latter also passed the defile, at a trot, in column of
divisions, the head of the column wheeled to the
left, and the whole then moved by batteries to their
right front, coming into position by batteries. This
complicated movement was carried out without loss,
since the enemy was completely disorganised, firing

only to make a noise, and laying up at the sky, so that all his missiles passed over our heads. But these are the only two occasions in all the battles and actions at which I have been present, when I have seen brigade movements attempted. The first, as I said above, I had reason to regret (I will speak of this later on); the second might have been executed by direct order to the batteries without any combined movement, and what is more, was not carried out correctly as a drill movement.

I lately saw in a pamphlet, written by a cavalry officer who is well known by the whole army for his practical excellence, the expression of a wish that the regulations might be so far simplified that particular stress should be laid upon those movements which are practicable in war, and that those which are intended to be used only in time of peace should be separated from them. There is some little irony concealed in this wish. If such a simplification were undertaken with respect to the artillery regulations, . the whole of brigade drill, with the exception of the formation for the march, and the advance in line, would be banished to the second category of evolutions. But I cannot advise that they should be excised altogether from the regulations. The work of the artillery during peace would, in that case, become too monotonous, and monotony must, if possible, be avoided, as it is the enemy of all delight in the service. Moreover, all general officers have not the time to inspect each individual battery, and they will therefore, in time of peace, desire to see the movements of larger bodies, as of several batteries brigaded together.

LETTER IX

ON THE RENEWAL OF AMMUNITION IN TIME
OF WAR

I SHALL to-day write to you upon a subject which will, in my opinion, be very wearisome to you, namely, the reasons why our artillery in 1866 often ran short of ammunition, and how this difficulty was got over in 1870. But I cannot excuse you, since it is of the very greatest importance that the expended ammunition should be replaced at the proper moment, for what effect on an action can a line of artillery produce when it has no more ammunition? You cannot even say to them, as a certain brave Saxon General said to the light infantry battalion at the battle of Sedan, when it had exhausted its ammunition: "Well, you have got your swords!"—so he spoke, but remained with the battalion in the foremost line of the battle until the ammunition came up. The artillery must therefore strive to arrange for the timely supply of ammunition with the same zeal as it devotes to the carrying out of its proper tactical employment. Many a Staff officer, who has worked out the details of arrangements in operations against an enemy, becomes angry and impatient when he thinks of the gigantic train

of the lines of ammunition-columns, which drags
like a log at the heel of an army-corps: he may well
say, "As soon as you begin to talk about lines of
wagons, I begin to feel ill." But it is of no good
to say this. They must be thought about.

It is true that the idea of these endless strings of
wagons which, slowly creeping on, cover the roads in
rear of the army (in 1870 each corps had 9 columns
of 27 wagons, each 20 paces in length), has little
to do with the poetical chivalrous picture which the
young warrior, burning to do great deeds, ordinarily
draws to himself of the coming "grand and joyous
battle." I was not therefore surprised when a young
man of rank, an officer of the reserve of the cavalry
of the Guard, who was assigned to me to do duty
with the artillery, and who asked to be appointed to
a battery of Horse Artillery, nearly fainted with
horror when I was compelled to tell him that he was
told off to the ammunition-columns. He was recon-
ciled to his fate later on, for he found an opportunity,
when he came into action, to get his horse wounded
by infantry fire, and to so distinguish himself that
for his very first battle his breast was decorated with
the Iron Cross.

Speaking generally, the views of glory, honour,
and chivalry, which in old days and in the Middle
Ages were judged by and founded upon strength of
body and skill in fighting with the sword, the mace,
the lance, and the morning-star, have experienced
a considerable change by the improvement of firearms. For all that is nowadays required in order to
combat an Achilles of Troy, or even Hercules with
his gigantic strength, is the same little, well-directed

bullet of ·36 of an inch, which would serve to knock over the most puny soldier.   Individual action plays but a very small part in modern war.   The infantry soldier lies in a shelter-trench or under a hedge, loading, aiming, and firing his shooting machine. The artillery takes even a less personal part in the action.   One man orders the direction and the nature of the fire, another sponges out the gun, another brings up the shell, another fixes the fuse, another lays, and yet another pulls the lanyard. And yet they all fight fully to the same extent as the cavalry soldier, who strikes bravely, sword in hand, like the old knights.   Chivalrous honour in the field now lies in the scrupulous, quiet, and precise performance of one's peculiar duty, notwith-. standing the stress of constant danger.   Thus, he who, through great risks, brings up ammunition into the firing line has just as large a share in it as he who is firing in that line.   What difference is there between the gunner who carries the shell from the limber to the gun, and the soldier who brings a full ammunition-wagon up to a battery which is in action?   You will allow then that the renewal of expended ammunition has as much to do with the fight, and therefore must be treated as of the same importance, as the shooting, the attack, and the tactical dispositions for the battle, and that we ought therefore to overcome that feeling of weariness, which is involuntarily connected with this subject, since the latter has already to struggle against so many terrible difficulties.

I have no accurate knowledge of the special arrangements which were made, in the wars at the beginning of this century, to secure the regular renewal of expended ammunition in an army in the field. But it appears to me probable that a renewal of artillery ammunition during the battle was seldom necessary (except, perhaps, at the battle of Denne-witz, during which Bülow sent an ammunition-column to Tauenzien), not at least when a battery went into action with its full amount of ammunition ; at any rate, the regulations for the renewal of ammunition which were in force with us in 1866 seem to point this way. There was plenty of time and opportunity to bring up the ammunition-columns after the battle, especially since the battles and actions did not follow each other at such short intervals as in our last war. Even the very energetic conduct of war of the first Napoleon did not produce such a rapid succession of serious actions as in the eight days' war in Bohemia, which lasted from the 26th of June to the 3d of July 1866, and the same point may be observed if we compare the three years' War of Liberation with the six months' war of 1870-71. We may add that, with B.L. guns, at critical moments, a more rapid consumption of ammunition may take place than was possible with M.L. guns, which required more time for each round. We may further add that masses of artillery are now brought earlier into action and are not kept back in reserve. Finally, moreover, much larger armies are now employed in war, and thus more ammunition is expended and calls for renewal. For the same reason the roads are now more choked by the larger masses of troops, and thus the advance of the ammunition-columns meets with more difficulties and hindrances. It

appears that in the beginning of the century this
need was sufficiently met by a certain number of
ammunition-columns which followed the army, and
by the addition of ammunition - wagons to the
batteries.   No well-regulated system appears to
have been laid down.   At least, when the Inspector-
General of Artillery, after the war of 1866, asked
two veterans of the war of 1813, who had retired
from the service, what was their opinion as to the
person to whom the direction of the ammunition-
wagons should be entrusted, one of them answered
that this should certainly not be left to the battery-
sergeant - major or to the quartermaster - sergeant.
His in 1813 were, he said, so faint-hearted that
they in every action fancied that the day was lost,
and so always retreated with the wagons.   The
other gave the same opinion, but for the reason
that his were such brave men that he could not do
without them when the battery was in action.

If our regulations with regard to the renewal of
ammunition in battle, such as were in force in 1866,
were to be based upon the experiences of 1813
to 1815, it would certainly appear that, in those
days, no battery ever fired away in one day the
whole of the ammunition which was carried in the
limbers and in the wagons, for these regulations
are limited to the renewal of the ammunition in the
limbers from the wagons of the battery.   As to
the replenishment of the wagons, it was considered
sufficient to lay down that the captain of the battery, in his report of the action, was to send in a
statement of the ammunition expended, and to
demand its renewal ; he would then receive instruc-

tions as to where he might obtain fresh ammunition. These regulations were limited to the case where the battery and the ammunition-store (now ammunition-column) were under one command.

The painfully minute control which exists in every branch of our military and civil administration, and which may well be, speaking generally, the cause of the excellence of our public servants, has, with time, introduced into this matter a precise rigidity which, when in 1866 it was for the first time in its existence set in motion, was the cause of very serious loss of time.

In that campaign the ammunition-columns and the batteries had to send in, at regular intervals, on a prescribed form, a "State of remaining ammunition," which was forwarded through the officer commanding the artillery of the corps, and in which the issues and the receipts must be made to balance. In accordance with this "State" the officer commanding the artillery of the corps sent in a demand to the officer commanding the artillery of the army, and the latter gave an order on the depot for field ammunition, whence the columns could draw the ammunition. Again, after each action, every battery had to send in with the report on the battles an extraordinary "State of remaining ammunition," in accordance with which the renewal of the expended ammunition was carried out by the columns. Although the amount of writing, which was the consequence of all this exactness, was much diminished by the fact that, before their departure from their garrison, the troops were provided with printed forms for this "State," you can still understand that so much office-work after an action not only was a great burden on a battery, but also became impossible of execution in the case when a battle lasted up to nightfall, and when the battery had to bivouac wherever it could in rain and mud, and had to push on the next morning at the break of day. For the report on the action had to be also accompanied by a plan of the ground, a list of losses, and a list of recommendations for honours. Thus several days passed before the officer commanding the artillery of the corps was placed in a position, by the receipt of the " State," to issue the orders for the renewal of the ammunition, and during all these days the battery had to wait. This matter took still longer in the case of the officer commanding the reserve artillery of the 1st army in 1866, for he had to send in a requisition first to the officer commanding the artillery of the whole army (since there was no officer in command of the 3d and 4th corps), and the latter issued an order to the officer commanding the reserve artillery of the army, who had under his charge the two brigades of ammunition-columns. The enormous number of the wagons of the main artillery reserve, which followed in rear of the army, delayed exceedingly the transmission of these orders, owing to the great distances which had to be traversed. Just imagine this main artillery reserve of the army, with its 16 batteries and 2 brigades of ammunition-columns, which, on the march, covered the road for a space of 27 (English) miles. This immense length of the column of march made it also extraordinarily difficult to transmit punctually the necessary orders for the execution of marches.

It might thus well happen that a battery four days after an action had not yet been able to replace its expended ammunition, since the ammunition-column had not yet received any orders, and so could not issue any supply; the battery might then have to enter on a new battle with four empty wagons, and might thus be soon compelled to cease firing for want of ammunition ; and yet with all this no one might have been to blame.

The regulations for the ammunition-wagons, which form an integral part of a battery, were yet more unpractical, as regarded the punctual replenishment of the limber-boxes during an action. These regulations laid down that the ammunition-wagons of a battery were to be divided into two "lines," of which the 1st, consisting of two or three ammunition-wagons and one store-wagon, was to follow the battery at a distance of 300 or 400 paces, while the 2d, which included the remaining wagons, was to remain out of fire, and thus at least 1000 paces from the battery. It was very difficult to carry out these regulations, even when a battery was acting independently, as, for example, in the case where a subaltern was undergoing his examination for promotion ; the commander of the lines of waggons, a N.C. officer, or even sometimes an old soldier, could not always receive in time the orders rendered necessary by the rapid changes of position ; nor was it always possible to find a man of that class who had the necessary amount of skill. Thus it not rarely happened that, when movements in retreat were worked out, the lines of wagons got in the way of the battery, or stopped up a defile, or found themselves considerably nearer to the enemy than the battery was. You can easily imagine how these difficulties grow into impossibilities when several batteries advance by the same road to a new position, or when other troops are also moving forward to the battle. Thus an unfortunate N.C. officer, in charge of a line of wagons, may find himself with his three or four wagons treated by a cavalry or infantry regiment, if he gets in their way, as so much train which has no business there, and will thus be hustled into the ditch. Imagine now an army-corps which is engaged, and which has all the batteries of the corps under fire. In rear of the batteries, at a ˙distance of 300 or 400 paces, stand the same number of little clusters of three or four wagons, painfully but unsuccessfully striving according to the regulations to find some " cover from the ground." At least 1000 paces in rear again are the same number of other little clusters of seven or eight wagons, which have received instructions to keep out of fire. Imagine then the arrival of the very slightest crisis in the action, and what an awful state of confusion there will be. I do not know if it really happened, but, according to the regulations which were then in force, the two lines of wagons of those batteries which at the battle of Nachod had to retire with the whole of the advanced guard, ought to have retreated quickly out of the zone of fire, and have thrown themselves head-over-heels into the defile of Nachod, right in front of the main body of the corps, and would thus have stopped the advance of the latter. If this did not happen, then all the leaders of the lines of wagons acted contrary to regulations.

I have reason to believe that these regulations with regard to the direction of the battery wagons, which were still in force in 1866, were not founded on the experiences of the war of 1813, but that long after that war they were worked out to the best of the ability of certain adjutants, who had never seen war. The authorities who sanctioned them did not perhaps attribute much importance to these regulations, since in the wars from 1813 to 1815 there was probably seldom any deficiency of artillery ammunition in action, and after the fight there was always sufficient time to provide for its renewal. I incline to this opinion on account of an expression of a former commander of my regiment, Colonel von Rohl, which he made when I was passing my practical examination for promotion to captain. He was a veteran of the War of Liberation, and was decorated with the Iron Cross. When he was in a good humour and felt at his ease he spoke with a strong Berlin dialect. He said that he was satisfied with the arrangements which I made, during my examination, for the renewal of the ammunition, since they were according to the regulations. " But," said he, "regulations are all nonsense. No one can conform to them in war. Two lines! Bosh! In war we always march with our wagons, and when the enemy opens fire then we say, 'Here, get the wagons out of the way!' and then we push on and open fire. And then we send some one to tell them to come on." I expressed my regret to the Colonel for having been obliged to learn that which was all nonsense, and asked what I was to do in order to learn what was correct. "My boy," said he, "do not work so much, it will make you stupider and stupider!" He was certainly not a scientific gunner.

The old regulations, of which we are speaking, also laid down that the renewal of expended ammunition (with the exception of case, which was to be at once replaced) was to be carried out as soon as there was a pause in the fire or the action; but that the renewal of ammunition was to be looked to, at the latest, when half of the ammunition in the limbers had been expended, that is to say, that only in this case was the supply of ammunition to be filled up during the action. But we found that this limit would be far too late for rifled guns. They can be loaded much quicker than the smooth-bores, and they will, if rapid fire be ordered, consume the other half in far less time than will be required to carry out the orders for renewal.

What the officer commanding a brigade was to do at first with his wagons, at the moment when the whole brigade of four batteries came into action under his command, the regulations did not say. And yet almost every day during the drill season whole brigades were to be seen working together, which would have been impracticable if three or four wagons had been following 400 paces in rear of each battery. What would have become of these groups of wagons at the word of command, "Advance from the right in column of divisions"?

When we, on the morning of the 3d of July 1866, were called to arms in our bivouac near Rettendorf, I was summoned to the railway station at Königinhof to receive my orders, and hastened

thither.   As I was about to start, the commander of
the 2d Field Brigade, Major von Miesitschek, came
up to me with the request that I would allow him
to march with all the guns of the batteries of his
brigade at the head of the column, and would permit
the whole of the wagons to follow in rear, saying
that unless I permitted this he could not command
his brigade as a whole in its advance against the
enemy.   Hurried as I was, I said as I rode off,
" All right, do as you like."   I bitterly repented
this.   For what happened ?

The orders given in Königinhof by the General
commanding the corps directed that the reserve
artillery should cross the Elbe at Königinhof after
the 1st Division of the Guard, and should be followed
by the 2d Division of the Guard.   After I had led
the head of the reserve artillery into Königinhof, and
begged the commander of the 2d Division to allow
them to go in front of him, I pushed on to Chotieborek, in order to make myself acquainted with the
position of the battle.   In the meantime the 2d
Division of the Guard had allowed the batteries of
the corps artillery to pass through the town.   But
when the Division saw nothing but ammunition-
wagons following (there were forty of them) they
mistook them for an ammunition-column and, burning for action and not being willing to follow the
"train" in their advance against the enemy, marched
off, forcing the wagons to make way for them, since
orders had been given that the ammunition-columns
were not to cross the Elbe.   In this manner the
ammunition-wagons of the batteries of the reserve
artillery were missing during the whole of the battle,

as they followed in rear of all and had then to find their batteries on the field of battle, in which they did not succeed until the action was already over.

If I had had them with me earlier, that is to say, if Miesitschek had held to the formation prescribed for a rapid march, in which each gun is followed by its wagon, I should then have been at 4.30 P.M. at Chlum supplied with more ammunition, and should have been in a position, without assistance, to stop the advance of the enemy's infantry, since General von Dresky is quite right when he says, "It is impossible to break the front of a line of artillery,"—always of course understood "when it has ammunition." But we were by no means in this condition, for many batteries had only a couple of rounds left. I therefore joined in the movement in retreat (which was made by our infantry, hard pressed by the enemy's overwhelming strength) on to the hill on which the northern part of Chlum stands, after which the advance of our 1st and 6th corps put an end to that of the enemy. But I learnt one lesson by this: "*Never again to allow the batteries to be separated from all their wagons.*"

If you also take into account that, in addition to the unsatisfactory regulations as to the supply of ammunition, there was also no order that a battery which had no more ammunition ought nevertheless to remain in the line of battle, you will certainly find it most natural that batteries which had no ammunition, and were therefore defenceless, should prefer to retire rather than see their guns serve as trophies to the enemy.

When I relate to you, in contrast to the method

of 1866, upon what principles the ammunition was replaced in the year 1870, I will beg of you to allow me to describe to you the manner of proceeding which the Guard corps employed, for I do not know whether all the corps managed it in the same way. The Inspector-General of Artillery after the war of 1866 replaced the useless regulations by others, under which more liberty was given in detail. But I am not quite sure at this moment how much was a matter of regulation, and how much was the result of the initiative of the troops.

I begin with the proceedings of batteries in action. On the march batteries never moved in any other formation than that prescribed for rapid marches. A wagon followed every gun, and was under the command of the No. 1. At the rear of the battery marched the store-wagon, the field-forge, and the baggage-wagons (all the wagons connected with the internal economy of the battery), under the command of the quartermaster-sergeant. No other formation was ever employed beyond the column of route and the advance in line. When the battery formed line, the wagon still followed its gun, and the four baggage-wagons formed a third line. When the battery was about to advance into its position for action, the command was given, " Form lines of wagons ! " The guns pushed on as soon as they came within reach of the enemy's fire. The 1st line of wagons followed close behind them ; this included three ammunition and one store-wagon. The 2d line, that is, the six other wagons, were collected from the whole of the brigade, placed under the command of an officer, and posted at

some point selected by the officer commanding the
brigade. When the battery unlimbered, the wagons
of the 1st line took up a position on the left of the
guns, on the same front and with the same intervals.
The brigades did not advance (with the sole exception, mentioned above, of the movement from its
first to its second position of the 2d Field Brigade at
Sedan) into their position under the individual
command of the commander of the brigade; but
one battery after the other, in succession as they
came up in column, moved up according to the
orders which had been sent to it by the officer
commanding the brigade. These were very simple.
He brought up the leading battery himself, and sent
orders to the other batteries to take up their positions
to the right or left of it. When the ground was
open and it was in other respects advisable, each
battery in succession came into action 200 or 300
paces nearer to the enemy than the position occupied
by that which preceded it. This latter mode of
proceeding Scherbening had thought out, and had
already in 1866 carried it out successfully at
Blumenau, for thus an enemy who is standing on
the defensive, and who is firing on the first battery,
is puzzled, not being able to fire with the same
elevation on those which follow it, and is obliged to
find his range anew. When once the position is
firmly established, then the more distant batteries
must be brought up into the foremost line, in order
that their field of fire may be as open as possible in
every direction. The moral effects of this advance
are also good, for it is not wise to allow some
batteries to remain at a greater distance from the

enemy than the others. This mode of proceeding
is possible only when taking up the first position,
and when, as at Saint-Privat, the ground is open
and not undulating.   At Sedan the hills stretching
between steep-sided ravines marked so distinctly the
positions for the artillery, that this manner of
approach in echelon with intervals of 200 to 300
paces was not possible there.

After this digression into applied tactics, let us
return to the question of the renewal of ammunition.

It was established as a principle that *the ammunition in the wagons should first be used, and that in
the limbers kept as a last reserve.* So long as the
permissible slowness of the fire rendered it possible
to do so, every shell was to be taken direct from the
wagon, with which object a wagon was posted in
rear of No. 2 and another in rear of No. 5 gun.
Ammunition was allowed to be taken from the
limbers only in two cases : to fire the first shot in a
new position before the wagons had come up, and
when a rapid fire was ordered.   But as soon as the
critical moment had passed, the limbers were as
quickly as possible filled up from the wagons.   The
numbers who had been brought up on the wagons
had to assist in this duty.` As soon as a wagon was
empty, the wounded and also the dead were placed on
it (for it is not wise to leave them long in the sight
of the battery), and it was allowed to return slowly
to the collected 2d lines of the brigade.   The third
wagon of the 1st line took its place, and one from
the 2d line was brought up as quickly as possible
to the flank of the battery.   The empty wagons
which came back from the front were sent by the 2d

line of the brigade, as soon as the 1st line of the ammunition-columns had reached their proper position, to be filled up from the latter.

I found in the battles of Saint-Privat and Sedan, when I rode along the line of batteries, and looked into the limber-boxes, that they were *all full*. And when at Saint-Privat we accompanied the infantry to the assault, the batteries reached the heights which had been captured between Saint-Privat and Aman-villers, and also the closer position near to Saint-Privat, with *full limber-boxes*. We soon found this fact to be most useful. From this moment it was not any longer possible, on account of the continued necessity for a rapid fire, always to draw ammunition from the wagons. But as soon as a rapid fire ceased to be necessary, the consumption which had taken place was made up from the wagons. Thus only were we able to manage that, in spite of the enormous expenditure of ammunition in this battle, it was not until late in the evening that here and there those of the heavy batteries which had been the longest in action (of the 1st and 2d Field Brigades, since the heavy batteries had less ammunition than the light) began to be embarrassed, and had to fire the last shell of the last wagon and the whole of the ammunition in their limbers. The 15 batteries of the Guard fired on this day 8000 to 9000[1] shells. But, as I shall describe to you later, the ammunition-columns relieved this embarrassment immediately, and in good time.

The posting of the wagons of the 1st line on the same front as the batteries has, it is true, this disadvantage, that the front of a battery is thus

---

[1] An average of about 100 rounds per gun.—*N. L. W.*

increased from 120 to 200 paces, and it is therefore
practicable only when, as at Saint-Privat, there is
sufficient space.   At Sedan we could not find room
for them.   But on the whole this mode of proceeding offers nothing but advantages.   Owing to the
greater extent of front the enemy is more enveloped
with fire.   The interval of nearly 100 paces from
flank gun to flank gun of batteries facilitates the
observation of the effect and the correction of the
elevation, and also offers a position for the escort
which the infantry furnishes.   You may think,
perhaps, that the wagons of the 1st line, when they
stand in the front line, will suffer greater loss than
they would if they were 300 to 400 paces in rear.
The contrary is the case.   In these days of rifled
guns the space from 300 to 400 paces in rear of the
battery is more dangerous than a position near to the
battery and in line with it, owing to the splinters of
shell which spread about in all directions.   The
enemy's rifled guns shoot so well that their shells do
not go sufficiently wide of the mark to hit the
wagons.   For the enemy does not lay on the
wagons, but on the guns which are firing at him.
Thus it arises that wagons posted near the batteries
and on the same front suffer less than they would
were they 300 or 400 paces to the rear.   During
the whole of the battle of Saint-Privat no wagon
was blown up, but only some limbers.

I have especially noticed the battle of Saint-Privat,
because in it there was the greatest expenditure of
ammunition.   In the battle of Sedan the 15 batteries
of the artillery of the Guard fired only 5000 shells.[1]

[1] About 55 rounds per gun.—*N.L.W.*

At no time during this latter battle was it necessary to call for the assistance of the ammunition-columns.

Let me now describe to you the arrangements for the renewal of ammunition by the ammunition-columns, and for the replenishment of the latter from the depots of field ammunition.

The nine ammunition-columns which followed an army-corps were divided into two lines, of which the 1st, consisting of two infantry and one artillery columns (this proportion was reversed after the battle of Saint-Privat), followed the corps at the distance of half a day's march ; while the 2d, consisting of the other six columns, was a whole march in rear. The officer commanding the column brigades marched with the 1st line, and received daily orders for his guidance from the officer commanding the corps artillery, who himself received them from the officer commanding the corps. The distance of the columns from headquarters made the transmission of orders a matter of great difficulty. For it is evident that, since the army-corps cannot until the evening, after the arrival of information about the enemy, either come to a decision or issue orders, it must be very difficult to send, during the night, 23 to 27 (English) miles (including the length of the corps on the march), in order to carry to the ammunition-columns the orders for the march of the following day. Aides-de-camp and orderly officers cannot conveniently ride 23 to 27 miles during the night, and then, for example, in the case where the corps, during the day, marches 13 miles, ride in addition these 13 miles before they return to headquarters. The regular direction of the ammunition-columns is

P

therefore only possible by establishing, on the principle of the experiences of the year 1866, a flying line of relays of orderlies between the headquarters of. the corps, the headquarters of the corps artillery, the headquarters of the commanders of columns, and lastly between them and their two lines of columns. These orderlies were relieved daily. These flying relays of orderlies were sufficient for the regular transmission of orders, but the columns had to struggle against innumerable difficulties, and to surmount tremendous obstacles. For in the rear of an army-corps the roads are claimed by the columns of train, the pontoon-train, the requisitioned wagons, the field hospitals, etc. In extraordinary cases, when we were about to begin to advance for battle, aides-de-camp were sent, who certainly had to ride considerable distances.

The leaders of the ammunition-columns were bound in addition to exert their utmost efforts to prevent the troops, when in action, from being left without ammunition, and in the case of a battle were expected to push on, on their own responsibility, without orders. The officer commanding the column brigades was instructed, as soon as he should know or hear that a battle was probable, to come without orders as quickly as possible to the officer commanding the artillery of the corps, if he could find him, in order to receive his directions as to where the ammunition-columns should be posted. These orders were then sent, during the action, to the divisions and the corps artillery, so that they might know where to send the empty ammunition-wagons to be filled.

But any regular daily direction of the ammunition-columns was altogether impossible when several corps marched one behind the other on the same road, since each of them with their combatant troops alone occupied nearly 14 (English) miles of road. In this case it was only possible to follow the instructions conscientiously, and to do one's utmost to follow on, and to gain touch of one's own troops as soon as possible, and, without waiting for any orders, to act on one's own responsibility. Allow me to tell you how well these gallant officers did their duty.

The railways were in 1870, at the time of the concentration of our army towards the west, so entirely taken up by the combatant troops, that at first only three ammunition-columns (one line) were sent forward after each army-corps. The orders regarding this matter were drawn up by the railway section of the General Staff at Berlin, and the officers commanding troops had nothing to do with it, nor any knowledge of it, since these orders were varied according to the movements of the enemy, which could not be foreseen. It was not until the troops joined their leaders that the latter had any power over their disposition.

We (the headquarters of the Guard) were disentrained on the 1st of August at Mannheim, remained there during the 2d, marched on the 3d to Dürkheim, and on the 4th to Kaiserslautern. Here, as we marched in, the three ammunition-columns of the 1st line were disentrained, after the cavalry division of the Guard and the corps artillery had left the railway. Now at least the 1st line of the ammunition-columns had come under my command. But its commander, Major von Heineccius, had not arrived.

He had received orders to march by road with the other six columns from Berlin to Wittenberg, where he was to entrain. We heard nothing more of these six columns until the 15th of August. The direction of even the first three columns was very difficult, as three army-corps were then marching on one road. The corps which followed us blocked up their way, and yet they were obliged to advance. There were thus often collisions between the various troops, and the columns scarcely found the roads free even at night. On the 9th of August, when the deployment on the French frontier had been completed, all the three columns could for the first time march regularly.

On the 15th of August a written report arrived from the commander of the ammunition-columns, which said that he had on the 14th reached Saargemünd with the six other columns. He entrained on the 6th of August at Wittenberg, and disentrained on the 8th at Mainz. No one there could tell him whither the Guard corps had been directed (and this direction might be changed any day), and he then marched, trusting to chance, through the Palatinate to Westen, where he found the track of the Guard corps. According to his report, he proposed to direct the columns on the 15th by Morhange on Verminy, on the 16th to Noményy, on the 17th to Dieulouard. If you follow on the map his march from Mainz to Dieulouard, you will agree with me that such forced marches by entirely newly-organised troops deserves so much the more recognition, as they had no orders and marched to the front on their own responsibility, moved solely by zeal for the service.

Early on the morning of the 16th of August the commander of the brigade, who had ridden on in advance of his columns, reported himself in Dieulouard to the General in command, and on the evening of the 17th of August the corps orders for the first time mentioned the 2d line of the ammunition-columns. It was a great piece of good fortune that, on the evening before the great decisive battle, the first regular conveyance of orders was possible even to the very last part of the corps which had left the railway, and that thus the renewal of ammunition was made sure.

On the 16th of August the General commanding arrived at Bernécourt, the 1st line of ammunition-columns at Manonville, and the 2d, as I said, at Noményy. The corps was ordered to march on the 17th to the Meuse, the 1st line of columns being directed on Apremont, while the 2d was expected to arrive in the evening at Dieulouard.

The events of the 16th made it necessary for the Guard corps to turn to the north on the 17th. The columns of the 1st line were therefore, by a modified order of 3 A.M. on the 17th, which was brought by an aide-de-camp, directed from Manonville on Limey.

The corps orders of the evening of the 17th August, which directed the corps to be collected at a rendezvous near Mars-la-Tour at an early hour on the following morning, gave instructions to the ammunition-columns that the 1st line was to be at 7 A.M. on this day at Sponville, while the 2d was to reach Thiaucourt.

On the 18th of August, soon after the first gun

was fired, the commander of the ammunition-columns came to me and asked for orders. They were first brought forward to Doncourt, and were there stationed close in rear of the troops who were engaged between Habonville and Batilly. Their position was reported to the divisions and to the corps artillery.

I enjoyed at the very commencement of the fight a feeling of perfect confidence, for I knew, from the results of the practice which they had just completed, that the batteries had learnt to shoot excellently, and that they would be irresistible and invincible if there was no lack of ammunition ; while the renewal of the ammunition appeared to be secured. During the long cannonade General von Colomier, who commanded the artillery of the army, came up and rode along the batteries, and informed me that he had assigned all the ammunition from the 1st line of my ammunition-columns, which had come up exactly at the right time by Sponville, to the batteries of the 3d and 10th corps, which two days before had fired away so many rounds that their own columns were not in a position to supply the deficiency. Fancy my horror! I was engaged in a very hot action, and yet in rear of me my source of life was cut off. But I cannot in my inmost heart think that the General was wrong. He had to provide for the renewal of the ammunition of the whole army, and what would have been the use of the batteries of the 3d and 10th corps without any ammunition? Could he possibly foresee which artillery would on this day require the greatest quantity of ammunition?

The order was the more annoying as the com-

mander of the column brigades had just ridden off
to take up his position between Habonville and
Batilly.   When he returned to me he gave me a little
consolation by his report, that he had also heard of
General von Colomier's order and had consequently
sent an order to Thiaucourt, that the artillery ammunition-column of the 2d line should come as quickly
as possible to join the 1st line.   But it was still
doubtful if it could march so far that day, since it
had only on the previous evening completed its
forced march from Berlin to Dieulouard, and had on
that very day marched to Thiaucourt, a distance of
13 (English) miles.   The latter place was 18 miles
from the field of battle.

(After having made his report this officer remained
near me in order to see where ammunition might be
needed.   He afterwards accompanied Prittwitz's
battery, which he had commanded in the war of
1866, up the heights of Saint-Privat, where it, as I
have already stated, was the first to come into
action.)

The performances of the columns exceeded my
highest hopes.   They had not waited for the order
to advance farther, but had set out on hearing at
Thiaucourt the noise of the gigantic battle.   Two
ammunition-columns (those of Planitz and Keudell)
marched direct to the field of battle, making their
way with the greatest energy along roads covered
with all sorts of carriages, provision-columns, field
hospitals, train, etc., and in the evening supplied the
batteries directly with ammunition, sending a wagon
or two to each.   They thus obviated the embarrassment which threatened us.   But this was made

possible only by the energy of the officers in charge, and by their independence of action.

At the break of day every care was taken to fill up the limbers and the wagons of the batteries, and between noon and 2 P.M. all the five artillery ammunition-columns were emptied.

I have already told you that this required no office work on the part of the batteries. They simply sent their empty wagons to the columns; there they were filled up, while the soldier in charge of the wagon named the battery for which he sought for ammunition, and gave a receipt on a prepared form. But the columns replaced for us something more than ammunition. The batteries had lost many (275) horses in the battle, and this loss the number of the spare horses was insufficient to replace. The ammunition-columns had to give us 200 horses, for their empty wagons could now be drawn by fewer horses, and it was left to them to cover the deficiency by requisition as they marched. They also had to fill up casualties in officers and men. Many captains of batteries had been killed or badly wounded. The four commanders of the artillery ammunition-columns, who belonged to the Field Artillery regiment of the Guard, had each to take over the command of a battery. In their place reserve officers of the cavalry of the Guard (who had been appointed to assist with the columns, and had thus learnt their work) were told off as commanders of the ammunition-columns. A certain pedantry, such as clings to every officer of long service, made me at first doubt whether these cavalry officers could well fill their positions. But it proved in course of time that they were most excellent in them. These gentlemen were in time of peace, by their position as landed proprietors, accustomed to manage men, horses, and harness, and had also the habit of acting independently and on their own responsibility, as they had now frequently to do when they were marching at a distance from other troops. But a fire-worker was attached to each column to look after and to keep account of the ammunition. I soon saw what essential service these commanders of columns were able to render to us.

When the columns had made up all our losses, they were ordered to fall back. The first of them set out during the afternoon of the 19th of August.

In order to describe the machinery by which the renewal of ammunition was carried out, I must now relate to you how the columns brought up the ammunition from home.

During the battle of Saint-Privat an officer on the Staff of General von Colomier had informed me that the reserve park of field ammunition for the 2d army had been pushed forward as far as Herny, to the east of Metz, and that there the ammunition-columns could refill. The whole of the five empty artillery ammunition-columns were directed to that place, and with them the empty half infantry column which was attached; for the infantry had in proportion used much less ammunition. But the commander of the column brigade remained with the three and a half infantry ammunition-columns which followed the army-corps. The Staff of this brigade now made up, according to the receipts received, the regulation "states" which showed the expenditure, the renewal, and the balance which remained of the ammunition, and these "states" were forwarded by the officer commanding the artillery of the corps to the officer commanding the artillery of the army, that the latter might instruct the field ammunition reserve park to complete the issue. A despatch was at the same time sent by the field telegraph to give warning as to the amount to be supplied. Thus not a minute was lost, and yet a most accurate account was kept. The control of expenditure in the batteries was managed by occasional inspection of the limbers and wagons, and it was thus made certain that they actually were filled up with ammunition.

But the replenishment of the ammunition of the columns did not go on so smoothly as you might think. They made their way by Pont-à-Mousson to Herny. What did they get there? Absolutely nothing! I believe that the supplies there may probably have been expended in making good the enormous consumption by the 1st and 2d armies in the three great battles around Metz, and may have been quite exhausted. You must not forget that we have now to take into account a number of guns and a succession of battles, of which in earlier wars there was no idea. So my columns marched on, and at last found in the Prussian fortress Saarlouis the ammunition which they needed. Thence they marched to the west, and heard that the Guard corps now formed part of the army of the Meuse; so they searched for and found its track, and hurried after it by forced marches. They did all this without

receiving a single order as to their march, for no one
with the Guard corps knew where they were. And
when do you think that they reached us? For my
part I thought that I was dreaming when, on the 29th
of August, I received a report that the first of these
columns had come up with the corps. On the 31st
of August, the evening before the battle of Sedan,
they had all arrived. The first column had thus
marched 200 (English) miles in 10 days, while the
second marched 230 in 12 days. But from each of
these totals one day must be deducted, having been
expended in receiving and packing the ammunition.

On the 1st of September the columns reached
the village of Villers-Cernay, whence already on the
evening of the 1st they in part carried out the
renewal of the ammunition expended. As I have
already said, we fired only 5000 shells in the battle
of Sedan, an amount not so great as the batteries
carried with them. But the bombardment of Montmédy on the 5th of September cost us nearly 4000
shells, and on the 6th of September all the ammunition-columns of the artillery were again empty.
They marched back again by Saint-Mihiel and Pont-
à-Mousson ; the greater part of them had to return
to Saarlouis, and thence to hasten after the army.
When we, on the 19th of September, arrived in front
of Paris, the first of these columns (that under
Räbel) rejoined the corps. It had between the 6th
and the 19th of September, that is, in 14 days,
marched over 320 (English) miles. This was a
most astonishing rate of march, and is made yet
more wonderful by the fact that they met with many
delays and stoppages, which all had to be made up

by a longer march on the other days. I did not ask how many horses they expended on the way, after having obtained them from the country by requisition. Nor did I ask any questions as to how often and for how long the escort of the columns had been carried on the wagons, or how many miles they had thus been able to get over at an easy trot. I was delighted that the ammunition was there, and that the columns were complete as to their horses and equipment. They had not wasted much time in reporting themselves to the commandants of the posts on the road, or in looking for quarters. They marched every morning and afternoon, while at noon they bivouacked and cooked, and passed the night as a rule in villages near the road, but unoccupied by troops, trusting for protection to the rifles of the infantry escort.

The later actions were not sufficiently severe to cause any particular difficulties in the renewal of ammunition. Also by that time the field ammunition-park had been pushed forward to Epernay.

Although punctual renewal of the ammunition took place in every battle at which I was present in 1870-71, I was nevertheless convinced that the quantity of ammunition which we carry, whether with the batteries or with the columns, is not sufficient. You cannot safely reckon, especially in the case of decisive battles, where such great masses of troops are collected to take part in the decision, upon the columns being able to make their way through the combatant troops during the very day of the battle. We must therefore fill up the limbers and wagons of the batteries with as much ammuni-

tion as they can possibly consume during the whole
length of a day of battle. We had not as much as
this in 1870. On the 18th of August we first came
into action about noon, and yet by the evening we
had to have recourse to the ammunition-columns, in
order to prevent embarrassment. I am sure that
our supply would not have been sufficient if we had
come into action in the early morning.

Moreover, I consider that the supply which was
carried in the columns in 1870 was not sufficient.
After the great expenditure on the 18th of August
all the columns were empty. If the consumption of
ammunition had been greater, as it might well have
been had we commenced the action at an earlier
hour, there would not then have been a sufficiently
large supply in the columns to fill up the batteries
in readiness for a fresh battle. But this necessity
must be provided for, unless the General's hands
are to be tied while the columns are bringing up
ammunition.

After the war the question arose as to how much
infantry ammunition should be carried in the columns,
seeing that during the war of 1866, as a rule, the
average expenditure per man was only from seven to
eleven cartridges, while in 1870 only a few infantry
ammunition-wagons had to be filled up when already
the whole of the artillery columns were emptied. But
no certain conclusions can be grounded on these
experiences, since the overwhelming effect of the
breech-loader in 1866 generally brought about a
rapid decision, so that the infantry fight was but
short; while in the year 1870 our gallant infantry
had generally to undergo in silence the long-range

fire of the enemy, so long as they (on account of the inferior range of the needle-gun as compared with the chassepot) were unable to answer it. In battle between two equally-armed infantries the expenditure of ammunition will be much greater than was that of our infantry. We must thus, in order to arrive at an opinion on this subject, abandon the consideration of our war experiences, and seek for some other foundation for our reasoning.

I have told you already (in *Letters on Infantry*) that when a company and a battery, both at war strength, placed side by side on the practice ground, opened a well-aimed and well-managed rapid fire, the amount of ammunition consumed by the two arms was in weight (and also in value) almost exactly the same. This fact as regards weight is decisive with respect to the replenishment of ammunition. If we suppose that both arms are engaged during the whole of a day in a warm, well-managed, rapid fire, then each company will expend the same weight of ammunition as one battery. An army-corps contains 25 battalions (100 companies) and 19 batteries ; the supply of infantry ammunition should therefore be five times as great as that for the artillery. But the latter arm expends a proportionally greater weight of ammunition in action, since it fires at longer ranges and for a longer time. The effective range of artillery may be considered as five times that of the infantry, and thus a battery will in battle use five times as much ammunition as a company. I consider then that we ought in future to have with an army-corps the same number of small-arm and artillery ammunition-columns.

If you now ask what should be the proportion of shell and case-shot, I will allow you to decide that on the ground of the consumption in 1870-71. During the whole of this war the batteries of the artillery of the Guard expended about 25,000[1] shells and one case-shot. And the latter was broken in transport.

If you feel that I have said too much to you about artillery ammunition, remember this : Artillery with open ground in front is invincible if it has ammunition ; without ammunition it is a burden to its friends, preparatory to becoming a trophy for its enemies.

[1] About 270 rounds per gun.—*N.L.W.*

LETTER X

HOW THE ARTILLERY "SAVED" ITSELF DURING THE LAST WAR

WE have still to examine another point, in which the employment of the artillery in the war of 1870-1871 compares favourably with that which obtained in the earlier war, namely, with reference to the system of retiring the batteries, which was the custom in 1866, either for the purpose of refitting or in order to avoid the infantry fire of the enemy. This was no longer done in 1870, and was the result of regulations and habits invented and prescribed during the course of a long period of peace, it having no foundation on the experience of war.

As regards "refitting," I refer you to the paragraphs concerning " Disabled Ordnance," which for the most part had no other object than to "save" the guns. The first example, which was continually practised, was that which consisted in lashing a spar under the axle-tree, and how great was the importance attached to the neatness of the various kinds of lashings! But how could this contrivance be possibly used, except to drag the gun to the rear, that is to say, to retire it? It was said, it is true, that a gun so fitted could be fired, and in order to prove this a blank cartridge was fired from a gun so prepared. But when once at "Instructional Practice" a shell was fired from a gun thus fitted with a spar, the latter broke like a toothpick with the recoil, amidst the general laughter of all the officers, who thus learnt something that they did not know before. The question as to where you are at once to obtain such a spar was solved by the regulations, which said that you were to cut down and prepare some tree which stood conveniently near. But the fact stares one in the face that more time would be taken up in this carpenter's work than would be required to bring up a spare wheel from the wagon ; but nevertheless the lashing of the spar was always a favourite exercise. I further recall to your recollection the system of lashing the gun under the limber, in order to save it, that is, to get it away in time. In the four campaigns of 1864, 1866, 1870, and 1871, I never saw any use made of a spar lashed to the axle-tree, or of the process of lashing the gun to the limber. I might almost dare to assert that no artillery officer ever saw either during these wars.

It is true that the regulations laid down that these operations were to be performed " whenever possible " in the line of battle, but it was added that guns which could not be " refitted " in that line were to be retired from it, in order that they might be made serviceable out of reach of the enemy's fire. The amount of retirement which would be necessary for this condition has been very much increased by the invention of rifled guns, and would now be about 2 (English) miles. Should a captain send away a single gun as far as this under the charge of a N.C.

Q

officer, he may reasonably fear that he will never see it again. It is, further, very difficult to tell beforehand whether it is or is not possible to refit under the fire of the enemy. This depends very much upon the effect of his fire while the work is going on, a matter which cannot be known beforehand. Thus whenever any gun of the battery, or most of them, required some sort of repair, the officer commanding the battery could, without breaking the regulations, retire "for the purpose of refitting."

There was also the disgrace which befell any one who lost a gun. Since the time of the War of Liberation this had been considered as a heinous fault. When Bernadotte hesitated to advance to Blücher's assistance and take part in the battle of Leipzig, since the movement demanded seemed to him too dangerous, he with reference to this subject plumed himself upon the fact that he had fought so many battles and had never lost a gun. It is perfectly right that a gunner should prefer to fall under his gun rather than lose it, since his country's eagle is engraved on the gun, while with his hand on his gun he swore his oath of allegiance, and the gun is his colours. But it is nevertheless better to lose a gun than a battle. After the war of 1866 different principles obtained with regard to this question. In 1870 and 1871 we lost guns in action, as we lost also one colour. And how great was the glory which these losses brought to the troops which suffered them. They are inscribed on the brightest pages of our military history. Thus it was received as a principle that the loss of a gun was in itself no disgrace, but that praise or blame should be guided by the behaviour of the troops.

After the war of 1866 it was laid down as a rule that no gun, in whatever condition it might be, was to be retired from the firing line for the purpose of refitting, and thus in the war of 1870 every gun remained in that line and was repaired with the stores from the store-wagon, which stood near the battery in the 1st line of battery wagons.

There was perhaps much temptation for many officers commanding batteries to follow the regulations, and with a praiseworthy regard for the preservation of their guns, to withdraw them out of action. I have already once directed your attention to the fact that the instinct of self-preservation, which is innate in human nature, never directly influences educated men, but speaks to their hearts under the guise of some plausible excuse, and thus gradually wins its way. But if an excuse is wanting, then it loses its force, for an educated man will before all do his duty. The need to refit, the want of ammunition, and the fire of infantry (of which I shall speak later), were such excuses, and very reasonable excuses they were. It is a difficult thing to fix the moment at which these excuses speak to the heart. This depends upon the toughness of the nerves. Many men who take part for the first time in an action appear to me like a party of people who bathe on a really hot summer's day in a very cold river. They leap with joy into the water, and at first delight with rapture in the delicious freshness. But after a little time some of them begin to shiver and long to get out, and so on with the others, some soon, some very

late.   It requires strong nerves and constant habit
to feel comfortable in water for hours together.   But
under all circumstances the whole party are happier
when they are dressing after their bath than they
were beforehand.

Our nerves in 1870 were the same as they were
in 1866.   But the regulations were different.   For
the first principle laid down was, that no artillery,
not even one gun, should dare to make a movement
to the rear, under any circumstances, except in the
case of a direct order to do so.   Consequently in
1870 I did not see one retire in order to refit.   There
were plenty of guns put out of action.   In the battle
of Saint-Privat, as I have already told you, when it
was a question of accompanying the infantry in their
attack, a total of three guns out of the batteries under
my command were altogether unable to advance.
They could naturally not come on with the others,
so remained where they were, but were there refitted,
and followed as soon as possible to the new position.
At Sedan one gun of mine became altogether un-
serviceable.   The gun had burst.   But the carriage
looked very pretty in the firing line.   I believe that
also in other corps in 1870 it never or seldom
happened that artillery or single guns retired without
orders to do so.

But before 1866 there were even regulation
movements, which directly taught us to " desert in
front of the enemy " ; forgive me the expression, for
I can find no other.   These movements were for
choice practised and learnt, since when they were
well done they looked very showy.   What else can
you call it when a battery of Horse Artillery, as soon

as the trail-eye in limbering up to retire had been dropped on to the pin-tail, went off when the " Trot " was sounded, while the gunners had to mount as quickly as possible and were hurried after the battery by the word of command from the captain : " Left turn—wheel—gallop ! "   Have you ever before 1866 seen a Horse Artillery battery at drill without this manœuvre being executed ?   Certainly it looked very lively and pretty as the gunners leaped on their horses with astonishing dexterity and then chased their guns. But think what would be the effect in front of the enemy of one little mistake.   I will only suppose that the captain has overlooked that No. 6 gun has not finished limbering up, and that he thus sounds the " Trot " prematurely.   Thereupon five guns and one limber trot off too soon, and the gunners give chase, while the enemy's shells flying after them add wings to the speed of the horses, who pass from the trot to the gallop and finally get out of hand.   In vain will the captain try to catch up the empty limber at least, for its horses can go as fast as his own.   Shouts and trumpet-calls cannot be heard on account of the rattle of the carriages, while the racing pace of the captain, who wants to catch up his limber, seems to the detachments a proof that he approves of this rapid retreat ; so on they go in their mad race for about two miles, until at last some obstacle offered by the nature of the country brings the battery to a halt. If then the dragoons, who accompanied him to the front, drag back to the captain with their lassoes the gun which he left behind, before he can give the order to go and fetch it, he has nothing left to do but to receive back his prodigal son from them with profuse shame and thanks.

I do not know, and I do not think, that anything of this sort happened to us in the year 1866 ; but I do know that after that war an order was issued that artillery, when it had received an order to retire, was to do so only at a walk, and was only under exceptional circumstances to move at a quicker pace, if it had to clear the front of an artillery line which was in action farther to the rear, and on the flank of which it proposed to come into action. In any case artillery when falling back *must retire over the first hundred paces, after limbering up, at a quiet walk.* The latest regulations contain also a similar order. This elegant desertion of a Horse Artillery battery in front of the enemy was thus abolished even from the drill-ground. It was no more seen during the period between the wars of 1866 and 1870.

Another still more elegant form of regulation quick movements in retreat was a charge made in open order by the mounted detachments, while the battery retired into a position farther to the rear. I must admit that I, when I was a subaltern, always took part in this charge with the greatest delight. After it was over the sounding of the " Assembly " recalled the detachments, and they raced over the 1500 paces or so which divided them from the battery as hard as they could go, spreading all over the drill-ground at headlong speed. They had to get all they could out of their horses in order to arrive between the guns in time, and not to find themselves in front of the muzzles when firing commenced. For hardly had the detachments reached

their battery before the first of the guns, which had
been loaded by the limber-gunners, was fired with a
roar, and all the spectators of the other arms lavished
their praises on the magnificent spectacle which they
had beheld.   Then my heart swelled in my bosom
and, excited as I was by the rapid joyous movement,
and flattered by the applause of my comrades, I
imagined myself to have played the part of a hero.
For this manœuvre was the crowning movement of
the drill of the artillery.   I never considered that such
a charge against an enemy was inconceivable, and
that were it possible it would be wrong, nor did I
remember that there was no particular reason to be
proud of having run away.   And yet this crowning
movement of our drill manœuvres did represent
a flight.

That such a charge in front of the enemy would
not be conceivable, and if it were possible would be
a fault, you will perhaps refuse to grant.   Well, I
will ask you, how far to my front shall I suppose the
enemy to be when I undertake this charge?   100
paces ?   In that case he will drive back my detachments and will rush in with them pell-mell among the
guns, which he will overtake, as they will not have sufficient start.   400 paces or more?   In that case I
shall retire with my detachments without charging, and
he will not catch me ; I shall thus not lose the half
of my men, nor weaken the effective strength of the
battery.   For you cannot suppose that the charge
can be successful.   If the enemy were so few in
number that the 48 mounted men of a battery could
defeat him in a charge, then a well-directed fire of
case, opened at a range of 200 paces, would so

decimate him that he would not reach the battery in any dangerous strength. Will any one ask the mounted men of a battery to join a cavalry line which is about to charge, with a view of reinforcing it? That would, in my opinion, be exactly as if the officer commanding a battalion were to dismount the half-troop of hussars, which might be attached to him, and to reinforce his line of skirmishers with them on the occasion of an attack on a village. It is true that this has been done, but only at *Kriegspiel* by some subaltern who has just received his commission. Under all possible circumstances the battery will destroy ten times as many of the enemy by its fire as it would by a charge of the gun detachments, and it will stop the enemy sooner by its fire than by the charge, if only the men will lay quietly. Since it is thus better to fire than to charge, it must be wrong to do the latter.

The order that artillery was always to retire the first hundred paces at a walk, made this show-movement also disappear between the wars of 1866 and 1870.

Since the Horse Artillery has had rifled guns, and the infantry has had long-range rifles, any such charge by the gun detachments is, in my opinion, absolutely impossible in real war, whether it be intended to cover the flight of the guns or not. These various charges by mounted gunners had their origin from one single instance in the War of Liberation. There was once a Horse Artillery battery which, while in action, found itself attacked in flank by a little group of hostile skirmishers, who had come up so close that the bullets, in spite of the short range of the

S.B. muskets, were taking effect on the battery.
According to the tactical views of those days, the
battery ought to have retired. But the captain was
a gallant fellow, and mounted part of his detachments
and with them drove off the skirmishers. He thus
rightly earned great praise. Later on he became
Chief of the Staff of the artillery (Von Jenichen), and
later still was the Inspector of the 2d artillery
district. He was indeed one of the most important
generals of artillery of his time. His ideas and his
actions were held as a standard in the artillery.
Thus was the charge of the gun detachments of the
artillery introduced in various forms. Naturally it
was not omitted when the celebrated Jenichen
made his inspection.

But in these days the dispersal of skirmishers by
such a charge is an absolutely impossible movement
in war, since these skirmishers can now annoy us at
a range of more than 1000 paces, and you would
not, I am sure, allow the detachments to be sent 1000
paces to the front, in order that they might cut down
a few skirmishers. The fire of the battery is more
efficacious and of more use than the swords of a few
gunners, while ten skirmishers could nowadays cope
with fifty mounted gunners, if the latter should
charge them.

As far as regards the employment of artillery as
such, it would be desirable that a gunner should
have no other arm than his gun, and should devote
all his energies to serving it well, and should see in
it his only source of safety. I could name to you
an officer in high command in the artillery (if he
had allowed me to do so) who was riding quietly to

and fro between his batteries playing with his riding-whip (which he carried because his horse had a habit of refusing), while the enemy's cavalry was charging the guns, and who, when his adjutant asked him whether he would not draw his sword, quietly answered, " I will take very good care not to do so, otherwise every gunner will draw his, instead of laying and firing, and then the cavalry will be sure to ride over the battery." But the charge died away under the fire of case at fifty paces from the guns. Unfortunately it is not possible for other reasons to march a soldier to war without a weapon by his side. Here or there on the march or in quarters, it is neces-sary to guard one's skin against hostile inhabitants of the country. Besides a soldier without a weapon would be a ridiculous object. General von Dresky wrote to me, in the letters which I have already quoted, that he, as he was hurrying to the battle of Vionville through narrow roads, sent two gun detach-ments of Horse Artillery to the head of the column, to turn off to the side of the road all wagons, etc., which hampered the advance of the corps artillery. If these detachments had not carried swords, you may imagine that they would not have succeeded in their purpose.

But there is no reason why they should therefore practise the charge ; it is only necessary for them to be able to ride and to handle their swords. It is moreover wrong to found a system of instruction for the time of peace on some single exceptional incident which may have happened in war, and thus to take up some of the precious and too short time allowed for instruction. It once happened that the Horse

Artillery which was under my command arrived at their appointed quarters, which were quite near to a fortress of the enemy, and found that there were no covering troops between them and the fortress. I do not know, and it does not much matter now, with whom the fault lay, that the troops which had been told off for this duty had not reached their position. As a matter of fact the major pushed forward picquets, vedettes, and patrols towards the fortress, until some hours later the other arms came up. But I have never on this account thought of proposing that, in consequence of this single incident, the Horse Artillery should, in time of peace, practise the out-post duties of cavalry.

General von Dresky makes the following narration: After the capture of Orleans on the 5th of September 1870, I received orders to operate up the river Loire on the right bank against Bourges. The corps marched on one road in the following order: 5th Division, corps artillery, 6th Division. They marched with large intervals in order to prevent checks. I followed the 5th Division at a distance of about two miles. On the 8th December 1870 we were drawing near to Gien, when we heard in front of us a fairly strong fire of infantry, which however soon ceased. I thereupon pressed on my march and soon reached Gien, through which the 5th Division had just passed. They had been fighting against franc-tireurs, who had posted themselves in the houses of the suburb which lies on the left bank of the Loire. The bridge over the Loire had been blown up, and the river was full of ice. The streets of the town ran partly parallel and partly perpen-

dicular to the Loire.   As I turned with the head of
the column into one of the latter streets, I received
a scattered infantry fire from the houses of the
suburb, probably from the franc-tireurs who had returned.   As I had no infantry with me, I could not
at the moment undertake anything in the narrow
streets of the town.   I suffered no loss, for the enemy
fired too high.   The outlet from Gien towards
Briare lies close to the Loire, which is here about
500 paces wide.   By the side of the river the road
is planted with high poplars, while on the other side
there are houses.   When I had passed the gate with
a part of the leading battery, the fire from the suburb
became so strong that we had some casualties, fortunately only from slight hits, and those mostly
among the horses.   The enemy shot very badly, and
the poplars gave us some cover.   I now ordered the
heavy battery which was leading the column to come
into action to its flank and to fire on the franc-tireurs.
After two rounds a house was set on fire and the
franc-tireurs disappeared, so that I continued my
march without any further molestation.

But no one will propose, in consequence of this
unusual situation, to issue a regulation, according to
which artillery should be practised in passing through
a town occupied by the enemy's infantry.

Perhaps you will shake your head and say that
it might happen that artillery would be obliged to
retire quickly from their position.   But you will
perhaps allow that when cavalry has come so close
that the very greatest haste would be necessary, it is
then too late to retire, and it is better to continue to
fire.   But if infantry suddenly comes so immediately

upon artillery? You do not surely desire that artillery should now, as it used to do, accept as a principle that it should vanish as soon as a couple of infantry bullets fall into a battery. It will, and can and must hold its ground, though the enemy's infantry come to within 1000, even to within 500 paces. It is at this very moment that it offers the best support to its own struggling infantry, and will perhaps so decimate the superior masses of the enemy that they will give way. But how, you may perhaps ask, if the enemy's infantry suddenly surprises the artillery and appears at a distance of 100 paces? In that case the guns can under no circumstances retire, for if they try to limber up and get off, the enemy will hit at least one horse in each team, and thus the gun will remain where it was and fall into the hands of the enemy. The only chance of safety for the artillery is to drive back the enemy by its fire, and it may perhaps succeed in doing this by its very last shot, when the assailants are only 10 paces from the gun. The 5th 4-pr. battery of the Guard did this near Rosberitz in the battle of König- grätz, when it was about to retire with our few companies, who had been driven back by the over- whelming strength of the enemy, and suddenly (as the report says) saw a mass of the enemy's infantry (a battalion or a division of two companies) rise out of a hollow in the ground in its front. The officer commanding the battery gave the order to fire case (we may add that the shells which were already in the guns were first fired, and bursting in the midst of the masses of the enemy produced even more effect than the case), and this fire in conjunction with the rapid fire of one company, which once again formed front, drove back the enemy for some distance. The battery took advantage of this moment to make a quiet and orderly retreat.

Moreover, artillery must never retire while a hostile attack is advancing against it. This is the most favourable time for good effect of fire. If the artillery has been ordered to retire, it must for this purpose take advantage of the pause which will ensue when the assailant has been stopped by its fire, and is wavering until he shall be ready to push forward again when he has been reinforced by fresh troops. But if the artillery receives too late the order from the general to retire (and without such an order it must not retire), so that it cannot withdraw quietly and in order, in that case it must give up all idea of falling back, and cannot be blamed if it loses its guns. It is better in this case to go on gloriously firing than to allow itself to be captured while flying.

Such were the principles which were laid down for the behaviour of the artillery after the war of 1866, and which were observed during the war of 1870. On these principles at Spicheren it held its ground on the Rothe-berg, and at Vionville stood fast in line in the centre of the action ; on these principles the guns were gloriously lost near Aman-villers [1] at the battle of Saint-Privat, and at Beaune-la-Rolande ; and on these principles we lost

---

[1] At Amanvillers more guns were put altogether out of action than fell into the hands of the enemy, since many batteries lost, according to their lists of casualties, all their men and horses who were in the firing line, and were later on supplied with others, thus remaining still fit for action as batteries.

no guns at Coulmiers,[1] though the battle went against us.

There were before 1866 many other regulations for the artillery which put forward in a too prominent position the necessity of saving the guns, and thus tended (more from fear of blame than from fear of the enemy) to make us too timid of holding our ground before the foe. Allow me to give you only a few examples. I possess an old *Handbook for Officers of the Prussian Artillery*. In this I find, at page 696, with regard to the choice of a position : " The ground within the field of battle which may be selected as a position for artillery, must give the power of free movement in all directions, *particularly towards the rear.*" If these regulations had been still in force in 1870, General von Bülow would not have dared at Spicheren to push forward the two batteries which secured the Rothe-berg through a wood-road, which was narrow and steep, and wound along under rocky precipices. In the same manner the position of Colonel von Dresky and his corps artillery at Vionville would have been contrary to regulation, since it stood immediately in front of the passage over a marshy ditch with but a small bridge, which was, moreover, under the fire of the enemy's chassepots. These two examples will be sufficient ; if I wished to cite them all to you I should be obliged to write an extraordinarily thick book, since I am convinced that three-quarters of all our artillery positions in the war of 1870-71 would fall under this category. But after 1866 the regulations were

---

[1] The batteries made use of a pause in the enemy's movement of attack for the purpose of drawing off and retiring.

altered. Nothing more was said of retreating. It became the most sacred duty of the artillery to crown quickly with their guns any position which the infantry had carried, and thus to make its possession permanently secure. In these cases nine times out of ten there was a defile in rear, and thus " free movement in retreat " was not possible.

But if it was no longer possible to save the artillery, then the handbook here and there offered an expedient. On page 812 you will find, on the subject of " the regulations for the surrender of a fortress " : " The artillery officer of the place will hand over by quantity and quality the contents of the artillery depots, and will endeavour to get a receipt for them." *Sapienti sat.*

Now this handbook is not a private work, as was in its time the handbook by Von Oelze ; for the note printed on the title-page—" printed for the use of the service "—gives it at least a semi-official character almost equivalent to that of a regulation book.

It will puzzle you, as it does me, how such regulations for the conduct of an arm which did so many noble deeds during the War of Liberation can have crept in. I can only find a solution for the puzzle in the fact, that the longer the peace lasted the more were the exercises carried on in peace taken as a standard, and the more were the experiences of war forgotten. During the manœuvres, up to the war of 1864, as you can well remember, it was considered the very greatest disgrace for the artillery to be captured, whereas on the other hand the other arms hunted passionately after the enemy's guns. A good soldier will gladly stake his all but not his honour. Thus the artillery never willingly placed themselves in danger of being taken. Holding such opinions, and besides also perhaps animated by the true spirit of administration, the authors of such regulations have written orders to the best of their ability, but such as were never founded on the experiences of war. For the authors, who lived during the nearly fifty years of peace, had never seen war. That the old veterans of the War of Liberation should have allowed such regulations to be printed is easily explained by their size. The handbook which I have mentioned has 871 closely-printed large octavo pages. What senior general of artillery could, in addition to his ordinary work, read all this with attention and correct it with care?

I must add that I have not divulged to you one of the mysteries of the artillery by speaking to you of the regulations contained in this book. It was for sale by the trade, and any one could buy it.

As regards the advisability of the artillery avoiding the zone of infantry fire, this was also taught to the arm during the course of the long peace, and orders on the subject were very distinct. "You are under infantry fire here," was one of the most severe reproofs which the officer commanding a battery could receive at the manœuvres. Artillery which was exposed to infantry fire was, at the manœuvres, obliged always to retire, whether it liked it or not. If the officer commanding a battery had said that he did not wish to retire, and that he considered that the moment had come for him to sacrifice himself,

R

he would simply have been told not to talk nonsense. Besides, the umpire always ordered the retirement, and the umpire must be obeyed, or manœuvres become impossible. After the fire of infantry had increased its range by the invention of the rifled breechloader, the artillery, before it had rifled guns (and thus especially in the sixth decade of this century), had to play a very discouraging part at manœuvres. It could scarcely advance far enough towards the enemy to obtain really good effect from its fire, before it came under the fire of infantry, and in this it was not allowed to remain. Even if it took up a position, it was quickly, according to the umpire, "driven out" of it by infantry fire. Thus it was hunted from position to position, and had in addition while it was moving to take care not to be captured somewhere or other by a squadron of the enemy. In those days the enemy's artillery was an object of far greater interest to the other arms than was their own. Their own artillery was not of much use to them ; on the other hand, they were obliged to defend it, and it was considered a matter of reproach to the other arms when their artillery was captured. But the enemy's artillery might at least be taken, and they might thus gain some distinction. Under these circumstances it was quite natural that officers of limited intelligence should when in difficulties say, "I would rather not employ artillery at all. I am always getting into trouble about them."

There were hundreds and thousands of cases, in the war of 1870-71, where artillery which refused to retire could not be driven back by infantry fire. Thus we may consider the decision of the umpires, that artillery should be compelled to allow itself to be driven back by infantry fire, as one of the most unnatural of all such decisions.   Such decisions are also ruinous in their consequences, since when they are constantly repeated during a long period of peace, all artillery officers who have not seen war end by believing that artillery cannot stand its ground under infantry fire, and the natural consequences of this will be that they also, as so many others have already done, will in war at once give way before the fire of infantry.   But officers who have not seen service will soon be in the majority amongst us.   Even now, as I write, fourteen years have already flown by since the battle of Saint-Privat, and politically everything looks so peaceful on our frontiers that we might easily imagine that no further war would threaten us during the present century.   It is therefore my duty to give warning in time, lest we should in the course of a long peace allow bad habits to grow up during manœuvres, which shall cause false ideas to strike root, and lest permanent decisions may be given, which obedient officers will observe at the beginning of a war, and will thus innocently bring upon themselves grave suspicion that they have too willingly withdrawn from under the fire of the enemy.

I repeat yet once more, and I cannot too often repeat : *Artillery cannot, generally speaking, ever be driven back by infantry, if it refuses to leave its ground.*   On the contrary, when the infantry fire is really hot, it cannot for the moment fall back, since too many of its horses will then be shot.   But nevertheless nothing is lost, so long as there are a couple of men left with each gun, who can load and lay quietly ; it can thus go on doing its full work until the last gunner is disabled.

I know well that an umpire at manœuvres cannot always attribute the victory to the artillery. Neither can he compel it to take flight if it does not wish to do so. He may give any decision he likes; for example, that it has been annihilated. But if it has carried out the tactical operations properly, and has behaved well from an artillery point of view, it should be praised for this and not blamed ; above all, it must not be loaded with shame. Only thus can artillery be prepared in manœuvres to be ever ready to sacrifice itself in war.

I cannot pretend that all umpires in manœuvres since the war of 1866 have acted in this manner as I could have wished. On the contrary, the decisions that artillery must retire when it comes under infantry fire were, between 1866 and 1870 (and even after 1870-71), as frequent and as stereotyped as they were before. But the artillery itself endeavoured to prove that it could stand under infantry fire just as well as the infantry could. In this also the original determination to hold out to the end came from the artillery itself, actuated as it was by the true Prussian soldier spirit. This is a proof that it was in no way a discredit to those men who commanded the artillery in 1866 if, they being without experience of war and trusting simply to the custom of the service and the regulations, the artillery of 1866 did not distinguish itself so much as did that of 1870. It was urged on in 1870 by the pressing desire to prove its equality with the infantry, which appeared to it to be rendered doubtful by the events of 1866. Thence arose, in contradiction to all the decisions of umpires up to that time, the heroism of the batteries on the Rothe-berg at Saarbruck; thence also the endurance of the collected batteries which Colonel von Dresky led at first into his position at the battle of Vionville; thence the words of the captain of the 6th light battery of the Guard (Ising), who was asked, after the battle of Saint-Privat, when his arm had been amputated, whether he was in much pain, and answered, " Pain! Not a bit! I should not have minded losing my other arm as well, since we have shown that we also can hold our ground under infantry fire "; thence also the order of one of the officers commanding the artillery in one of the great battles of 1870, when one of his subordinates drew his attention to the fact that the line of guns was under infantry fire, and that they must eventually be compelled to retire: " All right!—sound ' Drivers dismount!' Now we cannot retire."

I will not worry you with still more examples from military history, for they might in time weary you. Have they done so already? Let me only give you one fact drawn from statistics: If the surgeons who were employed in 1870 and 1871 would make a collected report on the wounded among the German artillery, saying how many were hit by the artillery fire and how many by the infantry fire of the enemy, I am persuaded that the result would show that 75 per cent were hit by infantry fire. This was at least the proportion in the batteries under my command, and I have no reason to believe that the other artilleries of our army showed less endurance.

Least of all did they do so on the Rothe-berg at
Spicheren or at Vionville.

If artillery wishes to "save" itself, it must kill its
enemy by its fire.   This is its only safety, as far as
I can see.   If acting thus it does not save itself, it
will at least save its honour.

LETTER XI

I CANNOT consider my remarks on the reasons for
the improvement of the arm between 1866 and 1870
as complete unless I mention a certain name, even
at the risk of being accused by you of wandering
from my subject. I have not as yet told you who,
but only what, was the cause of it. It is evident
that in an army like ours, in which discipline forms
the basis of existence, an arm could not be so generally and completely improved in less than four years,
if the desire for improvement had not found a very
strong supporter among those in high places. Though
the wish for improvement was felt by the greater
number of officers of the arm, and indeed by juniors
among these, yet the minority showed less of this
desire, and even some objection to the novelty. The
driving-wheel of reform, the soul of the movement
which seized the artillery after 1866, was no other
than the Inspector-General himself, General von
Hindersin. He certainly found in all parts of the
arm willing ears and ready hands, for the need of
such changes had made itself generally felt. But
Hindersin led the transformation, and directed it ; he

brought—and this was the principal point—all the many and frequently very divergent ideas on the subject to one conclusion, and it was he who hastened the matter. Whilst the very highest authorities were constantly at work to introduce, by means of orders and criticisms, a proper tactical employment of artillery, Hindersin strove by the development which he brought about in the arm to qualify it for the employment which it was proposed to make of it. It was he who forged and sharpened the sword, while the highest authorities taught how it was to be used.

This man, who stood at the head of the arm, was an original phenomenon. As the son of a poor parson, he had been well educated, as far as regarded his talents and his heart. But he had to fight his way through life under privations and toil. This had given him an iron strength of will, but all taste for social pleasures was thereby extinguished in him and he never applied himself to develop or refine his manner in society. (Among other matters it was a subject of pride with him that he never went to balls in any but ordinary leather boots.) During his laborious and most earnest career, which he began soon after the War of Liberation under superiors of the artillery of the old school, he had acquired their roughness of speech. Though he was educated in all kinds of science (he had mastered mathematics, physics, and chemistry, and could speak English and French), he yet cared nothing for the "science" of the arm, but set practical and tactical considerations before all knowledge. For himself, like Enke, he made a truth of the expression, "The day consists of twenty-four hours of duty," and he expected very much from others.

He was peppery and very violent, and his hot temper was increased by his impatience to get things done. This impatience had its origin in his conviction that he would not live to be old, since all his brothers and his father had died of heart disease at an age earlier than that which he had already reached. He expected this end daily. But he longed, before this should happen, to see the results of his work at the head of the arm. From this there resulted a haste which compelled a greater energy in those under him, and very much accelerated many improvements, though they sometimes suffered also from a too precipitate action. Very characteristic of this was an expression which he once made use of to one of his aides-de-camp, whom he had ordered to prepare a very comprehensive and difficult report, and whose face grew long as he thought of the magnitude of the task and of the number of days that he would have to sit over it. "There is no hurry," said the General, "you can have your dinner first."

Like all hasty men he was at the bottom very good-natured. He had a kind heart for the men and for his numerous family. But he did not think it soldier-like to show that he had a kind heart and a good disposition. For this reason he preferred to pose as being rough and unkind, even to his family. His eldest son died, after many months of pain, of a wound received at Saint-Privat. He said, "The young man is very much to be envied. A young officer cannot have a better death than his. In one hand he held the Iron Cross, in the other his mother's hand." He said this just as roughly as when he blamed some fault on duty. But a slight trembling of the chin betrayed the warmth of the feeling within him. After that his air became more stiff and more iron than ever, and he began to speak of matters connected with the service.

Hard as steel were the features of his broad weather-beaten face, with its large wide brow and moustache and whiskers of a light red mixed with gray, and stiff as iron the rigid attitude of his thick-set middle-sized figure. He seldom laughed, for anything humorous was strange to him. On the occasion of the representation of a comic play by some of the officers, he left the room suddenly with the loudly-expressed exclamation, "No, this is too silly for me."

He did not desire popularity, nor did he wish to be beloved, and he was not; but generally men feared him. The wit of the young officers nicknamed him "The marble guest."[1] His family knew the goodness of his heart, though he behaved so tyrannically to them. I could give you many touching examples of this, some of which I have heard related, while some I have witnessed. But such family details must not be told abroad.

Hindersin did not willingly give praise. He feared that praise might lessen the zeal of his subordinates. But when he was compelled to praise, he liked to weaken the force of his praise by something said either before or after. And as he was by no means a good speaker, it sometimes happened that he, after diminishing his praise as much as possible at the

[1] Referring to the Commendatore in "Don Giovanni."—*N. L. W.*

beginning of his speech, diminished it again at the end, under the impression that he had given a full amount of commendation before, and thus no praise at all remained. Thus he said once in a circle of officers, who were present at a lecture given by a young officer, which had afforded him much pleasure, " As I do not agree with all which has just been laid before us here, I find very much to object to in it." The officer grew pale, and asked me afterwards whether after these words he might venture to continue his lecture, which was intended to extend over several evenings. I asked Hindersin afterwards when we were alone what it was that displeased him so much in the lecture, since he had spoken so sharply about it. He was quite astonished, thinking that he had loaded the officer with praise. But on the next occasion he made the matter all right by thanking the young officer in the most friendly way, and by telling him of his approbation as he shook him by the hand. It also once happened to me to receive from him in a similar manner the most unheard-of rudeness, while he thought that he was assuring me of his approving recognition of my behaviour with regard to the affair in question.

Hindersin, without being really short-sighted or deaf, had not either good sight or hearing. I do not know whether it was on account of this, or because of his gloomy experiences, that he was distrustful. But he was full of mistrust of his subordinates and of the men, and this often showed itself in a very unpleasant way, while it was so much the less flattering for those who suffered from it, as he always spoke out without reserve. His principle was not only to inspect the troops, but also to lie in wait for them, for he thought it always possible that they might make an X for him in place of a U, and might not carry out his orders as he had directed.

He was once inspecting at practice some troops under my command. When I wanted to show him one special detail, he declined to see it, with the observation that he had seen it eight days before and was satisfied with it. But I had not noticed him on that particular day when I had carried out this detail. I therefore apologised to him for not having reported myself to him at the time, saying that I had not known that he was present. " You were not meant to know it," he said. " I was hidden in the wood and saw you through a field-glass. I wanted for once to see how you carried on when you were left to yourself."

At another time he had fixed the beginning of the inspection at 6 A.M. It was very hot weather during the longest days of summer. From sunrise, that is, from about 3.30 A.M., he stood on a hill in a wood and watched with his glasses the preparations, the march, and the mode of taking up the position, etc. Under cover of the darkness of the night he had ridden out there from Berlin without being observed. When he had been discovered in his hiding-place I rode up to him and reported that the brigade was preparing for inspection. " Do not report to me until it is ready to commence practice. I am not yet here officially. I like to take a ride in the early morning."

The construction of the batteries at his inspection

was always carried out at night. But he did not do as his predecessors had done, who were only present at the beginning of the construction, and then went home. He remained there the whole night, and made us open fire at daybreak from the battery, which had to be completed by then, in order that the construction might not be accelerated by any illicit means, such as he knew of. His day of inspection thus began on the preceding evening, as night fell, and lasted till the next afternoon. During it he showed great self-command and tenacity. At his first inspection after he became Inspector-General, at Magdeburg in the year 1864, he fell and crushed his foot, on which account the doctors forbade him to ride. But he rode through the whole of his inspection, though suffering the most terrible pain.

A man of this kind excites by his example indefatigable zeal among his subordinates. But any one who did not feel himself quite secure, or was conscious of the least omission or neglect, had reason to be afraid of him, for he might be certain that Hindersin would, as soldiers say, "catch him on a lame horse."

I cannot deny that intercourse with him was distasteful at first. But when, later on, I came to discover how honest his intentions were, I gladly associated with him, and knowing the excellence of the kernel, paid little attention to the rough shell.

For his intention was always honest. He feared nothing so much as to be unjust to any one. I could name to you one of his subordinates whom he considered to be useless. But he hesitated up to the day of his own death to act on this opinion, because

in his youth he had had a duel with this officer, and
dreaded lest his dislike and his objection to him
personally might influence his opinion of him more
than was just.

He was a man essentially of the old school, and
yet he supported every new discovery and every new
idea.   He even received novelties which he came
across with gladness and zeal, and used indeed to
lose his temper when difficulties appeared or when
such novelties were criticised.   But he never confused
the criticisms with the critic.   On the contrary, he
afterwards quietly pondered within himself upon all
that had been said, and when he was convinced, gave
up his former ideas at once.   But when, having
considered the whole matter, he came to the conclusion
that the new idea was correct, then he set to work
with that tenacity which alone can give life to
anything.

In order to be able to rightly estimate anything
new in his department, he not only had all fresh
discoveries laid before him, but he also attended all
the military lectures which took place in Berlin, and
was able sometimes to extract something worthy of
notice from even the most immature ideas of the
youngest officers.   During one winter he collected
together periodically at a late hour of the evening the
generals and field-officers of the artillery in the halls
of the School of Artillery, and had discussions carried
on before them by officers of the School of Gunnery
and of the Ordnance Committee, on the subject of
the latest inventions.   He perhaps asked too much of
their intellectual power, and soon had to give up this
undertaking, since he convinced himself that those

whom he wished to instruct were of too high standing
and too old to be collected together for instruction;
yet the endeavour showed plainly his restless energy.

One feeling directed and animated his every step
and deed.   This was his attachment to his king and
a boundless veneration for that sovereign who has
been our leader in war.   This veneration is indeed
universal and is felt by us all; it is thus no merit
nor does it need special mention.   But I have known
few men who have been so completely influenced by
it in their least actions as was General von Hindersin,
and who showed it, as he did, at all times and
seasons.

Such a man was thoroughly able to recognise our
deficiencies, to do away with them, and to carry
through our great transformation.

In the year 1864 he had the direction of the
artillery in the attack on the Düppel redoubts.   After
the victorious end of this siege he was named second
Inspector-General of the artillery.   The then first
Inspector-General was confined to his room by ill-
health, and was after a few months compelled to retire
from the active list; upon this his post was given
to Hindersin.

During the siege of Düppel the enormous superiority of rifled over smooth-bore guns became practically known to the world, as will be well remembered
by every one who was alive in those days.   But at
that time the introduction of rifled field guns had
suffered a sort of check.   A quarter of our field guns
were rifled, and they were 6-prs.   A trial battery
of 4-prs. had taken part in the war.   We had
not yet finally decided to introduce 4-prs. to

increase the number of rifled guns, or to abolish smooth-bores. Hindersin's first object was to altogether introduce rifled guns. At this time I came first in contact with this original man. He sought me out. My astonishment, that he so senior a general should make advances to me, a young field-officer, increased when he said to me that since his appointment as Inspector-General he could not sleep at night, and that I must restore his sleep to him. He thereupon developed his opinion that rifled guns must supersede smooth-bores, and that we must have none but rifled field guns. It was his duty to insist that rifled field guns only should be used in war. If he did not do all that he could in this direction, and if Prussia, having three-quarters of her guns smooth-bores, should be entangled in a war with a Power which had rifled guns only, she might probably lose a decisive battle. But the loss of a decisive battle might bring about the destruction and the annihilation of the Fatherland. If therefore he delayed in the least the introduction of rifled guns, he might by this omission be responsible for the downfall of the Fatherland. This thought weighed on him like a mountain and would not let him sleep. I was therefore to introduce him to His Majesty, in order that he might lay before him the reasons for the increase of the number of rifled field guns. It was easy for me to carry out his wishes. It was indeed my duty, as the aide-de-camp in waiting, to introduce to His Majesty all high officials who desired to see him.

Hindersin explained his reasons to the highest authorities. Many other personages took part in the discussion. Although many considerations which told against the total abolition of S.B. guns were urged (for it was considered that they could not be altogether dispensed with for the fire of case), and although, as I have already written, the United States of America, during the war which had just ended, had invariably made a quarter of their guns smooth-bores, very like our short 12-prs., yet Hindersin with his arguments succeeded in convincing the very highest authorities. In June 1864 followed the order to commence at once the construction of as many 4-pr. field guns as the manufactories were in a condition to supply. But you know that this, especially with such a material as cast steel, takes time. When then in less than two years, as Hindersin with his political far-sightedness had foreseen, we were engaged in a great war, in only half of our Field Artillery had S.B. guns been exchanged for rifled. We possessed, after a year and a half, at the be-ginning of the year 1866, eight rifled field batteries out of the sixteen belonging to an army-corps, namely, four 6-prs. and four 4-prs. As soon as the political complications with Austria in 1866 made an event-ful war probable, Hindersin kept in view the necessity of hurrying on the increase in the number of rifled guns. In accordance with the principles of adminis-tration of that date, it was considered necessary in case of war, in order to be able to replace possible losses, to keep in readiness a certain reserve of weapons, and therefore also of rifled guns. But Hindersin insisted on the argument that there must be a decisive battle in this war, and that if this decisive battle were won, it would not be necessary to

S

replace the rifled guns expended, since fewer guns would then be needed ; he thus obtained that all the available rifled field guns should be issued to the Field Artillery. So, shortly before the beginning of the campaign, two additional batteries of each army-corps were armed with 4-prs., and we had thus ten-sixteenths of our Field Artillery provided with rifled guns at the outbreak of the war. He was not the man to allow himself to be diverted by any objections from a determination which he had once made. Thus he met the objection that the batteries were not accustomed to the new weapon, with the answer that, however badly they shot with the rifled guns, they would make better shooting with them than the best they could make with smooth-bores. There was scarcely sufficient time to give the batteries superficial instruction, and each of them had but one day of practice with plugged shell. After this they left for the war.

Hindersin was again right. The one important battle in this war was indeed decisive. The hurried arming of the batteries with rifled guns turned out well. If you follow the numbers of the batteries in the official account, you will find that many of the 4-pr. batteries numbered 5 or 6 (these were those which had received rifled guns just before the advance) did right good work, or at least did not shoot worse than other batteries armed with rifled guns. Such artillery as in the war of 1866 was not employed in the various actions or in the decisive battle, was armed, at least the greater part of it, with S.B. guns. After the war of 1866 all the batteries which still had S.B. guns were, as quickly as means permitted, provided with rifled guns.

He showed the same iron determination as he had with regard to the introduction of rifled guns, with respect to the foundation of a School of Gunnery. At the time of the siege of Düppel he had already noticed that the troops did not make half as many hits with the rifled siege guns as they should have made according to the statements of the inventors. Some of the latter had been invited to be present at the siege. In every battery in which they had offered advice the shooting had at once improved. In the year 1864 also, at the time of his first inspection of the practice, he noticed that the troops did not develop the full value of their guns. He was the first who made the results of practice the main ground on which he formed his judgment as to the excellence of the troops. Whilst he was criticising the movements, the evolutions, the appearance, the behaviour, etc., the range reports were prepared, and as soon as he had these he said, " And now, gentlemen, we come to the most important point on account of which we are here, namely, the number of hits." Then he had the results of the practice read out, and went on drily : " According to the statements of the Experimental Committee there ought to be so many per cent of hits. To-day we have only so many per cent." All the officers' faces grew long, for the results were terribly bad. But he said drily and curtly, " The figures tell their own tale. I have nothing to add. This must be changed."

Speaking privately to the officer commanding this or that battery, he would comfort him with the

information that the other batteries throughout all
the artillery shot no better. Then he added, "How
is it that the infantry can hit? Because they have
a School of Musketry. I will also have a School of
Gunnery for the artillery."

And from the beginning of his career as Inspector-
General of Artillery he, like the Roman orator who
added "cæterum censeo" at the end of each of his
criticisms, at each interview with the higher authorities
added, "I must have a School of Gunnery."

His bitter criticisms on the bad shooting of the
troops produced a number of theories and proposals
as to how the fire of rifled guns should be directed,
should be corrected, and should be observed. He
always answered, "What is the use of all this to
me? I must have a School of Gunnery."

The first beginning of such a school was but
small. A special staff could not be at once created
for it. For this it was necessary that it should be
included in the estimates and be voted by the
Chamber. The systematic opposition of the majority
at that time would vote no increase of the Budget ;
it had indeed created the so-called " Situation without
a Budget." But this did not prevent Hindersin from
bringing about so much as he considered to be
absolutely necessary. He formed a School of Gunnery of volunteers, for after he had emphasised the
need for such a school, and had expressed his opinion
that every officer would gladly sacrifice something to
make it possible, he appointed the first students to
the School of Gunnery, and these all joined and
gladly incurred the necessary expenses. This fact I
have, I believe, already mentioned. In this first

School of Gunnery old field-officers and old and young captains, after the English fashion, served with their own hands light field and heavy garrison guns, in order to acquire the necessary skill in practice.

But this naturally was not enough. It was very soon seen, as every artillery officer now knows, that in addition to the correct service of the guns by the gunners, the principal difficulty lies in the accurate observation of the effect of the fire, in making the proper corrections, and in directing the practice. In order to learn how this difficulty is to be overcome, it is also necessary to learn to command, and thus a School of Gunnery must have troops available for this purpose.

The victorious war of 1866 brought the " Budgetless Situation " to an end, and the Chamber again granted money. Funds for the formation of a School of Gunnery became available. You have seen from my former letters how, by this entirely personal creation of Hindersin's, the power of shooting of the artillery was developed, as was so astonishingly shown in 1870. I have also already told you how, after the School of Gunnery had existed for some years the practice of the troops was perfected in conformity with that School, and was everywhere carried out on a system founded on a fixed basis. But some time passed before such a fixed system was arrived at. At the beginning scientific propositions flowed in from all sides in profusion, and many errors had to be abandoned before the right way was found at last. I will only ask you to recall to your recollection the " Practice on a sliding scale," and other similar complications. Though Hindersin was decided that the system must be not only mathematically exact, but must also be simple and easily intelligible if it was not to be neglected at the moment of danger, he allowed the School of Gunnery to a certain extent to try anything however complicated, until they were themselves convinced that it was unpractical.

It was very wise of him to thus restrain his natural impetuosity, since he could not know himself which system would turn out to be the best. But in order to be able to form an independent judgment with regard to the system to be preferred, he spent from choice as much of his time at the School of Gunnery as he was able to spare from the other duties of his position. There he might be seen the whole day long, a silent witness, on the practice-ground at practice, in the lecture rooms at discussions, at instruction or listening to criticisms. He disturbed no one, and spoke to no one, but every day he took away something home with him in his head. Thus he allowed the School of Gunnery to work out its system for a certain time. I have already told you how the true instruction of the troops in shooting, the " course of practice," was in 1868 first organised in a manner suited to the distinctive character of rifled guns. I will here only remark how prudently Hindersin acted in permitting the School of Gunnery to do its work for a while, before he set about a change in the practice course. He had thus not only provided a certain number of instructors for each regiment, but had also awakened among the troops in general a feeling of the necessity for such a change, and thus found not only obedience but also a readiness which met him half way. This went so far, that when he, in the beginning of the year 1868, invited the brigades and the School of Gunnery to send him propositions with regard to new regulations for the course of practice, his message crossed the specific proposals on the same subject which were being forwarded to him.

From this date he, at his inspections, insisted with iron severity that the troops should shoot as well as possible, and thenceforth he judged of the condition of excellence of the troops by their power of making rapid and orderly marches over long distances to the field of battle, by their advance in accordance with the drill regulations into the firing line, by the number of hits on the target which they obtained, and by the accuracy of their turn-out.

It would be difficult for any artillery officer, who had no experience of this period of transition, to sufficiently estimate the great service which Hindersin rendered. Since at the present day, when there is perhaps no officer commanding a battery or field-officer who has not been at least once through the School of Gunnery, it is hard to conceive the condition of obsolete and senseless pedantry from which the arm had to be delivered before it could be fully and freely developed.

You may easily imagine that this was not carried out without some severity. That a man of such harsh manners, and who in addition was so distrustful by nature, should in this matter have hurt the feelings of many, was only to be expected, while that he sometimes made mistakes as to individuals was only human. For this reason he was not beloved but was only feared by the troops. But he did not wish to be beloved.   He desired only, as long as he lived, to work out and to carry through whatever he had determined to do.

In addition to his interest in practice Hindersin set a great value on the war-game.   He had the war-game systematically and officially taught at the School of Gunnery, and at a later date made it a part of the service training of the troops.   The war-game is certainly only a game.   It will always be more or less unlike the reality according as the person who directs it has less or more experience and practical sense.   But at any rate it teaches the value of ground, how to read maps, and how to take into consideration the respective conditions which affect the various arms.   Since in this game artillery officers have to employ all arms, the part which artillery has to play in combination with an army is made clearer to them.   They will gradually come to learn of themselves, without any necessity for instructing them on the subject, that artillery can only be an auxiliary arm, whose dependence upon the army is the first condition of its value ; thus the war-game serves to extend the circle of ideas of gunners, to remove their tendency to look at only one side of things, and to annihilate the old spirit of caste.

Hindersin took up everything which his subordinates proposed for the improvement of the arm.   It happened once during the harvest, at the time when, after the end of the manœuvres and when, since the reserves have been sent home, the artillery for want of men can do no drill with horsed guns, that he noticed some officers and N.C. officers riding across the fields, and learnt that they were riding about the country for the purpose of looking for positions suitable for a supposed battle and with the object of discussing the question with each other.   He went home at once and had the matter systematically worked out.   From that time reconnaissance-rides became a branch of service duty.

Since I am writing to you about Field Artillery only, I shall speak but superficially of Hindersin's action with respect to garrison artillery.   But I beg your attention to the following : Under his direction the garrison artillery, which received but a stepmotherly care from the brigades of artillery, were formed into independent regiments of artillery.   He changed the whole spirit of this arm, which, up to that time, had considered the acme of their efficiency to consist in daily performing the regulation exercises in the drill-bastion with guns which never changed their positions, and in daily firing at the same target, and which were not even allowed to learn anything about any other work in the fortress in which they were quartered than the bastion in which they drilled.   He made these troops carry out the attack and the defence in the neighbourhood of their fortress.   If you think of the necessary details of this you will realise what a great service he thus rendered.   In 1869, at Hindersin's instance, took place the first " Extended Exercises in the Attack and the Defence of Fortresses."   These exercises were as yet in their infancy, and in embryo.   They are now amplified into a system.   No regiment of Foot Artillery, as these troops are now called, could imagine the possibility of a drill-season without some such exercise, which forms the conclusion and crown of the

whole.   Before Hindersin there was no such thing!
He saw the necessity of it and he created it.

Consider, further, that at this time also took place
the actual substitution of rifled guns for all the old
S.B. garrison guns (with the exception of those which
were required as flank-guns), and what an enormous
amount of matériel had thus to be changed ; think
of the difficulties which this matériel raised merely
by its existence and its mass ; and finally, take into
account that at this very time the general regulations
for the artillery, field and garrison, had to be altered,
and that Hindersin controlled every syllable of them
and had each order tested practically in his presence
before he sanctioned it, and then you may get some
idea of the gigantic energy which this man displayed
during the seven or eight years that he was at the
head of his arm.

"No one is happy before his death," said the
Grecian sage.   Hindersin is dead, and we can now
say that he was one of the happiest of men.   His
life, his actions, his work, and his end were all
enviable.

He personally had no other thought or aim than
the improvement of the artillery.   It stood the proof
well in the war of 1870-71.   It performed so
many and such important services that its praises
were on every tongue, and it took among the other
arms a generally recognised and proud position.
Hindersin was able to say to himself with delight
that this was in the main his work.   He saw the
fruits of his labours, and when the victorious year of
1871 came to an end, he laid himself down and took
his rest in death.

His presentiment that he would die of heart disease did not deceive him. He said one day as a farewell to a person who had been spending the evening with his family, "The next time that you cross this threshold will be at my funeral." It was true. His interment took place eight days later. He died on the 23d of January 1872

LETTER XII

WHEN I finished my last letter, I thought that I had satisfied your curiosity and had so fully answered your question as to the manner in which so great a transformation took place in our artillery between the war of 1866 and that of 1870, that I should have no more occasion to address you on subjects connected with Field Artillery. But you now ask yet more, and wish to know my opinion as to the manner in which Field Artillery should be employed now that it has so much extended its sphere of effect, that at a range of 5500 yards it produces very good results with common shell, has considerable effect with shrapnel at 3800 yards, while at from 2200 to 2800 yards these effects may be described as annihilating, if we take the results of practice on the ranges as a basis for our observations. If you wish to prove this statement, buy the regulations for 1877, which can be obtained from any bookseller, and in which you will find tables showing the power of the guns.

I was not very desirous to enter further into this question, because in the first place I have been nearly twelve years away from the arm, and can give no accurate information concerning its present character, since I do not know its secrets, and cannot thus offer a decisive opinion on it. I might answer you by saying, the old man belongs to the past, apply to the young for news of the future. In the second place, I might observe to you that I have in ten letters examined into the changes in the principles of the employment of Field Artillery which have, between 1866 and 1870, resulted from the perfection of the precision of guns and from the enlargement of their sphere of effect, and which were well proved in the war of 1870-71. I might add that further improvements will not necessitate any change of system, but only a farther advance on the path which we have proved. Lastly, I might in the third place remind you that I have already, in the year 1869, in a lecture before the Military Society of Berlin, disclosed my opinions on the subject of the employment of Field Artillery in combination with the other arms since the introduction of rifled arms and guns ; a lecture at which you were present, and which came out as a pamphlet at the booksellers ; and I might add that my experiences during the war of 1870 and 1871 have given me no occasion to change these opinions. But having read this pamphlet once more through, I convinced myself that it in some of its details is no longer quite in accordance with the present organisation of our army-corps, in two divisions, one corps artillery and (eventually) one cavalry brigade or division (whereas formerly we spoke of the advanced guard, the main body, and the reserve) ;

and that it in many places gave certain numbers as maxima and minima, which are now no longer in accordance with the extension of the sphere of effect of guns and of infantry arms. I was thus compelled to altogether remodel this pamphlet in order that it might be of use at the present time.

I will therefore, following the line of thought of the pamphlet, inquire as to what changes the improvements effected in firearms since our last war must necessitate in the employment of our Field Artillery. To my great regret I shall in this be often obliged to abandon the mode of procedure by induction which I have employed in all my earlier letters to you, when I founded my statements upon facts and drew my lesson from experience ; whereas I must now walk in the deductive path of logic, which, failing experience, indulges in speculation. But it is not possible for me to do otherwise, since we have no experience of the new field guns in war. This process of deduction is very dangerous, and has too often led to unpractical speculations, which have at a later date faded like dissolving views before the force of fact, since even the most accurate logic is often very far from the truth, for when "a system is prepared with words," then "all theory is dim," etc. etc.

We must first lay down the sphere of effect of the arms from the statistics of our practice grounds and of the practice reports.

The effect of infantry fire begins when the sight is raised to 1700 yards, is of some importance at 1300 yards, and continues to increase up to 500 yards, at which range it may be already called "decisive," while from 200 to 300 yards and less it is annihilating.

The effect of artillery is already noticeable at 5500 yards. The effect of shrapnel begins at about 3800 yards, and at from 2000 to 1500 is decisive, while at from 1100 to 1000 yards and under the effect of artillery is absolutely annihilating; always provided that its field of fire be open. Since shrapnel with the time fuse set to zero have become so murderous in their results, the effect of artillery at very short ranges, which had been diminished by the former inferiority of the case for rifled guns, has now again become annihilating.

The effect of cavalry has in the main continued to be confined to the "*arme blanche*," and is thus absolutely nil in a frontal attack against infantry or artillery which is intact and is well supplied with ammunition, when the ground is open and commanded by distant fire. But cavalry with respect to both the other arms has preserved all its destructive power in cases where it can succeed in surprising them, or when they have no more ammunition, or when they are in any way disorganised.

The effect of artillery will even more than formerly be affected by the greater or less degree of good laying, by the greater or less accurate judging of distance, by the observation of effect, by the due use of corrections, and by the power to see the enemy, indeed by all that which gunners include under the expression "the regulation of fire" (*Einschiessen*). But this "regulation of fire" will become gradually more and more difficult as the length of the range increases, and will at last be

problematical, since it will finally at the longest
ranges be very hard to see sufficiently well even
with the best glasses.   The more accurately and the
farther the gun carries, so much the more necessary
will it be to lay, to observe and to correct it carefully, and on that account the more seldom will a
shot be fired in haste.   But it will also be so much
the more important to come into position very early,
earlier than the enemy, in preponderating numbers,
in order to gain the time which is required for laying
quietly and for the systematic regulation of the fire,
and in order to engage the enemy with superior
force.   On the other hand, the very long ranges at
which artillery can in these days commence to fire
and to produce an effect, and at which it will therefore, as a rule, commence the action, have called a
new element into existence, which deserves the
greatest attention, since it favours the assailant,
and therefore us, who since the time of the great
Frederic have preferred the offensive.   It can ninety
times out of a hundred be safely reckoned that at a
range of from 3000 to 5500 yards from the enemy's
defensive position the ground will somewhere offer
positions to the artillery of the assailants, which they
can take up unseen by the enemy, since they will be
favoured by cover, by the light, by the character of
the weather, or simply by the distance, and thus
the attacking artillery will not be observed until
they themselves open fire.   As a rule, therefore, the
assailant will always be able to come into action.
Already in 1870, though the range of our guns was
then less than it is now, I met with no cases in
which the artillery fire of the defenders ever in the

least jeopardised our coming into action and opening fire. We alone have, so far as I can state as a witness, destroyed batteries of the enemy while unlimbering, before they commenced firing, and that was at Sedan. But that was at a distance of from 1200 to 1600 paces, say from 1000 to 1200 yards, and with an enormous preponderance in the number of guns.

Hurried firing against stationary targets, and want of system in practice against moving targets, are now, on account of the greater accuracy of the guns, still more ineffective than they were. Still more prominent than formerly is the need to allow artillery the time required to fire every shell with deliberation (but not with pedantic slowness). Extremely hurried, unaimed fire has no effect at all. The roar of the guns, when it is only a roar, gives courage to the enemy. Though we, with our matériel of 1870, tried to carry on the artillery fight at ranges under 2500 paces (since when we were beyond this distance the action drew out into a protracted cannonade), yet in these days when the mighty shrapnel can carry 3000 yards, the artillery fight must, whenever the ground offers a free and open field of fire, be commenced at from 4500 to 5500 yards. This need not prevent us, in cases where such a thing is possible, from pushing forward under cover into a position nearer to the enemy and from coming into action there at the beginning, for it must always be considered as a first principle to advance under all circumstances as close as possible to the enemy.

Decisive effects from artillery can be expected

T

only at ranges under 3800 yards (the regulations say under 2500 yards). But this range is still so great that one may easily be deceived with regard to the observation of fire, while the enemy can find cover from view, and thus we shall be compelled in most cases to advance to considerably shorter ranges as soon as decisive action is desired. Indeed the fire of guns is not even now absolutely destructive except at ranges between 1600 and 1000 yards or under.

When engaged with infantry, artillery should, if it has the choice, at first take up a range over 1600 yards. But in the course of the action it must not hesitate here and there to expose itself to the fire of infantry at 1100 to 1200 yards. Artillery fighting alone (unsupported by the other arms) should avoid advancing nearer than this to unbroken infantry. But against disorganised infantry or in combination with the other arms artillery must not shun the very shortest ranges, especially when acting on the defensive; for since we have such a tremendous missile as the shrapnel with the fuse at zero available for the shortest ranges, we may hope to drive back the enemy with this fire alone, even though he has pressed on up to the very muzzles of the guns.

The duties which artillery has to fulfil are the old ones, such as you learnt during your time at the Military School:—(1) To commence the action; (2) To lengthen out the fight; (3) To prepare the decision; (4) To draw off the enemy's artillery fire from the other troops; (5) To pursue the beaten enemy; (6) To form a rallying-point for the other troops.

In order to fulfil all these duties satisfactorily, it

is absolutely necessary that the officer commanding the artillery shall continue in permanent communication with the officer commanding the troops, and shall keep himself always acquainted with the intentions of the latter. I have already, on an earlier page (Letter VII.), written to you once on this subject. The officer commanding the artillery will therefore, as a rule, either receive orders direct from the officer commanding the troops, or will at least know his general intentions, and will thus be able to act in accordance with them without orders.

Only in the case when the officer commanding the troops is engaged in an action against an enemy who holds his ground so strongly that the general is obliged to bring forward his last reserves and to join in person in the fight, will it be necessary for the officer commanding the artillery to work out his part of the action from his own head. But in that case his duty is simple. He must make haste to occupy the captured position as quickly as possible with his guns, since only the thunder of the guns can give a permanent character to the occupation of the position.

Up to the present the artillery fight which precedes each crisis of the battle has not been considered as of a decisive but only as of a preparatory character, or at the most it has been held to mark the development of the action. It will probably be otherwise in the future, since shrapnel and double-walled shell produce such a murderous effect, that the fight may be considered as decided in favour of that side whose artillery has overcome that of the enemy in the artillery fight and can now turn the full weight of

these projectiles on the other arms of the enemy.
The artillery duel will thus form the beginning of
the decisive action, as soon as it is carried out with
more favourable effect from shrapnel. It will therefore be more necessary than ever to bring up
masses of artillery, and to be as soon as possible after
the beginning of the action so superior in number
over the enemy's guns that his artillery shall be
beaten down. In this case nothing can be more
fortunate for us than to see the enemy's batteries
come up in succession, and thus allow themselves to
be destroyed in fractions, since we shall then without
any loss to ourselves crush them one after the other.
The more accurately and the farther artillery can
shoot, the more urgent is it that it shall be brought
into action as early as possible in the greatest possible
number. In accordance with this system of the
employment of masses, I recommend as a principle
that artillery should never be employed by batteries,
but should always be brought upon the scene by
entire brigades.

This principle of using artillery in brigades of 3
or 4 batteries is also necessary for reasons connected
with the direction of fire, the concentration of the
destructive fire of more batteries against the decisive
point, the observation of fire, and the correction of
laying. The only exception must be in the case of
attaching artillery to an infantry or cavalry brigade,
or to an advanced or rear-guard of such small strength
that more than one battery cannot be detached to it.
It must further remain always a first principle that
artillery shall avoid ineffective cannonades at too
great distances, but urgent necessity will often compel

us to allow the artillery fight to take place at exceedingly long ranges. Besides, the artillery fight of the present day would be effective at ranges at which during the war of 1870 the fire of guns was considered as a waste of ammunition.

This is why in the future many battles will work out quite differently to what they did formerly. The range-tables of our rifled field guns, according to the regulations of 1877, go up now to 7700 yards, or to more than 4 miles. At this range half of the shell fired will fall on a space 15 paces wide. Thus if, for example, a battery of the defenders stands in the prolongation of a road which is 15 paces wide, it could at a range of more than 4 miles fire on troops which might be marching on that road with such effect that it would not be advisable to permit them to continue to move by that road. In this case the assailant would be obliged to commence his artillery fight at a very long range, in order to disengage his marching troops ; and it may thus happen that the fire of artillery will be received and answered, and even an artillery fight may be begun, before the heads of the infantry columns of either side have come in contact, whereas up to the present time in most cases the first rifle shots from the advanced antennæ have opened the ball. But the greater the range is at which the action begins, so much the thicker is the veil which hides from us the dispositions of the enemy. In order to clear away this veil artillery is brought into play. The enemy will then at least betray himself by his artillery, and a cannonade will take place, during which the assailant will be able to reconnoitre and decide upon his plans.

Thus the increased extension of the sphere of effect of guns will lead to a yet earlier employment of the whole of the artillery.

As soon as the assailant has decided as to where and how he will attack, the commander of his artillery can, in accordance with this decision, advance to within shrapnel range for the decisive artillery fight ; he must also endeavour to work out the decision of the artillery fight at the very point where the decisive infantry attack will take place at a later hour.

From all this it results that the introductory cannonade will continue for longer than formerly, since it will be begun at longer ranges. The decisive fight between the two artilleries will certainly last a shorter time, on account of the very great effect of shrapnel fire, but it would be well to begin it later, in order that the infantry, the real army, may have time to come on to the ground and to deploy, so that the energetic action of the infantry may be immediately combined with the decision of the artillery fight, and may profit by its results before the enemy's artillery has recovered itself and is again ready for action. Then the artillery will follow its infantry into close action, will support it there, and lastly will secure the possession of the captured position, and will from it take part in the pursuit.

Allow me to illustrate these general ideas by concrete examples. Imagine a strong line of our newest field guns in position on the heights of Lipa (field of battle of Königgrätz). This line will command the high road as far as the heights of Dub, with an average of 50 per cent of hits, and will compel the assailant, if he wishes to use the high

road for his columns of march, to begin the introductory cannonade from the line of heights to the
west of Mzan-Dub-Ober-Cernutek, in order to draw
off the enemy's fire from his columns. On the 3d
July 1866 the artillery of the assailants was able
and had to advance as far as the Roskos-berg, in
order thence to fire on the advanced batteries of the
defenders at the Skalka wood and near Sadowa;
and when these had been drawn back into the main
position of Lipa, the range from the Roskos-berg to
that place was too great for the artillery of the attack,
for fire at such a range would have been only a waste
of ammunition.

In the present day an artillery action carried on
from the great line of guns at Gravelotte against the
position Point du jour—Moscow Farm (about 2700
yards)—must quickly be decided, owing to the murderous effect of shrapnel. On the 18th of August
it lasted during the whole battle, without either of
the artillery lines giving way.

When I delivered my lecture I was able to lay
down as a principle that, considering the sphere of
effect of our guns, the fire of artillery at a greater
range than 2500 paces would only be a cannonade
tending to prolong the action. At the present day
at such a range as this an artillery fight must very
soon be abandoned by one or other of the sides
engaged.

The Horse Artillery also will be obliged to change
its mode of procedure when it acts in support of
cavalry in a cavalry action. It was formerly received
that Horse Artillery, even when it trotted up in good
time, had at the most from a quarter to half an hour,

while its cavalry division was deploying from order
of march into order of battle, in which to prepare
the attack ; and from this it was argued that it
ought, without troubling itself about the fire of the
enemy's artillery, to direct its guns on the cavalry of
the enemy as soon as it saw them.   In the present
day the increased sphere of effect of artillery has
lengthened the time for the preparatory fire.   On the
other hand, the murderous effect of the shrapnel of
the enemy's artillery on our cavalry makes it now
imperatively necessary to first cripple that artillery,
after which we may turn our fire against the enemy's
cavalry.   This will moreover be naturally the case
when the cavalry are well led on both sides, since, in
consequence of the very long distances at which each
side must remain from the other, some accidents of
the ground are sure to give greater opportunity of
concealing the cavalry from the sight of the enemy's
artillery.   This need not prevent us from firing with
at least a part of our guns on the enemy's cavalry,
in the case where they allow themselves to be seen
within effective range.   For we must not overlook
the fact that it is of the first importance to fire on
the cavalry, and that if they give way the enemy's
artillery will fall into our hands.

     This principle must also be adhered to in the
case where artillery assists in an infantry action, and
the artillery must not allow itself to be deceived by
the very great length and the increased importance
of the artillery duel, which will always commence an
action, into the belief that this artillery duel is their
principal duty.   Their main purpose is, and must
always be, to defeat the enemy's army, that is, his

infantry, and to this end the artillery must always contribute, as far as lies in its power, whenever and wherever the opportunity arises.

The foregoing remarks concerning the future employment of artillery leads us to another most important point, namely, the place which it should occupy in the order of the march. For it is natural that troops acting on the offensive should be employed in succession according to the order in which they arrive. Even if the artillery, especially with its present mobility, were allowed, as soon as it was pushed forward, to trot past infantry on the march, the distance at which it marches from the head of the column (and this is the first scene of their action) must not be so great that too long a time will elapse before it comes up in sufficient masses, so that the masses of infantry may not have to wait under the fire of the defenders, and to suffer from its effects.

Artillery must, therefore, march *as far to the front as possible.* The reasons for this, which were already of importance in the war of 1870-71, have now by the extension of the sphere of effect of fire increased in number and consequence. " How far to the front," do you ask? Well, I will give no exact instructions, but will confine myself to the following remarks.

The general in command will be more anxious than ever to push forward his whole artillery early into action, in order to reconnoitre the enemy and to draw up his plan under cover of a cannonade carried on by the greatest possible number of guns. Until this has been done he will not bring forward any other troops than those needed for the purpose of reconnoitring the ground and of affording an immediate escort to the artillery line. It may even be said that up to this time the presence of more troops than are needed for these duties will be disagreeable to him, since they will be uselessly exposed to the enemy's fire, and he does not at present know whether he may not perhaps prefer to direct them on another point. While, for example, his guns were in action near Dub on the line of hills to the west of Mzan-Dub-Ober-Cernutek, the enemy's dispositions might cause him to decide to direct the main body of his infantry on the enemy's right flank in the direction of Cernutek and Hnewcowes, and it would be much more convenient for him if at the moment when he came to this decision, the head of this main body had just arrived at Milowitz, rather than that it should have already begun to deploy at Dub.

Thus the first artillery position can at the commencement be covered by infantry on the road by which it advances only. The other flank (if it takes up a position on one side of the road, otherwise both flanks) must at first be scantily covered by cavalry.

But this escort will be ample at first, since the enemy's position is still at a distance of almost four miles, and it will thus be sufficient to reconnoitre the ground, so that the troops may not fall into an ambush.

The small effect of the artillery fight at very long ranges will induce the assailant, as soon as he has a sufficiently numerous line of guns in position, to push forward nearer to the enemy, even though he does not desire to open a decisive artillery action at shrapnel ranges. Returning to our former example, the artillery line will soon advance, either simulta-

neously or in two echelons, to the line at Mzan-Roskos-
berg. It will in this case often happen that the
artillery will be in front of its foremost infantry.
Its closer neighbourhood to the enemy brings it into
greater danger, and it is then most necessary to take
care that all the ground in front and on the flanks is
minutely reconnoitred.

Even in the days of the less powerful earlier
rifled guns the great artillery line had frequently to
hurry on in front of its foremost infantry. I will
remind you of the first advance of Von Dresky, with
the corps artillery, over the bridge at Vionville, while
Flavigny was still in the hands of the enemy. The
official account informs us of a similar movement by
the whole of the corps artillery of the 9th corps,
when it advanced into position between Verneville
and Amanvillers at the beginning of the battle of
Saint-Privat, in the course of which it fell into an
ambush of the enemy's infantry and suffered severe
loss. When the Guard corps in the same battle
were pushing forward into the fight, and the 1st Field
Brigade was advancing in echelon with the corps
artillery, we were for some time in action nearly a
mile in front of our infantry line. The right of the
line of guns rested on the Hessian division, but for a
long time the regiment of hussars of the Guard at
Saint-Ail was the only support which we had on
our left flank.

Colonel von Dresky writes concerning his position
on the 18th of August: "I should wish to give
warning against carelessness in reconnoitring positions, such as I was guilty of at Verneville. The
position which I chose had a wood on its right. In

the heat of the fight I neglected to ascertain that it was occupied by our troops. I discovered later on, at the moment when my batteries were taking up their position, that the wood was still held by the French. How easily they might have seen me, and in that case it would have been all over with the corps artillery of the 3d corps. I have thus learnt always before advancing to a selected position to have all cover on the ground on both flanks explored by N.C. officers or trumpeters, and to leave these men in observation until the ground in question has been occupied by our own troops."

We must also here mention the artillery position of the 5th and 9th corps on their entrance into the battle of Sedan, which was so far in front of their infantry that its left flank was at first covered by cavalry only.

Such isolated advances of the great artillery lines of the assailant will become more and more frequent as the sphere of effect of artillery increases in size.

The eventual advance of the infantry into close action will relieve the exposure of its position, and it can then proceed to work out the decision of the artillery duel.

I have already given you my opinion so clearly as to how the artillery should support its infantry in the attack, when I wrote to you about infantry, and especially on the subject of an attack over open ground, that I should only repeat myself if I said more about it.

I believe that I have now sufficiently developed my opinion as to the future mode of employment of artillery in the field. If you take into consideration what I have written earlier as to the result of my experiences in war, you will yourself be able to construct a system for the employment of artillery in connection with the other arms. For my part I am an enemy of all systems and plans, and prefer the tactics of the moment.

Of what I have already said as to the detail of artillery I wish to put the following forward into prominence : (1) Artillery *must seek for the crown of its efficiency in learning to shoot well,* with all that belongs to that ; (2) Artillery must *in its exercises direct the whole of its attention principally to rendering itself capable of being in position in masses at the proper moment ;* that is to say, *it must be able to get over long, very long distances, even many miles, at a fast trot either in column of route or as a battery in line ;* (3) *On no account whatever* should it be made a point that *the first shot be fired as quickly as possible after unlimbering.* No time need be lost about this, but *the most important point is that the first shot shall be well laid and well observed ;* so that further corrections may follow ; (4) If, as I believe, the extension of the sphere of effect of artillery will result generally in an earlier commencement of the artillery fire ; if the artillery duel will tend to increase in importance and in severity ; if, as is probable, the artillery will also remain in action until the last stage of the infantry fight, and will even have the last word in the pursuit, it must be that in future *artillery will expend a larger amount of ammunition* than it did in the last war, and it is a matter of the first importance *that the ammunition shall never fail, and above all that it shall not do so at critical moments.*

I might hold forth at greater length concerning this last point, uninteresting as it is. I must strongly advise that the 1st line of the ammunition-wagons of the battery (3 ammunition-wagons and 1 store-wagon) be considered as an integral part of the guns when in action, and that it shall always follow them in the closest possible connection. When the captain of a battery first gives the order to unlimber on a position, he must then decide on which flank (or in rear of the battery) these wagons shall be placed.

But even the battery wagons of the 2d line should not go too far from the battery, above all they should not leave it too soon, as when they are early separated from it there is always some danger that they will not be seen again during the whole battle. At the time when the officer commanding a brigade points out their position to his batteries, he should order the wagons of the 2d line to be collected under an officer, and should direct them where to remain.

If you remember that, according to regulation, the interval between each gun in rapid firing is laid down as from 6 to 8 seconds, and that thus the whole of the limbers of the battery will be empty in less than half an hour, you will own that great inconvenience (that is to say, the want of ammunition) may arise, unless the wagons of the 1st line have been placed so close to the battery that during slow systematic fire every round can be taken from the wagons, and thus the limbers can be kept intact for the rapid fire. For if half of the limber ammunition has been expended in slow fire, while at the same time the wagons of the 1st line are at some distance from the battery (which may in the course of the action easily cause an interruption of communication between them and the battery), and if then suddenly a crisis necessitates a rapid fire, the battery will be defenceless in less than a quarter of an hour.

The 2d line of wagons ought also not to leave the battery too early or to go too far, since thus the communication between them and the renewal of the empty wagons is always secured and will not be interrupted by other troops. I nowadays read in many works, such as *Studies* and other meritorious productions, that the author, in the case of a mere march in war before anything has been heard or seen of the enemy, assigns to the 2d line of battery wagons a different place in the column of march to that occupied by the batteries, for example, in rear of the advanced guard or even in rear of the whole division. Others even propose to canton them in quite another place to the batteries, as soon as " War-cantonments " have been taken up in the immediate neighbourhood of the enemy. I cannot therefore help fearing that now, after thirteen years of peace, unpractical measures are being again thought out which, when they are applied in war, will have the most mischievous consequences. Only think of the 2d line of wagons marching in rear of the division, and thus from 2 to 4 miles from the batteries. The batteries receive the order to trot forward into position, and accordingly trot from 2 to 4 miles. The 2d line will soon be nearly 8 miles from their batteries, since no battalion will allow them to pass it. The infantry is also advancing into action, and will not permit its road to be blocked up by these " ammunition-columns." Thus it probably comes about that the batteries, as

happened to mine at Königgrätz, do not see their
ammunition-wagons again during the whole battle.

I must mention another circumstance. The larger
expenditure of ammunition, which we foresee, makes
it probable, and even certain, that we shall be obliged,
in a battle of only moderate violence, to draw ammunition for the artillery from the ammunition-columns
during the action. In the battle of Saint-Privat we
had to expend shell from the ammunition-columns,
though we did not fire our first shot until after noon.
Should a battle begin in the early morning of a
summer's day, it would be impossible in future to
count, as I have already shown, upon being able to
make the ammunition in the limbers and wagons of
the battery suffice for the whole day. Rapid firing
would consume this amount in less than two hours.
It is true that a rapid fire for two hours is not
probable. But the ordinary rate of fire (15 to 20
seconds between guns) will expend it in from 4 to 5
hours. Though a battery may not be firing during
the whole duration of a battle, yet arrangements must
be made to allow that the ammunition may be
expended in from 6 to 8 hours, and that within that
time it may be possible to fill up the gun limbers
with ammunition from the columns. The battery
wagons of the 2d line are there with the object of
bringing up this ammunition from the columns.
These columns march 4 miles, or half a march, in rear
of the troops, and are thus at least 8 miles behind
the head of the column. They will at the earliest
have reached the post assigned to them in from 3 to
4 hours after the beginning of the action, and soon
after that the empty ammunition-wagons of the 2d

line of the batteries must be with them in order to be refilled, since much time will be taken up in packing, in the march, and in re-packing. But this will be impracticable if the 2d lines march in rear of the troops, even should they succeed in finding their batteries in the battle, and in establishing communication with them, since this will itself, even under favourable circumstances, take from 3 to 4 hours. It is therefore imperatively necessary that the 2d line of wagons of the batteries shall, during every march in war, remain an integral part of them, until they know where they themselves will take up their position, and are accordingly in a condition to decide where these 2d lines shall be posted.

I must now speak of one point which refers specially to artillery ; I have indeed often mentioned it to you, but I cannot refrain from referring to it now that I have the opportunity, for I consider it as very important. I mean that under no circumstances must a battery be permitted to retire merely on account of want of ammunition. If a battery has no ammunition left, then it must remain silent standing under fire. Do you think that this sounds somewhat tyrannical and cruel? I quite agree with you, but it must be so. Von der Goltz's battery did so at Königgrätz by their captain's order, and in the year 1870 it was a regulation. It is, moreover, astonishing how quickly a battery which has no ammunition supplies itself, when it is compelled to remain silent under fire. Von der Goltz, sword in hand, "annexed" ammunition-wagons which did not belong to him, but which could not find their batteries. And what harm did that do? The ammuni-

U

tion at least did injury to the enemy, instead of wandering uselessly about. Moreover, each battery which is under fire will gladly assist its neighbour, if the latter runs short of ammunition, and this help can only tend to its own advantage. Imagine the case where a battery has expended all its ammunition, while its neighbour has two full ammunition-wagons, that is to say, enough to fill the limbers of all 6 guns. If the latter gives half, namely, one wagon or 15 rounds per gun to the battery which is without ammunition, it can then reckon upon being able, at least during the time required to fire 15 rounds, to fire on the enemy with a double number of guns. By the time these 15 rounds have been fired, some fresh stock of ammunition will perhaps have arrived. But if it gives no ammunition, then its neighbour cannot co-operate with it, and the battery which still has ammunition runs a risk of being overwhelmed by the enemy, since it has only 6 guns. We are thus compelled to assist our neighbour with ammunition when he requires it, not only because he is a comrade, but also by the instinct of self-preservation. But why did not this take place in the case of Von der Goltz at the battle of König-grätz? Because his battery was a 6-pr. battery, while those on his right and left were 4-prs. This will not happen again, since we have now but one calibre for the whole of the Field Artillery. Which is most truly a blessing!

With reference to the distribution of the artillery among the various units of the troops, a strong artillery would appear to be desirable in the case of advanced and rear-guards, in order that it may be able quickly to get good effect from its fire. In the year 1870 two batteries at most were attached to an infantry brigade which was sent forward by a division as the advanced guard of an army-corps. I do not think that if these were increased to three they would be too many. It is certainly true that then only one battery will remain with the other brigade. But I think that our divisions are too weak in artillery. They might very well have 6 batteries, organised in 1 regiment of 2 brigades of 3 batteries each. Such an organisation would facilitate the transition from the peace to the war establishment, since thus each regiment would remain complete in time of war. It is true that this would imply an increase of our artillery at the rate of 2 batteries per army-corps. It has been already stated, as an objection to any increase of the artillery, that infantry wastes quicker than artillery does, and that thus a disproportion would arise. But all generals have ever endeavoured, when their infantry has been inferior (either in number or in quality), to give it a strong artillery as a support, and thus to overcome the evil. Moreover, if we look at our neighbours, an augmentation of the artillery appears decidedly advisable. If this augmentation of 2 batteries per corps is not sufficient, as it possibly may be, then the regiments of divisional artillery must have brigades of 4 batteries each.

Another objection has also been urged to the augmentation of the artillery, namely, that it is a serious thing to increase the train of the army. Now, dear friend, if any one after the days of Vionville, Saint-Privat, and Sedan can still call artillery "train" and not combatant troops, I really cannot argue with him.

When a division acting alone pushes forward an advanced guard, which consists of only one regiment of infantry, then you cannot well attach more than one battery to it. More is not necessary, since the division with its main body will then be nearer at hand, and can quicker support the advanced guard with its artillery. If I could have my wish, and each division might receive a regiment of artillery of 6 batteries, then a detached brigade of infantry would as a rule receive a brigade of 3 batteries. But not more than 1 battery could be given to detached regiments of infantry.

The breaking up of batteries and the detaching of single divisions must be entirely avoided. The reasons for this which I set forth in my pamphlet in 1869 have increased in weight since the guns have improved.

As regards the Horse Artillery in their connection with cavalry, I have already, when I wrote to you on the subject of cavalry, stated and established my opinion that in the interest of the artillery it is most desirable that the brigade should not be broken up, but that a complete brigade of artillery should be permanently told off to a cavalry division. This ought to be done on all grounds, for reasons connected with tactics, organisation, and administration. No other arm is broken up on mobilisation into units of the size of a company or a squadron. Least of all ought this to be done to that arm which is the hardest to lead, and which has the most difficult tasks to fulfil.

The old principle also that Horse Artillery ought to avoid action with artillery is done away with now.

Already in 1870 some Horse Artillery batteries which were attached to the corps artillery took a foremost part in the artillery fight, since they were able to get into position earlier than the others ; for example, Von Dresky at Vionville. The Horse Artillery batteries of the cavalry division also took part in the artillery action as soon as it developed into a battle ; for example, at Vionville, Saint-Privat, and Sedan. The cavalry division had no need of its Horse Artillery during the battle, for it is only called upon to charge where the infantry and the artillery have already prepared a way for it. Only in the case where a cavalry division operates alone does it require the aid of its Horse Artillery. For this reason in the Guard corps the Horse Brigade was attached to the cavalry division whenever the latter was sent forward alone. But as soon as a battle took place the Horse Brigade was recalled to the corps artillery.

The more accurately the artillery shoots, and the more destructive is the effect of its fire, the more necessary is it to bring quickly into action a number of guns superior to that of the enemy, and so much the more serious would it be if we were compelled to leave the Horse Artillery of the cavalry divisions standing idle with their divisions through the whole battle until the moment of the charge, and thus to weaken the fighting line of guns by that number of batteries.

To the last letter which I wrote about cavalry you sent me the answer that if a whole brigade were attached to a cavalry division the latter would become too clumsy, as the brigade would be like a leaden weight hung on to it. This is quite true in theory, but in practice it is by no means the case. Three pounds are certainly heavier than two, and therefore three batteries must also be heavier than two. But this is not altogether correct, for three batteries can trot as fast as two. A cavalry division fully equipped for detached duty has many other leaden weights to draw after it, all of which fetter its flight, as, for example, field hospitals and provision-columns. On the other hand, the addition of one battery creates no new impediment. If only the mounted detachments be kept well closed up, if the brigade be employed as a principle only in mass, then it makes no differ- ence, as far as regards the mobility of the division, whether there be two or three batteries. But it makes a great deal of difference as regards the fight- ing strength of the division. In war no division would find three batteries too many, rather it would possibly find them too few. Did not General von Voigts- Rhetz at once increase the Horse Artillery of the 5th cavalry division to 4 batteries?——with these Major von Körber at Vionville surprised the French camps. They will only be found to be too many in peace, when no one knows exactly what to do with them.

But care must be taken not to scatter the batteries among the cavalry brigades. These brigades are not organised for independent action, and should never be employed independently. If as an excep- tion a brigade be intended to fight without other troops, then a battery may be attached to it. But it should be laid down as a rule that the whole brigade of artillery should always be employed as if it were a single battery.

For my part, when a brigade of cavalry is sent forward as an advanced guard by a division, I would not as a rule attach a battery to it. A light cavalry brigade of this description is frequently intended only to see and to annoy the enemy, and should alternately appear and disappear. In this duty artillery may easily be a burden to it. But if it is intended to fight, then a battery should be attached to it. The necessity for this will be governed by the news of the enemy, the character of the ground, and the object which it is intended to fulfil. If the situation and the orders of the cavalry brigade are changed, a battery can be sent after it. We did this during the war. The cavalry division at first pushed forward its dragoon brigade without artillery. When the dragoons drew near to the Moselle, and were thus placed in a position to be obliged either to occupy or to defend defiles, a battery of Horse Artillery was sent after it. I can very well imagine a case in which the whole artillery brigade would be sent forward to the advanced guard. Suppose, for instance, that a defile is barred by a comparatively weak detachment of infantry, which is also supported by some artillery, and that it is desired to drive the enemy quickly away ; in this case we should prefer to make use of the fire of a superior force of artillery, instead of causing disproportionate loss to the light cavalry, who would have to dismount and fight on foot.

If a division has to cover and reconnoitre two roads, it will push forward along each a light brigade or a regiment of cavalry, while one or two cavalry brigades will follow in rear of the centre. Here also will march the brigade of Horse Artillery, which will be sent forward as a whole in case it may be necessary to overcome opposition by the enemy. In the case where there are three roads, one regiment will march on each. A heavy cavalry brigade at least will follow as the main body, and with it will march the brigade of Horse Artillery.

The same principle should be observed in the case of a detached cavalry brigade. Whether a Horse Artillery battery is to be attached to it or not, must be decided by the nature of the task allotted to it.

The behaviour of Horse Artillery in action, in conjunction with, or in opposition to, cavalry has become simpler in character in proportion as its fire has increased in range and accuracy. It will, as a rule, have to occupy but one position until the cavalry fight has been decided, and this ought to be as close as the ground will permit to the enemy's artillery; it will thus overcome this artillery after the shortest possible action. It will then fire on the enemy's cavalry, remaining, however, generally in the same position. But it is a very much more difficult thing to recognise and to take up this position at the proper moment. For this reason the artillery must be commanded by a field-officer, who should remain in attendance on the officer commanding the division up to the moment when he has to lead his batteries into position, and who should not be required to trouble himself about the interior details of the batteries, but should solely be occupied in carrying out the views of the officer commanding the division. When the artillery commences firing, the position of the officer commanding the division will in general be near to it, since from this elevated point he can best give his orders. The officer commanding the Horse Artillery will thus be close to him, until the moment when he will personally join in the action with his last reserves. The officer commanding the artillery has then presented to him a most difficult problem which he must solve for himself; is he to hasten after the divisional commander in order to make victory certain, or is he to remain in his position, in order to check a pursuing enemy with his fire, and to give his own troopers a point on which to rally?

I will now enter upon the question of a special escort for artillery. You know that I strongly object to a permanent special escort. As a general rule, the artillery should be posted in such a manner that it is covered by the character of the action itself. But since a brigade of Horse Artillery will ordinarily stand and fire on one flank of the division, the outer flank of the artillery must itself be covered. If the artillery position is well chosen, this outer flank will not be in much danger. Its safety will be sufficiently secured if orders be given to a section of cavalry to push out its scouts to such a distance as will ensure the artillery from a surprise. If a special escort strong enough to fight were taken from the cavalry division, the latter would be deprived of too large a portion of its force at the moment of decisive action.

LETTER XIII

CONCERNING THE PROPOSAL "THAT ARTILLERY
FIRE SHOULD NOT COMMENCE AT AN EARLIER
MOMENT THAN SHORTLY BEFORE THE INFANTRY
FIGHT ; BUT THAT IT SHOULD THEN AT ONCE
BEGIN AT SUCH A RANGE THAT ITS EFFECT WILL
BE ANNIHILATING."

I WAS prepared for your first objection ahd for the
question connected with it. One is inclined, taking
into account the murderous effect of Field Artillery,
to come to the conclusion that the destruction of
the enemy will in these days take place in a shorter
time than was formerly required, and that thus,
supposing that the infantry attack is intended to
follow immediately after the completion of the
artillery fight, the commencement of the latter must
be deferred until the infantry have arrived sufficiently
near to the enemy to be able to make use for their
assault of the moment when the artillery has produced its most favourable effect, in order that the
disorganised enemy may not have time to avoid
this assault or to recover from his disorganisation.
I have many times heard these ideas expressed, and
one of the most important works of recent times,

dealing with the leading of artillery, favours this opinion. This even precisely states the time which will be required, and assumes that, in order to successfully carry through the artillery duel, it should take place at a range of 2000 metres, and need last only a quarter of an hour, while the same amount of time will suffice to shatter the enemy's infantry. From this the conclusion is drawn that the artillery fight should not begin until half an hour before the moment at which it is foreseen that the attacking lines of skirmishers will mask their own batteries.

Before I examine into the details of this idea, I must beg of you to look back with me as far as the time of the Romans. The great battles between the triumvirs, in which they fought for the empire of the world, did not as a rule end until the defeated army had been entirely destroyed. In those days, as history tells us, 100,000 corpses of one army alone covered the field of battle. In later times battles continued to grow less and less bloody, in proportion as more murderous weapons were discovered, and the range of missiles increased. Since gunpowder has taken the place of arrows and lances, losses have been considerably reduced. Frederic the Great, in his history of the Seven Years' War, calls the battle of Prague one of the most bloody of that century. He gives the loss of the enemy at 24,000, including 5000 prisoners, and his own at 18,000 combatants, "without counting Marshal Schwerin, who alone was worth 10,000 men." The Austrians numbered 61,100 combatants, the Prussians had 64,000 who took part in the battle. The number of killed and wounded was thus on each side about 30 per cent of the combatants.   The battle, according to the king's statement, lasted from 9 A.M. to 8 P.M.

In the two days of the battle of Aspern 75,000 Austrians (according to Höpfner) fought against more than 80,000 French. (This latter number gives the strength of the French after the losses of the first day of battle.) The Austrian official return gives their loss in killed and wounded as nearly 20,000. Napoleon's bulletin gives his losses at only 1100 killed and 3000 wounded, but Höpfner, after searching into all sources of information, puts the losses of the French at 42,000 combatants besides prisoners. Since these losses must be divided between two days, the battle of Aspern was less bloody than the battle of Prague.

Höpfner gives the strength of the Austrian army at Wagram as about 124,000 men, and its losses at less than 24,000. How many Napoleon actually lost in this battle out of his army of 180,000 men cannot be ascertained. The bulletins again acknowledge 1100 killed and from 3000 to 4000 wounded. In any case the two days' fight at Wagram was not nearly so bloody as the battle of Aspern.

I do not know whether I have selected the most bloody battles of the Napoleonic wars, but I think so.[1]

---

[1] In Colonel Home's work on tactics the losses in the following battles are given :

    Prague—64,000 Prussians lost 16,000.
          74,000 Austrians lost 8000.   Total 24,000—$\frac{1}{6}$.
    Wagram—150,000 French and
          130,000 Austrians lost a total of 24,000—$\frac{1}{12}$.
    Compare with these—
    Eylau—85,000 French lost 30,000.
          75,000 Russians lost 25,000.   Total 55,000—$\frac{1}{3}$.
    Salamanca—90,000 English and French lost 30,800—$\frac{1}{3}$.
    Borodino—250,000 French and Russians lost 80,000—$\frac{1}{3}$.

                              N.L.W.

At any rate at Leipzig the allies in three days
lost only 49,000 out of 330,000 men—about one-
sixth, and therefore from 5 to 6 per cent per
diem.

One of the most bloody fights of this century
took place on the occasion of a sortie from Fredericia
in the year 1849, when the army of Schleswig lost
25 per cent of its strength. This was one of the
last actions fought principally with smooth-bore
guns and muskets. Since then all armies have been
provided with rifled guns and rifles. Of all the
battles which have been fought, in which both sides
were armed with such weapons, undoubtedly the
most bloody were that of Vionville-Mars-la-Tour on
the 16th, and that of Saint-Privat on the 18th of
August 1870 ; in each of these battles the Germans
lost a larger percentage of killed and wounded than
did the French, and according to the official account
this loss amounted in the former action to 16,000
out of 80,000 combatants, and in the latter to a
little more than 20,000 out of 210,000, that is to
say, one-fifth and one-tenth of the men brought into
action. In all the later battles and actions the percentage of loss was very much smaller. Thus we
see that, the greater the perfection to which weapons
of war are brought, and the longer their range, the
less bloody are the battles. This fact is so well
known and generally recognised that, more than
twenty years ago, the inventor of a new fuse, in the
preface of the work in which he described his
invention, grounded his assertion that his invention
was a benefit which he offered to humanity, on the
fact that by it he improved weapons of war, and

that in consequence of this improvement battles would become less bloody.

When I, in the presence of these historical facts, hear in these days the opinion expressed that, in consequence of the latest improvement in artillery (the use of shrapnel), its effect will be so much increased, that in less than a quarter of an hour one or other of the combatants must be destroyed, I feel myself obliged to examine the reasons why, up to the present, battles have been less bloody in proportion as weapons have been made to shoot farther, more accurately, and with more deadly effect, in order to arrive at a decision whether the newest improvements of our weapons of war may not perhaps have the opposite effect. The results of inventions which have enabled us to shoot at long ranges are, in the first place, that battles will be begun at long ranges. Then, according to the result of the distant fight, we shall pass on to the contest at short ranges. But when this result makes it probable that this latter contest can have no favourable result, the great distance between the two armies allows that one which considers that it has no chance of victory to draw off the greater part or the whole of its forces from any further action. The longer the ranges of projectiles, the easier will it be to arrange for a retirement at the right moment. This will be equally true whether we consider the action of small bodies in a battle or the action of the army in the main contest itself.

In the days when the short Roman sword was the principal weapon of an army, combatants who had once come in contact were unable to escape from each other. The battle came to an end by the destruction of one side or the other. In the year 1870 we fought at such long distances that Bazaine on the 18th of August, after Saint-Privat had been stormed and his position thus made untenable, was able to retire unmolested with his entire army. In Saint-Privat itself only were the combatants closely engaged, and thus the defenders of this village were all either killed or made prisoners.

Now you will perhaps say that an artillery which is well led should not fire at too long ranges, but should strive for decisive action at shorter ones (that is to say, that it ought to quickly commence that artillery duel which is to be fought out with shrapnel at 2000 metres in 15 minutes), and that if the infantry are called upon not to waste their ammunition at excessive ranges, the same claim may be made upon the artillery.

On this subject I will relate the following from my recollections: No one in his time has ever so severely blamed artillery for firing at too long ranges as I have myself. In my lecture of the 18th March 1869 I said that decisive effect could be expected from the artillery fight at ranges under 2000 paces only; that fire at 2500 paces could be nothing but a cannonade to gain time; and that at from 4000 to 5000 it was a waste of ammunition; and when the war of 1870 broke out I ordered the batteries under my command to avoid as far as possible opening fire at more than 2000 paces. Soon after we received orders from the officer commanding the artillery of the army not to fire at a longer range than 1800 paces. I went into action on the 18th of August with a firm intention to observe this order,

and my batteries made all haste to get forward
within decisive range of the enemy. They even,
when the Guard corps first came into action, raced
against each other in their advance towards the crest of
the position of Saint-Privat, which was at first held by
the enemy's advanced batteries. But what happened?
These advanced batteries drew back into their main
position, and the movement of my batteries to the
front was brought to a halt by the imperious voices
of 3000 chassepots, carried by the thick advanced
line of skirmishers of which I have spoken above.
We thus found ourselves at the foot of the rising
ground, while the enemy's artillery, on which it was
our first duty to fire, was at a distance of 2200, 2800,
and 3200 paces. What were we to do? To go
closer meant to go over to the enemy. To retire
with a line of 54 guns (for we had as many as this
in action) would have meant that we gave up the
contest at this point as lost. To stand silent and
to allow the enemy's artillery and infantry to open a
combined fire upon us over open ground would have
been folly, and would' in addition have been asking
from the men more than man can give. Thus we
had nothing left to us but to carry on the fight,
against our own wills and against superior orders, at
long ranges. General von Colomier, the originator
of these orders, rode along the batteries during the
artillery fight. I made my excuses with regard to
the long ranges at which we were firing, and showed
him the thick chain of skirmishers of the enemy.
He approved of my dispositions and warned me
against a too rash advance, in consequence of which,
he told me, nearly the whole of the corps artillery of

the 9th corps had been horribly "wiped out" on the right of the Bois de la Cusse. I was to avoid such a catastrophe. Thus circumstances were stronger than our will. We could not select any shorter ranges until, at a later hour, the battle further developed itself, and the infantry took part in it. Along the whole front of the battle the artillery fight was carried on at similar ranges. The great line of guns of the 1st army at Gravelotte stood at a distance of from 2500 to 3200 paces from the enemy's position, and Von Dresky says that on this day he fired from his position on the enemy's batteries at a range of 3300 paces.

The comparison with the infantry is not altogether sound. We certainly expect the infantry when acting on the offensive not to open fire too soon, but we do so only in cases when we can keep the enemy, against whom it is advancing, under the fire of artillery from another direction. But no one will in these days expect infantry to advance over open ground quietly, without firing a shot, up to within 500 metres of the enemy's infantry standing intact in position. On the contrary, when I wrote to you about infantry, we came to the conclusion that during this advance the artillery fire (of shrapnel) must cover the infantry, and when the former is not available, that its place must be supplied by volleys from other bodies of infantry at a range of about 1000 yards. Artillery can certainly by the long range of its fire facilitate the advance, without firing, of infantry up to short distances, but the converse cannot be true, since the range of infantry is less than that of artillery. For the latter arm there is no

X

auxiliary which has a still greater range, so that it must itself furnish the long range fire under cover of which it may advance at the favourable moment to within the decisive ranges required for the artillery duel. Moreover, the principal reason why it is the duty of infantry to economise their ammunition when acting on the offensive does not apply to the artillery; this is the impossibility of bringing up ammunition during the continuance of the attack. Artillery can renew its expended ammunition even while the cannonade is going on.

Let us try to imagine what a fight would be like, similar to those of which I have seen so many, but with this difference, that the ranges at which formerly we carried on the delaying cannonade are now those at which decisive action will take place, and at which the artillery duel will in a quarter of an hour result in the destruction of one or other of the two sides. I cannot, then, understand how it can be possible for artillery, acting on the offensive, to wait before opening fire until within half an hour of the moment at which the infantry begins an energetic fire of skirmishers (say at 500 yards from the enemy), and to at once open this fire at 2000 yards. The infantry cannot make its way up to within 500 yards of the object of the attack without any pause or delay, as if it were marching on a road. It must move extended in lines of skirmishers, etc., it pushes forward on a broad front over obstacles of all kinds, and may perhaps have to advance by rushes, and the greatest distance which it can thus be expected to get over in half an hour will be about one half of what it would march in the same time, or

say 1500 yards. Thus at the moment when the
artillery, half an hour before the expected fight of
skirmishers, is beginning the artillery duel at a range
of 2000 yards, the infantry must also be about 2000
yards from the enemy, and so will be about at the
same distance as the artillery. How can the two
arms, without firing themselves, get so near to the
enemy, whom we must suppose to possess similar
weapons to ours, and who can therefore open a fire
of shrapnel on our advance at a range of 3700 yards ?
Will the infantry endure so effective a fire without
some of its leaders calling out in anger, "What is
the use of our artillery if it cannot keep that of the
enemy from us ? Get on, you artillery, and go on
firing !" Should the artillery abstain from firing,
with the result that its own infantry, crushed by an
infernal fire, may cease to advance, and that thus the
assault may fail ? Or should the artillery advance
alone in front of the infantry to within 2000 yards
of the enemy and begin the action ? In the first
place, it would thus fail to follow the principle which
we are discussing, since it would open fire more than
a full hour before the entrance of the line of skirmishers into the fire-fight. Moreover, it is doubtful
whether artillery, when acting entirely alone, *can*
advance directly to within so short a distance. Only
on very exceptional ground can an approach entirely
under cover to within 2000 yards of the enemy
be possible, unless indeed the enemy has chosen his
defensive position very badly. When this is the case,
and especially when one can under cover, and thus
by surprise, reach a position so near to the enemy,
the assailant will then certainly endeavour to occupy

it at once.   But if some portions of the line of
advance are exposed to effective shrapnel fire from
the enemy, how can the artillery advance against the
enemy's guns, which are firing without suffering any
annoyance, quite quietly, and as if on the practice
ground ?   If, moreover, there are obstacles in front
within range of this fire, then such an immediate
advance to within 2000 paces becomes absolutely
impossible.

In order to make my meaning quite clear, I will
again refer to the simple concrete situation on the
plan of the battle of Königgrätz, which I have used
in a former letter as an example.   Let us then suppose that the defender has posted his artillery from
the hill of Lipa to the hill numbered 733, on the
west of Langenhof, and thus almost along the road
which runs from Lipa to Stresetitz.   He has destroyed
the passages over the Bistritz, which is as much in
flood as it was on the 3d of July 1866.   The
shrapnel fire of the defenders ranges 3700 yards,
and thus up to Zowetitz, to the tile-manufactory near
Sadowa, and to Kopanina.

The assailant advances from Klenitz, and proposes
to make a front attack.   (We will suppose that on
both sides the flanks are prolonged by other troops.)

How can we make it possible for the artillery of
the assailant to take up its first position at 2000
yards from the enemy ?   It cannot advance over the
passages of the Bistritz, which have been destroyed,
and are besides under the shrapnel fire of the defenders.   Therefore these must be first occupied by
infantry.   But are the infantry who are told off for
this duty to advance the last 500 yards down to the

EXAMPLE 309

Bistritz under the undisturbed shrapnel fire of the defender? Do you believe that it can do so, if the effect of shrapnel is so murderous as we are led to think by the results of practice? I do not. Nothing then is left but to place batteries on the Roskos-berg and near Mzan, and to open such a shell fire upon the enemy's artillery that it will be compelled to leave the infantry alone. But this will not prevent single batteries from making use of small pieces of cover, for example, in rear of the tile-manufactory by the little wood near the sugar-factory, or wherever any cover may serve, and there finding a position, from which they can open a fire of shrapnel in order to assist the fire of common shell. It is very likely that on account of the length of the range more than an hour will elapse before any result is gained by this fight, and it may even take much longer if they do not succeed in quickly finding the range. I have already told you that our tables of practice show it to be by no means unlikely that the defender, firing from Lipa, will hold the high road as far as Dub so completely under fire that infantry moving on it must abandon their column of march; in this case the position of this infantry will imperatively demand that the artillery near Lipa shall be "contained," which will necessitate the assumption by the assailants of an artillery position near Dub before that on the Roskos-berg is occupied. It is clear then that altogether the artillery of the assailants must continue firing for from two to two and a half hours before their infantry can think of gaining possession of the Bistritz and of restoring the passages.

Here again the very strongest determination to

restrain as a matter of principle the fire of the artillery until the artillery duel can be commenced at a range of 2000 yards, will be brought to nought by the force of circumstances. The logic of facts moves by very different paths to those followed by the logic of even the most correct theoretical deductions.

I now come to the principal argument against the proposed system, that the fire of artillery shall only begin at the moment when the decisive artillery duel commences at a range of 2000 yards, and that this moment shall not be more than half an hour in advance of that at which the effective fire of infantry will begin. Who can promise you that any decision can be arrived at in less than a quarter of an hour? Can you be sure that your artillery will find its range quickly? May it not perhaps during half an hour or more make bad practice, thinking all the time that it is hitting the mark? In time of peace artillery has plenty of practice and a simple system of quickly finding its range. It is then so easy to observe the effect of the fire. When the smoke of the bursting shell hides the target, the shot is too short; when the target is visible in front of the smoke, the shot is over. The third, the fifth, or at the very latest, the seventh shell must hit. So say many gunners, judging by their experiences on the practice ground. But in war the ground sometimes plays the officer commanding a battery some very comical tricks. If in front of the target there be a slight depression of the ground, which is not noticed from the battery, and the shells striking and bursting in this cannot be directly seen, the smoke from them as it rises and grows thinner allows the target to show so clearly through it, that the observer is convinced that the smoke is in rear of the target and that he has shot over. If such a depression exists 500 yards in front of the target, it may very well happen that the battery may take the mean of its trial shots at from 500 to 600 yards too short, and may thus fire away the whole of its ammunition without result. I was once present when, in time of peace, one of the most practised instructors at the School of Gunnery steadily continued for this reason to shoot 500 yards short of the target. I once saw in action a considerable line of artillery, which was engaged near to me, firing for several hours too short, and this went on until I remarked it and informed them of it. The enemy had posted his guns on the farther edge of a plateau, in which there were some deceptive depressions, while our artillery was induced by similar appearances of the smoke to believe that they were standing close to the nearer edge.

There are certainly other means of observation. The captain of the battery may stand with his field-glass to his eyes on the windward flank of the battery. If we suppose this to be the left flank, he knows that every burst of a shell which shows to the right of the target was produced by a short shot, while any which show on the left of the target must have burst over it. This is all very simple and easy. But even in time of peace it sometimes happens that the gun is laid on the wrong target, when the enemy is represented by a line of guns, and when one of our guns has taken the wrong one of the enemy's guns as its mark ; in this case the observer will be deceived and will judge from false premises.

But in war many other disturbing elements come in. The smoke from one of the enemy's guns may envelop that of our shell, so that the latter cannot be observed. If the enemy is being fired on at the same time from many directions, it is possible that a shell from another battery may be mistaken for one of our own, and from this a false conclusion may be drawn, leading to the waste of many rounds. After some time it is observed that we are trusting in a faulty observation, and then we have to begin to find the range anew. But in the meantime the enemy's fire will also have become more lively, and he will have succeeded in finding his range. You try to observe a shot, but the smoke from the burst of one of the enemy's shells passes over your field-glass, obscures the view, and perhaps dirties the glass. You clean it with your glove and order another shot to be fired. At this moment your horse shies at a shell which passes close to him, and instead of observing the shot, you congratulate yourself on not having lost your seat. Then a shell falls into the middle of the team of a limber and bursts there, and the horses break loose and rush at you, just as you want to observe your shot. The enemy's shells fall thicker and thicker. Your detachments begin to hurry. The elevation is not given or corrected so carefully as it was, and thus any observation becomes valueless.

I am now relating to you my personal experiences at the battle of Sedan, when I brought up the first two batteries of the corps artillery. They were posted behind a hedge and some trees which, as I hoped, might hide our position from the enemy. But our

first shells burst in the boughs close in front of the
guns.   We then had to fell these obnoxious trees.
This took us about a quarter of an hour.   Then
happened all the difficulties which I have just narrated,
while the enemy was firing hotly on us.   I had nothing
left to do but to first cease firing all along the line,
then to lay every gun accurately and to order the
batteries to fire salvoes, so that I might get more
certain results from a group of six bursts.   This
rough mode of range-finding, which had been at an
earlier date suggested by Colonel von Scherbening
(who at this very moment was killed by a shell), was
quite successful.   We began to hit ; the enemy's fire
became hurried and ineffective, and we soon got the
upper hand.   But more than an hour had passed
before we were able to hit.   The range was, unless I
am wrong, 3200 paces (about 2700 yards), that is
to say, about the range proposed for the murderous
artillery duel which is to bring about a decision in a
quarter of an hour.

After our line of artillery had got the upper hand
of the enemy, I betook myself to the other batteries
in order to see if they were hitting the mark ; I was
in that mood which inclines us to interfere a little too
quickly.   "Captain," said I, " your shell are all over !"
The captain laughed and said that, on the contrary,
they were all short.   I pointed out to him the burst
of a shell far in rear of the enemy.   "That is not
one of mine," he said decidedly.   But I desired him
to give 500 paces less elevation ; he did so, and I
saw that he had been right.   I then allowed him to
find his own range, which he very soon did.   What
struck me was that he never looked at the target, but

only at his battery, on the flank of which he stood.
I asked why this was, and the captain answered, " The
one-year volunteer Klopsch is watching the flight of
each shell, standing to windward of each gun as it is
fired, and gives me a sign which we have agreed
upon after each shot." You may observe that there
are many ways of finding a range. If each battery
had a one-year volunteer with eyes as sharp as
Klopsch's, there would be no difficulty in finding the
range. But there is no general, fixed, and certain
receipt for doing so. Practice is the only one that
I can recommend, and the rules of the School of
Gunnery are only a useful guide.

It was a poor consolation to me to find that I
and my batteries were not the only ones during the
war who made such mistakes in observation and
correction. I have already told you how I myself
saw a neighbouring line of artillery continue for some
time to shoot short. General von Dresky writes as
follows with regard to the part which he played on
the 18th of August 1870 :

" I had another interesting experience, which proves
how in spite of a field-glass it is easy to err in one's
observation of the target. It appeared to us that the
four French gun-batteries, which we fired on at first
on the 18th of August and which stood in front of
Montigny-la-Grange, were posted in rear of embrasures
cut in a garden wall. We could see only the flashes
of the guns and these appeared certainly to come out
of embrasures. On these flashes we accordingly laid.
On going over the ground, however, two days later,
we found that the batteries had been standing in
front of the wall, since there we came across dead

gunners and horses and a quantity of splinters of wood ; we found no embrasures in the wall, but what had appeared to us as such were only branches which hung over the wall. The range from our position on the 18th to the wall was about 3300 paces (2700 yards). The wall was very much broken down by our shells, and if thus a good effect was obtained against the enemy's battery, it was principally due to the fact that the enemy's artillery stood so close in front of it, to the natural spread of the shells, and to the considerable number of rounds fired by us (about 1200 shells)."

I could name to you many officers of artillery, well taught at the School of Gunnery, who have related to me similar experiences, but I have not their permission to make use of their names, and think besides that I have already told you sufficient. You will also find it quite natural that there should be some difficulty in quickly picking up the range at a distance of from 2000 to 2500 yards, if you think that 2000 yards is almost a mile and a quarter, while 2500 yards is a mile and a half. Place yourself on rising ground, look at some point which is from a mile and a quarter to a mile and a half distant, and imagine that there from behind an undulation of the ground, or from behind a hedge or a village, you see the flashes of guns of which the shells reach you ; imagine also that you can see nothing more of these guns, and that you begin with trial shots, in the observation of which you are constantly disturbed. You will then certainly not wonder that one makes mistakes, or that one may shoot and observe for a quarter of an hour, or even for a whole hour, before getting the range. At any rate you will agree with me in this, that it is impossible to count with certainty upon being able to come victorious out of the artillery duel within a quarter of an hour after the first shot. But what will you do supposing that the artillery duel at from 2000 to 2500 yards is not so decisive as you could desire, or worse still, if it ends unfavourably for our artillery? The officer commanding the troops, who, trusting to the expectation which the gunner has urged upon him with regard to the result of this fight, has counted on an artillery duel of a quarter of an hour and a fire of artillery for a quarter of an hour on the enemy's infantry, will say to the gunner (according to what you tell me is the present system): "I can give you half an hour; at the end of that time I shall be so near the enemy with my skirmishers that I shall mask your fire." Well, the gunner opens fire at from 2000 to 2500 yards, and at the same moment the infantry commences its advance from the same distance, where it has already (naturally under cover) formed for the attack. At the end of half an hour the infantry is 500 yards from the enemy's infantry. But the artillery has made an error. It has not yet succeeded in finding its range. The infantry then, if in general under these circumstances it has been able to get as far, finds itself, at the moment when it masks its artillery, in face of the as yet unassailed position of the enemy, and will receive the combined fire, not only of the enemy's infantry, which is intact, but also of at least a part of the hostile artillery A catastrophe is yet more certain when the assailant's artillery has got the worst of the artillery duel, in place of being victorious, whilst the infantry, counting on victory, have been advancing against the enemy. Thus the artillery risks not only its own existence but also that of the infantry, if it fails to realise the expectation which induced it to withhold its fire until the opening of the artillery duel at a range of from 2000 to 2500 yards, and to reckon with certainty upon a decision to be brought about by less than half an hour of artillery fire.

In the face of such a risk the officer commanding the troops will refuse to embark on such a dangerous speculation, especially if he has already had unpleasant experience of it. He will simply order the artillery to contain that of the enemy, as soon as the latter annoys his infantry, and later on to prepare his attack, when he is ready to make it. In this case the artillery fight will be carried on in the same manner as formerly, except that the ranges will be longer. It will commence with a "cannonade," by which I mean a more or less ineffective fire, which must be opened in order to draw the attention and the fire of the enemy's artillery upon our batteries, and thus to prevent it from annoying the advance of the infantry. I have already shown that this cannonade, owing to the power of modern guns, must according to circumstances be commenced at 5000 yards or even at a greater distance. Then the officer commanding the troops will decide where he proposes to make his real attack. When he has made up his mind on this point, the artillery will advance up to the edge of the zone of shrapnel fire (about 3500 yards), and will endeavour to obtain the advantage in the combat with common shell.

The moment of time at which this advantage becomes palpable will be the earliest at which the officer commanding the troops will be in a position to determine when he will commence his attack. This also will be the moment at which the artillery can first resolve to engage in the decisive artillery duel; for this purpose it will advance by successive fractions, without ceasing its fire and making use of any cover which the ground may afford. If as the result of this duel the defender's artillery is silenced, then the moment will have arrived for the officer commanding the troops to let loose his infantry, which has awaited this moment in the order of attack; the infantry will thus first reach the enemy half an hour after the end of the artillery duel. It will carry out its advance of from 1500 to 2000 yards under cover of the shrapnel fire of its artillery, which should be used to shatter the enemy's infantry; for this purpose the artillery should advance by successive fractions in company with its infantry, as indeed I have already told you in my *Letters on Infantry*.

Thus the increase of the range of artillery not only does *not* make it advisable to delay later than formerly the opening of the artillery fire, but will also, as a general rule, make it absolutely necessary, whether we like it or not, to open the cannonade at an earlier moment than was the custom; and it will also last longer. This is indeed only natural, since the farther a weapon throws, the longer the range at which one will begin to use it. Yet I still hold to my old principle as a true one, that ineffective cannonades at enormous distances should not be permitted, while if the enemy is foolish enough to waste his ammunition at such ranges, we may be glad of it, but should not imitate him. But if the enemy begins to *hit*, then we *must* answer. Ranges will tend to increase owing to the improvements made in guns, and whereas a cannonade at a certain range was at one time a waste of ammunition, fire at the same range may in the future have a decisive effect. For this reason the artillery fight of the future must begin at ranges at which in former years there could be no question of such a combat.

On the other hand, the improvements in weapons of war will make future battles less bloody. For whenever the result of the artillery fight outside of the zone of shrapnel fire tends to be unfavourable, the officer commanding the troops will, three times out of four, be in a position to avoid decisive action, since he will still be nearly two miles from the enemy.

LETTER XIV

SHOULD ARTILLERY AVOID IN FUTURE THE ZONE OF INFANTRY FIRE?

YOUR second objection also has not surprised me, for I have often heard it said that artillery, since it now at 2000 yards obtains an effect with shrapnel which would not be sensibly increased by a nearer approach to the target, has no need to go closer than this to the enemy, and that it exposes itself to altogether unnecessary loss when it advances into the zone of infantry fire. It ought, they say, on the contrary, to avoid the enemy's infantry fire. I have already written on various occasions that I am of the opposite opinion, and I have previously named the circumstances under which, as I think, artillery, whether on the offensive or the defensive, should not hesitate to enter the effective range of the enemy's infantry. In order to give the bases for my opinion and to combat the theories put forward by you, I will point out some considerations into which I have not sufficiently entered, and which have reference to this subject.

The first of these considerations is the danger that at a range of 2000 yards, when the two infantry lines have closely approached each other, we may confuse friend and enemy, and may fire on our own troops.

I once had an opportunity of comparing, after a battle, the official reports of the captain of a battery and of a major of infantry. The captain wrote : " At 3 P.M. I took up a position at the point where the road from M. to L. and N. forks. I opened fire upon a battalion of the enemy which was retiring from S. on N., and continued firing until it disappeared in a hollow road. I observed three hits ; range 2500 paces." The major reported : " I marched from S. on R., in order to take part in the action which was going on around that village. At 3 P.M. I received the fire of artillery from my rear. Before the battalion could find cover in the hollow road near R., three shells struck it." Could two reports agree more closely ? The range from the fork of the road to the beginning of the hollow road from S. to R., when measured on the map, was exactly 2500 paces. And this terrible mistake was made by a very steady and very gallant captain, and that at a distance of only 1900 yards.

General von Dresky writes to me as follows concerning the part which he took in the fight of Le Mans : " On the 12th of January at daybreak the corps artillery of the 3d corps received orders to support the attack on the heights of Champagné. By great good luck we found an excellent position in this most close country, which was besides full of obstacles and incapable of being commanded from any one point. We were about to open fire upon some troops which were plainly visible against the snow, when an officer, who had a particularly good field-glass, declared decidedly that these troops were Prussians. In order to make quite certain I sent

Y

forward my aide-de-camp with two mounted orderlies, who returned with the information that they were indeed Prussians. The French had already abandoned the heights of Champagné."

(The range from the position near the Les Morinières Farm to the heights of Champagné near the Les Rumaldières Farm is 2100 yards. See the official account, Part II., Plan 29.)

It is true that errors of this kind in firing at one's own troops happened even formerly, in the days of smooth-bore guns and muskets. Götz von Berlichingen tells us that he lost his hand by a shot from his friends. I take it for granted that you remember that in the battle of Wagram the two divisions of Bernadotte's corps fought for a considerable time with each other. But in the latter case the mistake was principally due to the uniforms, since one division consisted of Saxons and the other of French. But up to the time of the introduction of rifled weapons such mistakes were very rare. They have now become much more probable, owing to the long ranges at which such weapons are used ; and the longer the ranges the more must they be guarded against. For nothing has such a demoralising effect upon troops as receiving the fire of others of their own troops in their rear, while they are engaged with the enemy in front. I have met with this circumstance in two different battles. The men, it is true, did not think of flying, but they bowed under a resignation which paralysed all activity, such indeed as gains possession of men when they have to say, "It is all over!" One of my officers commanding a battery once even gave the order : "Open fire to the rear!" and wanted to return the fire. You may imagine what a terrible confusion would have arisen if he had done this. By good luck I heard the order and prevented its being put into execution. When I, remembering the impressions which I then felt, picture to myself the case of attacking infantry which is engaged in very hot close fighting against the enemy's infantry, perhaps even is in the last stage of the assault on a village, and which receives a destructive fire of shrapnel from its own artillery, a catastrophe appears to me to be inevitable.

Imagine yourself now on some point in open ground, which seems to you suitable for an artillery position in battle, and picture to yourself an infantry fight wavering backwards and forwards, at a distance of from 2100 to 2700 yards (or say about a mile and a half), around a village or a wood, and ask yourself whether you can with certainty decide that this advancing column of infantry, or that swarm of skirmishers charging in, is composed of friends or enemies. Would you dare, if you commanded the artillery, to open fire on them with shell and shrapnel? If you take into consideration at that moment the natural spread of the shell, the differences in the time of burning of the fuses (of which some are sure to be defective in manufacture), and the very great variations of some shell from the normal trajectory (which are sometimes far in excess of the mere want of accuracy of the gun, and may be ascribed to an error in laying, but which here and there are sure to arise),[1] you will, deterred as you will be by the thought of the awful consequences of such a shell,

---

[1] Our gunners call such shots "Deserters."

prefer not to fire at all. In that case the whole of the artillery must stand inactive (for we suppose that the enemy's artillery has been altogether silenced) while the infantry is engaged in the decisive struggle, instead of, as they should, throwing into the scale of victory the heavy weight of a destructive fire of shrapnel.

In order not to repeat myself I will refer you to what I wrote, at the time when we were in correspondence about infantry, concerning the share of the artillery in an attack by infantry over open ground. I then explained to you that artillery, when it advances into the zone of the enemy's infantry fire, is not exposed to destruction, provided that this fire is held in check by the fire of our infantry. It would certainly be mere folly to advance artillery to within 600 or 800 yards of a position (a village or wood, etc.) held by infantry, unless the latter were under the fire of infantry from an even shorter range. But at a range of over 1000 yards the fire of infantry ceases to be annihilating, and it will be even less effective if our infantry holds it in check at a range of 500 yards. In the war of 1870 the French infantry was armed with weapons which have since then been but little improved upon as regards range and accuracy. Yet Von Dresky with his Horse Artillery was able, at a range of 1600 paces (1200 yards) from Flavigny, to cross the bridge of Tantelainville, and left only one gun behind, while that very soon rejoined him. I was also able to retain in position the whole of my line of artillery of 54 guns from 2 to 5.30 P.M., although a thick line of the enemy's skirmishers lay 1000 paces in front of us and fired at us unceasingly. And when the infantry fight became really warm, the batteries did not avoid even shorter ranges, but fought shoulder to shoulder with the infantry, in some places even in the firing line.

Again those batteries were not destroyed which pushed forward into the heaviest fire of skirmishers at the assault of the Geissberg at Weissenburg, and at that of Elsasshausen at Wörth. Of course the artillery suffered some loss. No loss, no victory. But as I have already remarked, the men in a battery are not so closely packed as they are in a firing line, and thus the losses are not so heavy. And after all, is a gunner more valuable than an infantry soldier? Are they not both soldiers in the same army? Is not as much time and care expended on the training of an infantry soldier as upon that of a gunner?

I have once, at the manœuvres, seen a line of artillery which remained in their position at 2700 yards from the enemy, when their infantry pushed on into close combat, for the reason that the next position, which was separated from the first by a deep valley, being only 1000 yards from the enemy, appeared to be too near to his line of skirmishers. So the artillery stood there inactive, far in rear, and when even the reserves of the infantry were thrown into the action, and thus came within 500 yards of the enemy, the guns were over 2000 yards in rear of them, and hardly seemed to belong to them. The defender took advantage of this interval. Two squadrons went rapidly forward, under cover of woods and ravines, turned the flank of the artillery, charged it from the rear, and captured it. This made me think, what can the officer commanding the troops do if he is obliged to leave his artillery so far in rear? Ought he to leave two battalions as an escort and thus not only dispense with the aid of the artillery, but also weaken the very infantry attack? I further thought to myself, how can it be possible to bring up a couple of guns or so from this artillery at the proper moment, in order, as at Weissenburg and at Bazeilles, to break down at any cost some obstacles in street-fighting; for this artillery is a mile and a quarter away. How can artillery which has been left so far behind manage to get up at the right moment, in order to secure the position when it has been captured, and to crush the advancing reserves of the enemy after the infantry has won the victory?

I felt quite sure of one thing: even on the ground of its own safety the artillery cannot remain farther to the rear than some few hundreds of yards behind the last lines of battle. If it is intended to effectively assist the infantry fight and to secure at the proper moment the advantages which the infantry have gained, the artillery (either as a whole or in part, according to circumstances) must not be more than a few hundreds of yards in rear of their advancing skirmishers; circumstances may even arise which will compel it to push forward into the most advanced line of skirmishers.

Up to the present I have offered to you all the reasons which quiet consideration shows to be of value on tactical grounds to prove that artillery must not always avoid the zone of infantry fire.

But the chief argument of all, which I have left to the last, is based deep down in the human heart.

How can you expect a gunner to watch his comrades of the infantry charge in at the last and hottest crisis without longing to be with them? Would you ask him to play the part of a spectator "in order not to expose himself" at the moment when the decisive struggle is fought out; a struggle which, if it be carried on without his aid, will cost twice as many lives among his comrades of the infantry as would be the case if he fought with them; a struggle which, without him, may lead to defeat, to the destruction of all, whereas with his help it must end in victory? Hold to your rule, if you please, that artillery is to shun the zone of infantry fire. Some individuals may here and there take advantage of it, and feel themselves "justified" by its provisions. But the man of courage will, at the critical moment, despise these rules. He will go forward and help, and will not ask what are the regulations.

When we before Saint-Privat, to our great surprise (for I had been ordered to fight a delaying action), saw our infantry move out from their cover and advance to the attack, and when our fire on the village was masked by the infantry as they moved forward, we did not remain for a moment inactive in our position. I was immediately between the corps artillery and that of the 1st Division of the Guard, and was talking to the two commanders. With one voice we all three cried, "Now we must manage to advance." I gave an order to both officers that each battery was to push on in succes-

sion as its fire was masked. But many batteries
had already limbered up to advance before the order
reached them. Prittwitz's battery of the divisional
artillery did so, and advanced at a gallop up the
height. It certainly suffered some loss. It reached
the hill with at first only three guns, but its first
shot brought the advancing reserves of the enemy
to a stop. It is true that Generals von Pape and
Budritzky sent their aides-de-camp and asked for
the assistance of the artillery, but these officers
found the batteries already in motion. What would
have been the end of that struggle if the artillery
of the Guard and of the 12th corps had thought
that they ought to shun the zone of infantry fire?

One of the highest military authorities of the
present day said once in his criticism on some
manœuvres in which the artillery of the attack had
avoided the zone of infantry fire: "That is of no
use. The artillery may shoot as far and as well as
it likes, it must at the last go in."

To "go in" is the expression of a manly heart.
Even if cool reason says that artillery ought at such
moments to remain in rear, the heart would drive it
in. A soldier should work with his head and his
heart. Artillery which goes straight against the
front of an intact and strong line of infantry, and
advances to within a few hundred yards of it, works
with its heart but without its head, and would be
annihilated. Artillery which leaves its infantry in
the lurch, in its effort to avoid the zone of infantry
fire, shows plenty of head for its own interests, but
no courage at all, and would be useless.

Up to the present time I have spoken only of

the behaviour of artillery in the offensive. The measures to be adopted by it in the defensive may be very easily deduced from those employed in the offensive, and are theoretically much simpler, though practically far more difficult to carry out. I have fully stated my opinion, that when on the defensive opportunities will often arise to fire with very good effect at very long ranges. This is plainly shown by the example which I have worked out on the plan of the battle of Königgrätz, and in which the artillery of the defenders, firing from Lipa at a range of 5400 yards, would compel the assailant as far away as Dub to leave the road with his columns of march, and either to find cover or to assume the order of battle. It would be a great error on the part of the defender if he let slip this opportunity of firing on the assailant with 50 per cent of hits, since he would thus cause him delay and loss, and it must be the principal object of the defender to cause delay to the assailant.

But when we come to examine the question whether artillery should avoid the fire of infantry, the situation when on the defensive may appear very different to that which exists when acting on the offensive, and it may seem that artillery on the defensive should absolutely avoid the fire of infantry, since if it does not its horses will be killed by the assailant's infantry, and it will thus lose its power of movement, and will therefore on the farther advance of the assailant be irremediably lost. I am certainly of the opinion that, where it is in any way possible in the occupation of a defensive position, the fore- most line of skirmishers should be pushed somewhat

more to the front than the line of artillery, in order
that the latter may not be too much exposed to loss
at the very beginning of the infantry fight. But I
think that a distance of 500 yards will be sufficient
for this. If the lines of skirmishers are pushed forward
500 yards to the front, they will hold back the
enemy's infantry at a distance of at least another
500 yards from the guns, and at this range of 1000
yards the enemy's infantry will not do much harm
if they are properly received by our skirmishers.
This distance of 500 yards in front of the artillery
seems to be, on the other hand, the minimum in the
case where the artillery is placed in such a position
that it must fire over the heads of its own skirmishers ;
and this not on account of the safety of the artillery,
but in order to secure the infantry from the splinters
of their own artillery, if by any chance shells or
shrapnel burst in the bore. Thus 500 yards will be
the normal distance to which infantry when on the
defensive should be pushed in front of their artillery.

It is scarcely necessary to say that this distance
will depend very much upon the character of the
ground. It may be that at the foot of a low undulation, which affords an excellent position for
artillery, some building almost as strong as a fort
may be found ; as, for example, the Château Ville-
taneuse in front of St. Denis ; this would of course
be occupied with infantry, even though it were 1000
yards in front of the artillery line. On the other
hand, the skirmishers will not be posted more than a
few hundred yards to the front in cases where the
line of natural objects (such as patches of wood,
farms, etc.), which may serve them as cover, do not

extend farther to the front, while beyond them the ground is open. I can even imagine an excellent defensive position, in which the foremost line of skirmishers is on the same front as the guns. It all depends upon the character of the ground. But if I had a free choice (as, for example, supposing I had to dig shelter-trenches on the bare brow of a hill which sloped to the front) I should advance them, as I said, 500 yards in front of the artillery line.

From this it follows that artillery, when on the defensive, will not always be able to avoid the effect of infantry fire, since however well its own firing-line, which is posted 500 yards in its front, may occupy the attacking skirmishers, some few infantry bullets, either accidentally or intentionally, will reach the artillery at a range of more than 1000 yards, and even up to one of 1600 yards.

We have further to consider the question whether artillery on the defensive should hold its ground in the case where the assailant's infantry drives back its skirmishers, and is advancing so close to the artillery line as to threaten its safety.

In order to answer this question I will first consult the drill regulations for the infantry, and on page 148 I find the following : " For this reason the occupation of advanced points, which it is intended to defend only for a time, does not in most cases offer much advantage ; it is rather preferable as a rule to use the forces which are to be employed in carrying out the scheme of the defence, not perhaps at one moment, but at any rate on one and the same line."

According to this the regulations condemn the system of pushing forward light troops, which must be withdrawn when the enemy makes a serious attack; and, moreover, the infantry which is thus posted in front of the artillery will, as a rule, stand on the very spot where it has decided to carry out its principal struggle.

If it gives way and falls back from this line, it will do so because it will have been thrown back by the superiority of the enemy. But such an advantage to the enemy is not conceivable, at any rate in the case of our infantry, until after a long and very hot fight, and in this fight the artillery of the defence will have suffered such loss in horses, by the enemy's shell and shrapnel fire and also by the bullets which will occasionally fall among them during the infantry fight, that it will no longer be able to reckon with certainty upon being able to make a rapid change of position to the rear. And such a movement must be made rapidly owing to the dangerous vicinity of the enemy.

But still more important and serious is the moral effect which will be produced by the retirement of the guns at this moment. The infantry will have brought up its last reserves (this it must do, for by the regulations the whole force, which is available for the attainment of the purposes of the defence, should be pushed forward into the front line); it is, however, giving way before the superiority of the enemy, and its cohesion is loosening every moment on account of the losses among its officers and men. If at this instant the artillery joins in the movement in retreat, the temporary check will develop into a total defeat. Even if it has been possible to commence the movement of the guns, the enemy's infantry fire will kill many of the horses belonging to the retreating guns, and a great part of the artillery will fall defenceless into the hands of the enemy, since no line of artillery will remain in action which might form a rallying-point for the infantry, on which they might assemble and re-form, and be thus prepared for fresh combat.

What would have happened at the battle of Vionville, if the great line of artillery, which stood on the front first taken up by the corps artillery under Von Dresky, had retired out of the zone of the enemy's infantry fire, instead of offering, as it did, a rallying-point to the infantry when they were driven back by the double or treble numerical superiority of the enemy, in rear of which they re-formed their strength for a renewed advance? Should we have obtained a victory at Beaune-la-Rolande if the artillery had shunned the zone of infantry fire? The nearer the enemy's infantry approaches to our artillery, the more certain will be our fire, the flatter the flight of the whistling shells and their splinters, and the more destructive the rush of the shrapnel through the ranks of the foe ; and should the latter push forward even up to the muzzles of the guns, their fire will beat him back at the very last moment. What will it matter then if the artillery has for a time become unable to move owing to its loss in horses ? It has no need to manœuvre, it has only to continue to fire, and with its fire to sweep back the enemy and maintain the position. Von Dresky is quite right when he says, in the letter which I have quoted, that artillery is impervious to a frontal attack, and acts as a reserve appointed to receive troops which have been driven back. It is thus still less desirable in the defensive than in the offensive that artillery should avoid infantry fire ; and this more especially when their own infantry has been driven back. The arguments in favour of this statement have only gained in force in consequence of the improvements in artillery since 1870-71, for, with its shrapnel and its new pattern of common shell, artillery can now count with more certainty than ever upon the impenetrability of its front.

You will say perhaps that I have here stated a principle well known to all and disputed by none. But I have read lately in essays and pamphlets by very excellent authors, with whom I agree on almost all points, so many regulations for the artillery dealing with movements in retreat and changes of position to the rear, even when acting on the defensive, that I begin to fear lest in the course of a long peace we may, through a system of clever deductions, become again too scientific, may abandon simple downright movements for newly-invented and cunning manœuvres and evolutions, and may again leave in the background the main point—moral effect. One of the best of the new works—*The Conduct of Artillery in Manœuvres and in Action* (Hanover, 1883) —shows with an exactness which is beyond contradiction the importance of "finding the range." As this importance has increased artillery has tended to become more stationary. It can produce no effect while it is on the move, and when it has ceased to move it loses the time necessary to find the new range. It is one weak point of the attack that its artillery must manœuvre, that is to say, that it must advance from one position to another. The defence must take advantage of this weak point, and must pay the greatest regard to the source of its own strength, namely, the absence of any necessity to move its artillery.

This does not imply that the defender's artillery is never to cease firing during the artillery fight ; for instance, it may do so if that of the assailant begins to gain an advantage over it, or in order to economise its fire, with the object either of allowing the enemy's batteries which wish to advance to more decisive ranges to rush too far to the front, or of being in a position to aid in the repulse of the decisive infantry attack. But in most cases it will be sufficient for this object to draw back the guns a few paces in rear of the crest on which they are posted ; no very great power of manœuvring is needed for this. When in action at long ranges it will be sufficient to merely cease firing. When I at Sedan made one of my lines of artillery cease firing, in order that I might, as I passed from gun to gun, see that they were properly laid, the enemy soon after ceased to fire at us. I be-lieve that he thought that our guns were abandoning their position ; it was at a range of about 2700 yards.

You will perhaps remark that artillery cannot remain for ever standing on some defensive position when the officer commanding the troops has ordered a retreat. But when a retreat has been ordered the artillery ceases to have any independent power over its movements, and it would be well in such a case to avoid exposing artillery to effective infantry fire, for the officer commanding the troops cannot choose a more unfavourable moment for deciding upon a retreat than one when his artillery is under the fire of the enemy's infantry. Even at manœuvres a mixed force cannot move in retreat so quickly as a company, to which the captain simply gives the order, " Right-about-turn !" The proper dispositions must be made and the necessary directions must be given for the retirement of any mixed force. In war the officer commanding the troops, before he draws back his forces, must decide as to the direction to be given to his trains, his baggage, his field hospitals, and sometimes his ammunition-columns. If the artillery suffers from effective infantry fire while these movements are as yet uncompleted, it is then usually too late for an orderly retirement, and the retreat will take place in disorder and with great loss. Any guns which may have lost horses after being limbered up will probably fall into the hands of the enemy, before they can be unhooked. For this reason the decision to retire must be arrived at, either before the enemy's attack has progressed so far that the infantry is hotly engaged, or after an attack has been repulsed, and while the assailant is making his disposition for a fresh assault. (See the remarks on this subject in my tenth letter.) In that case the officer commanding the troops will first send back his artillery into a new position, from which it may delay the advance of the enemy, and where their fire may serve as a signal for the other troops, that here is the point on which they are to re-form. But there is an exception even to this rule. When, for example, the enemy has not yet attacked, and the defender's artillery commands a defile through which the assailant must pass, but which he is unable to traverse so long as the artillery remains in its position.   In such and in similar cases the artillery will be left to the last in front of the enemy under an escort of cavalry, until all the remainder, the train as well as the infantry, have obtained such a start of the enemy that the latter cannot catch them up on the same day.   But even in this case the artillery must not remain so long in position that it is exposed to infantry fire.   In such and in similar cases, it is necessary sometimes to gain time by a heavy cannonade by the artillery of the rear-guard, which should be reinforced under certain circumstances even by the whole of the corps artillery.

LETTER XV

ON SOME ARTILLERY QUESTIONS OF THE DAY

1. ON reserve-artillery.

As I have already said, the improvement of the fire of artillery has resulted in the abolition of reserve-artillery, and I believe that the further improvements made in the arm since the last war have strengthened the reasons which induced us to bring as much artillery as possible into action immediately at the beginning of the battle, and to hold back no reserve of artillery; all this you have exactly understood.

But you, on the other hand, make the observation that the artillery duel, owing to the murderous effect of shrapnel, will so entirely destroy that side which is worsted in it, that, if it has kept no reserve-artillery, it will have no more guns available for use during the close combat of the infantry; but I must, with respect to this, beg your attention to the fact that the artillery duel, if it really does prove so destructive, will probably lead to the annihilation of that side which puts the smallest number of guns into position. A single additional battery which can outflank the enemy's line and can bring a flanking or an oblique fire on it, may at the very commencement of a combat, carried on at effective shrapnel ranges, turn the fight to our advantage, and then, according to the experience of the School of Gunnery, when we have once begun to gain the upper hand, and make use of our advantage to concentrate our fire properly, the destruction of the enemy will soon follow. We have heard it said that it will take only a quarter of an hour. Even if it were so effective, I still doubt, as I have already written to you, whether this duel will resemble the well-known fight between two lions, who each devoured the other, since I think that fire will generally be opened at first on either side at very long ranges, and that battles, according to the nature of things as already shown, will tend to become less bloody as the improvement in weapons of war progresses. But if it be so effective, this is an additional reason for artillery to make the greater efforts to bring all its guns at once as quickly as possible into action, as soon as the assailant has decided that, and where, he intends to attack, or as soon as the defender sees the attack develop. Then if, of two equal forces of artillery, one holds a third back in reserve, the other two-thirds will be quickly destroyed by the superiority of the enemy, who can thus later on be still more easily ready for the other third. Now you say that according to this logic the other arms ought also to retain no reserves, and should not even form several lines of battle, but should strive to advance with all their force in the front line. But the comparison is not altogether just.

Why do the other arms use several lines of battle and reserves? (i) In order to receive and to collect troops which have lost their cohesion, so that they may regain their organisation and become fit for action, since infantry and cavalry which have become disorganised in battle are not only of little use against fresh and intact forces in close order, but are even defenceless before them. (ii) In order to take advantage of any disorganisation amongst the enemy and to destroy him. (iii) In order to keep troops in hand, in case some unforeseen accident may render necessary their employment on some new point of the field of battle. The two first reasons have no existence for artillery. The last loses its value in proportion as the sphere of effect of the arm increases. When the artillery had to advance to within 1000 paces of the enemy in order to produce any effect, when it could easily come into action within 400 paces of an enemy, who might threaten it with infantry and cavalry, then no one could count with certainty upon being able to use that artillery at any other point, if it had been once sent into the fight ; it had then to be considered as "expended." But the longer the range of artillery the less is it "expended," and the more it still remains, even when in action, at the disposition of the general. It can now limber up and be used in another position. During the combat of the Guard corps in the battle of Sedan, we were obliged in the middle of the action to "extend to a flank." Roon's battery was standing on the right flank of the 3d brigade, and was ordered to move to the left flank of the division. It limbered up to retire, passed at a trot in rear of the other batteries, and took up its position on their left ; and all this in an effective

fire of chassepots, for the captain was hit by a
bullet in the abdomen shortly after the guns had
been limbered up. In the same battle the whole of
the Horse Brigade trotted from the extreme right
flank to the centre, came into action there, and later
on trotted back to the right flank; the 3d Horse
Artillery battery went to the extreme right. The
2d Field Brigade of the corps artillery was able,
without difficulty, to move from its first position on
the right of the 1st brigade into its second on their
left. Even if the enemy's fire were much hotter
than it then was, it would be possible to dispose of
a line of artillery in action, provided only that the
position gives some little cover. When the fight is
taking place at a still longer range, it is only necessary
to cease firing and to draw back the guns a little;
then the enemy cannot see them and also ceases his
fire on them (as I have already told you, the enemy's
artillery at Sedan ceased firing shortly after I had
ordered my guns to do so); and then they can be
set in motion. With regard to artillery which is
employed at the shorter shrapnel ranges in a very
hot artillery duel, it would naturally not be desirable
at such a moment to find employment for it in any
other position. For the very heat of the fight offers
the best evidence that it is in the exact place where
it is most needed.

We may add that the greater the power of artillery,
the less is the necessity for it to move in order to be
available for use in some fresh direction. Even the
guns which we used in the war of 1870 were sufficiently powerful to be able, when standing in the
centre of the front of an army-corps, to give aid to

any part of the action of that corps, by merely turning
their fire upon the spot in question without themselves
changing their position.   From the position in front
of Saint-Privat which the artillery of the Guard
occupied, those batteries which stood in the centre
were able to fire across the high road on masses of
the enemy which were moving against the left flank
of the corps, as well as later on to shell the enemy
on our right flank as he advanced against the Hessian
division.   At Sedan in a similar manner it commanded
from one and the same position the extreme right
and left flanks of the corps.   Since the sphere of
effect is now still more extended, artillery will be
able, without moving, to aid on a yet wider front.
An army-corps must therefore always endeavour,
wherever possible, to bring the whole of its artillery
into action.   If artillery, for which there is room in
the position, is held back in reserve, the officer doing
so will act in a manner similar to those strategists of
former days who, as at Halle in 1806, placed their
strategical reserves outside of the theatre of war ; but
at last Napoleon taught them that it is impossible to
be too strong on the field of battle.

This will not altogether hold good in the case of
an entire army.   No field gun has at present sufficiently long range to be able, from one and the same
position, to command the battle front of a whole
army.   It might therefore in this case appear desirable
to have a reserve of artillery available, in case it might
be necessary to employ exceptional strength on one
or other flank of the army.   But an army composed
of many corps will hold in reserve a certain number
of entire army-corps, and will thus find a sufficient

reserve of artillery in the batteries of these corps. Thus in the battle of the 18th of August 1870, the 3d corps, which was otherwise not engaged on that day, sent forward its corps artillery into the position at Vionville.

Finally, with regard to your last argument in favour of the retention of a reserve, namely, that, owing to the tremendous effect of the artillery duel, there is some danger that, after a battle, no artillery will be left for another day, I would merely remark that this only proves the necessity of winning the first battle. If you lose that, all those of your guns which have lost their detachments and teams by the fire of shrapnel will fall into the hands of the enemy. If you win, I will show you how to make up a new artillery to replace that which you have lost. You will have lost only horses and men, for your guns will not have suffered from the shrapnel fire. We will take for the guns the horses of the ammunition-wagons, which, being now empty, can very well be drawn by one pair each, and we will form new detachments from the escort of the same wagons. After the battle of Saint-Privat the ammunition-columns of the Guard corps gave 200 horses to the batteries. Von Dresky must have filled up his Horse Artillery batteries in the same manner after the battle of Vionville, since they then lost 75 per cent of their horses, and were nevertheless available for action on the 18th of August (two days later).

2. On finding the range from a position in rear.

The second artillery question which you allude to, namely, " Finding the range from a position in rear," has already occupied much of my attention. I believe that great results are expected from it. The undeniable truth, that that artillery which first finds the range will obtain the superiority in the artillery fight, has led to the following suggestion : You begin to fire at a very long distance, simply to find the range ; when this has been done you open fire on the position which you propose next to occupy for the decisive artillery duel ; by subtracting the latter range from the former you find the distance of the new position from the enemy ; you then hasten on at a very rapid pace, perhaps with your guns loaded and your tangent-scales set, into your new position, and there at once begin the artillery duel with guns for which the elevation is known, against an enemy who has to commence by finding his range. For example, I am firing at the enemy at a range of 5000 yards ; I see a hill on which I propose to take up a closer position ; I find by firing at it that the range of that hill is 3000 yards ; I then know that this position is 2000 yards from the enemy.

I own that this idea has in it something so enticing, that I was at first much taken with it. But the more I considered its practicability, the more was I convinced that it could seldom be possible to make use of it. In the first place, I would simply observe that the nearer of the two positions is either in the possession of the enemy, in which case we cannot occupy it, or it is held by our troops, in which case we cannot fire at it ; therefore this process is limited in practice to an exceptional combination of circumstances, which will have enabled us to fire at the new position, before it has been occupied by our troops, and while it was still in the position of the enemy.

Either this must be the case, or we must have at least time to send an order to our troops, who are 3000 yards away, to direct them to open out and leave a space free into which we may throw our shell: and it is further necessary that the enemy's infantry shall fail to take advantage of this opportunity to return quickly and reoccupy the ground in question. Again, the new position must lie directly in the line of fire of the first position, otherwise the calculation will be incorrect. Furthermore, the front of the enemy's artillery must lie exactly in one and the same straight line, and our new position must for its whole length be exactly parallel to the enemy's front, otherwise the range for the guns on one flank will differ very much from that for the guns on the other.

But, granted that all these conditions may be fulfilled, I have still some more questions to ask:

(i) Supposing that we fancy that we have found our range to be 5000 paces, but have been deceived by the very great distance; what then? Say that we have judged it to be 300 yards longer than it is, and yet thought that we were hitting, which at a range of 5000 yards is easily possible; when we go in to 2000 yards we shall have 300 yards too much elevation, and shall suffer from the enemy's fire without producing the least effect upon him, since we shall steadily shoot over his head instead of doing him injury.

(ii) Supposing that the enemy's artillery, which, when seen from a distance of 5000 yards, appears to be standing in one straight line, has really every battery at a different range from us; what then? In that case we shall have found the range of a single battery and shall be crushed by the others.

(iii) If, as you advance at a gallop, at a racing pace, or even at a trot, you fail to find the spot to which you took the range; what then? And this may easily happen, for ground at a distance looks very different to what it does when you are on it. I will only ask you, who are an ardent sportsman, to recall your experiences when partridge shooting. You shoot a bird; it falls among the potatoes, close to that yellow flower. You walk up to it, but when you get there you mistake another yellow flower for the right one, and you search for half an hour without result. How do you propose to search for half an hour, with your brigade of artillery at a gallop, for the spot on which you wish to unlimber? The enemy in the meantime will have knocked you to pieces.

(iv) The new position, when seen from the rear, appeared as if you could there get on good terms with the enemy. When you arrive there you find that the enemy cannot be seen from it; what then? You will wander about with your tangent-scales set wrong, under the enemy's fire, looking for some position to take up; this is the worst thing that can happen to you.

(v) In the new position at the range which you have ascertained only one battery (or perhaps only one gun) can find room. The character of the ground is such that the other guns must be posted farther to the front or to the rear; in short, the range which you have found is valueless. It suits only one battery; the others do not hit, and suffer accordingly.

All these difficulties will tend to absolute failure

of effect on our part if we, as has been proposed by
certain Hotspurs who are full of this idea, advance
with shrapnel in the guns, with fuses which must
have been already set, for the first rounds, under the
circumstances mentioned above, will be altogether
ineffective. With common shell in the gun, the
tangent-scale can at any rate be re-set, if we are
obliged to unlimber at some spot other than that
which we selected ; but the setting of the time-fuse
for shrapnel cannot be altered when once the shell
has been placed in the gun.

Let us now again take a practical case. Let us
return to the battlefield of Königgrätz and to the
situation which we have so often considered. The
artillery of the defenders is standing on the heights
of Lipa, that of the assailants on the Roskos-berg,
and the latter has found its range as 4000 yards.
The infantry of the assailants has occupied the
passages of the Bistritz and the wood of Skalka,
and has pushed on into the Hola wood. This
infantry has been told that their artillery intends
to find its range from the spur which runs from
Cistowes to the Skalka wood, and that therefore the
infantry is not to occupy this spur. It is believed
that there is a point on the spur about 1780 yards
from the Roskos-berg, from which it will be possible
to fire on the enemy at Lipa. The range of this
point is found. A poplar stands there, showing up
clearly, which must prevent any unfortunate error.
There is no question of advancing at a gallop, for
the Bistritz must be crossed. But near the Skalka
wood a passage is found, which lies in a dead angle,
since it cannot be seen by the enemy at Lipa. You

cross there, form line, and advance on the poplar on the front of a brigade. Can you really see the enemy from this point? And if one battery can see him, can the others do so also? Read the description of this spot in the account of the battle of Königgrätz, and notice how often our batteries had to change their positions, because they could not get a good view of the enemy. In this particular case the wings must advance in a half-circle in front of the centre, in order to be able to fire. But the guns are loaded with shrapnel, of which the fuses have been set. There is then nothing else to be done but to fire the guns into the air, and thus to betray our position to the enemy, before we can open an aimed fire.

I can perfectly well imagine a case where it would be possible to find a point which might be fired on beforehand and the range thus found, and which might afterwards be occupied by our infantry, and then properly reconnoitred. A position might be found there which would be under cover of the hedge round a village or of a hill, etc. The approach to it might also be well covered, so that the enemy would not see the guns as they moved up into it. But such a position would seldom afford space for more than one battery. This battery should be taken there, but with the guns unloaded; standing unseen by the enemy, we might first study the position, and when we were quite sure that all was right, we might commence an unexpected and rapid fire of shell, or perhaps an immediate fire of shrapnel. I think that such a battery might produce a surprising effect, and even, if favourable circumstances concurred, might exert a decisive influence on the course of the artillery fight. But you will allow that for this the concurrence of many favourable circumstances is absolutely necessary, and that thus this manœuvre will not as a rule be practicable. In 99 cases out of 100, especially if it be attempted with a great artillery line of more than one battery, it will fail, that is to say, it will result in the destruction of the advancing line of artillery.

Do you know the everyday expression in Berlin, " It is a capital idea, but that is about all "?

3. On the use of salvoes by batteries.

There is a notion which finds some favour, that immediately after unlimbering in the position near the enemy, which is at any cost to be taken up at a gallop (even though in doing so two-thirds of the guns are left behind), a salvo of shrapnel should be fired ; but this will certainly lead to nothing but a useless waste of ammunition.

I am in general a declared enemy of artillery salvoes as a system of fighting. A battery has to load, set its tangent-scales, lay its guns, fire, observe and correct each shot, each of which duties has to be performed by a different man, while they must all be correctly carried out if it is proposed to hit ; it thus forms such a complicated technical machine, that only from the strictest pedantry and the most steady supervision of the execution of each duty can the best possible results be anticipated. As soon as, instead of a quiet calm, haste and precipitation arise, and as soon as the detachments feel that they are not looked closely after, mistakes will begin ; this is true of the practice camp, but is still more true when

they are in front of the enemy.   Suppose that out
of a battery salvo only one shot hits the mark, whom
is the captain of the battery to hold answerable for
the failure?   He does not know, after the salvo,
which of the six guns has been properly laid.   But
when shot after shot is watched by the captain, and
when he can make the gun which is concerned
responsible for each "deserter," then the detachments
take far more trouble in loading correctly, in setting
their tangent-scale and fuses, in laying, etc. etc.
Only thus can the captain obtain that command
over the fire which makes men say, "He holds his
fire in his hand."   Believe me, I speak from experience, it is hard enough now to keep one's fire under
control.   It is only necessary that a gun shall
miss fire, or that the firing number shall be killed
at the moment when the word "Fire!" is given, or
that any such interruption shall occur, and another
gun will fire immediately, and then, unless the
captain intervenes with the severity of a Draco,
independent firing at once takes place, such as is
not recognised by our regulations, such as, unwatched,
uncorrected, and often unaimed as it is, has no result
except an impenetrable cloud of smoke.   I trust only
to that fire which works pedantically from one flank,
where the captain stands to windward with his field-
glass to his eye, watches each shot, and can intervene
whenever a "deserter" occurs, since no shot is fired
until the preceding shot has been marked on the
target.   This is also the object of the regulations,
since it is there laid down that the shortest pause
between two guns is to be from 6 to 8 seconds,
while in 6 to 8 seconds the shell will traverse the

longest range (2500 to 3000 yards) at which, in my opinion, rapid firing ought ever to be employed. No more shells are thrown against the enemy by the use of salvoes than would be the case if a rapid fire were used, since well-laid battery salvoes cannot be fired quicker than with an interval of from 36 to 48 seconds; thus the regular quick fire from a flank sends just as many shells into the enemy's ranks, with this advantage, that they are more likely to hit, and that when shrapnel are used, and it has been found necessary to change the elevation or the range, shrapnel shells which have been loaded beforehand, and of which the fuses, previously set, will not admit of correction, need not be fired except in a few cases.[1]

Of all these causes of failure which I have quoted against the use of salvoes by artillery, it is very likely that many have also exercised an influence on the fire of common shell at the time when the captains of batteries under my command carried out comparative practice at a moving target with salvoes, and fire from a flank, and, as I have already mentioned, did not hit with the salvoes.

For this reason, when I hear or read of the great expectations which have in many cases been aroused as regards the effect of battery salvoes of shrapnel shell in the artillery fight, I cannot free myself from the very greatest apprehension lest we are in this giving ourselves up to a most serious illusion; serious, not only because the awakening will exercise a

---

[1] This is a little obscure. The author presumably means that, as all the guns will not have been loaded, it will be obligatory, supposing that the fuses are set for the wrong range, to waste only those shells which may have been already inserted in the guns.—*N.L.W.*

depressing moral effect, but also because these
salvoes, which will produce no injury to the enemy,
will leave the batteries for the moment defenceless,
and they will have to begin at last to find their
range, while the enemy will thus get a decided start
of them.   Our foes in the war of 1870-71 had
formed similar illusory notions concerning the effect
of the mitrailleuses.   They produced here and there
a most terrible effect.   In one of the fights at Le
Bourget the two Horse Artillery batteries of the
Guard lost 22 horses by one discharge from a
mitrailleuse.   But in most cases their fire was despised
by our men.   This may also be the case with salvoes
of shrapnel.   Here and there, especially if fired
quietly and with forethought, they may produce a
considerable effect.   But in most cases they will
cause only a waste of ammunition.

I also, as I have already told you, have used
battery salvoes in war, not for their effect, but simply,
at Sedan, as range-finders.   We did not then hurriedly
fire and load again, but worked very quietly, while
each gun of the battery had to be looked over by
the captain himself, so that no mistake should be
made.   Later on a salvo of the whole of the guns of
the corps artillery and the 1st Field Brigade was fired,
but only as a prearranged signal to General von
Pape that he might advance with his infantry against
the Bois de la Garenne, since we did not intend to
fire any more on it.

The regulations also mention the battery salvo as
being of use in order to furnish a fixed point for the
observation of fire, when the observation of single
shots is too difficult.   It does not mention salvoes as

a system for use in action ; on the contrary, it gives a warning against undue hurry in firing.

I am very much pleased with a proposition which is made in the *Conduct of Artillery in Manœuvres and in Action*, of which I have already spoken. This is as follows : A brigade should allow its batteries to fire salvoes with their tangent-scales set at different elevations, for example, the first battery at 2000 yards, the second at 2200, and so on, in order that soon after the commencement of the fire a fixed point may be obtained from which to learn the range. But I would not allow the brigade to hurry forward with loaded guns and with the tangent-scales ready set, nor would I permit them to open fire hastily, since such measures tend to make the detachments restless and to hurry the fire too much. And I should employ this mode of proceeding only in cases where the artillery, without being observed by the enemy, has taken up a position behind cover which hides it from view, where the laying of each individual gun can be quietly supervised, and where thus the accurate direction of the salvo can be guaranteed. The decisive ranges for the artillery duel (2000 to 2500 yards) are still so great that in almost any country screens may be found for some guns ; these it may be possible to reach unperceived, so that the commencement of our fire will give the first warning which the enemy will receive of our presence, especially if his attention has already been attracted by other artillery firing at longer ranges.

4. The occupation of a position in echelon.

The occupation of a position by a large artillery line in echelon of batteries, concerning which you

2 A

ask my opinion, is now very much in favour in cases
where the wind blows from a flank and drifts the
smoke of one battery close in front of another, so
that the observation of its fire by the latter is rendered
very difficult.   Such a direction of the wind is
certainly very annoying.   I found it most disagreeable at Sedan.   But we could not there place ourselves in echelon, since the shape of the hill fixed
our position for us.   This will often be the case.

At the beginning of the battle of Saint-Privat,
Scherbening, as I think I have already stated, advanced with his batteries in echelon with an interval
of 200 paces, as he had done before with success in
1866 at Blumenau.   This was not on account of the
direction of the wind, but in order to mislead the
enemy as to the proper elevation.   When we stood
firm in our position, and had settled our observations
and corrections, and since we for the present could
advance no farther, the other batteries came nearly
into line with the leading one, in order to give a free
field of fire to all the batteries, and also because it
has not a good moral effect when part of the batteries
remain farther from the enemy than the rest.   I am
therefore of opinion that, even in the very rare cases
where the nature of the ground will permit artillery
to take up a position in echelon, this measure should
only be adopted as a temporary expedient and should
then be used with great care.

5. On diagonal fire.

I entirely agree that we ought to endeavour to
bring enfilade or oblique fire to bear upon the
enemy's artillery line.   Nothing produces more effect
than enfilade or oblique fire, since every shot tells,

even when it is laid too high. Splinters and shrapnel bullets whistle through the whole length of the line among the guns, limbers, horses, and men. The moral effect of this is tremendous. On the heights of Chlum in the battle of Königgrätz I had in front of me a number of guns far superior to my own, but they did not produce nearly so much effect upon us as did one or two batteries which stood between Sweti and Rosberitz and fired on us obliquely from the left. For this reason our every effort must be directed to outflank the enemy's position, even if this can be done on one flank only. On that flank we shall quickly get the upper hand, and can thence (so to speak) roll up the enemy with fire, since we shall be gradually able to use more and more guns in oblique fire against the other parts of the enemy's line.

But when it is proposed that, in order to be able to make use of oblique fire in a duel between two artilleries standing directly opposite to each other, the artillery on one flank shall fire, not on the enemy which is immediately in its front, but on his other wing, I give it as my opinion that this would be a measure which would ask too much of human nature. Besides, the necessary observation and correction of fire, being on the diagonal of the field of battle, would be so difficult of execution that the effect would thus lose more than it would gain by the oblique direction of the fire. Moreover, in the case of an extensive field of battle such a co-operation in the management of the fire would lead to considerable friction, and if by any misunderstanding a part of the artillery did not follow the rules prescribed, another part would be crushed by the enemy. With regard to this I feel that such a management of the fire is too fanciful, and is too far removed from that simplicity which one must strive for in war. The officer commanding the brigade should assign its target to each battery, and this will as a rule stand straight in front of the latter ; as for the rest, I consider that the brief and excellent orders concerning the management of the fire which are to be found in the regulations are quite sufficient.

6. On cover for limbers and guns.

Former orders have laid down that the limbers should make use of cover near the batteries. The most recent regulations say nothing about this point. I have never in all my campaigns allowed the limbers to quit their regulation position in rear of the guns. My reason was, that even the nearest available position was too far from the guns. Cover for the limbers which is 10 paces from the left flank of the battery is certainly very close indeed. But if the captain places his limbers in rear of it, the limber of No. 1 gun is 110 paces from its gun. The number who has to bring up shell after shell to the gun has thus 220 paces to run between each round. Even when the limber stands in its regulation position this number is very hard-worked. Supposing that a battery fires 100 rounds per gun, as has often happened in a battle (at Solferino many batteries of the French army fired over 300 rounds per gun), then, if the limbers are posted 10 paces from the left flank of the battery, the number who brings up shell to No. 1 gun has 22,000 more paces to run than have the other numbers. It will also be very trying to his nerves to be compelled to run the whole length of the front of the battery as it stands under fire.

The case is somewhat different when another source of ammunition takes the place of the limbers. For this reason I consider the proposition made in the pamphlet which I have often before referred to (concerning the *Conduct of Artillery*) to be very good for such defensive positions as one is determined to hold, but not for such as one intends to occupy for a time only, as, for example, rear-guard positions.

The proposition is as follows : To post the limbers on the flank of the battery, and in their stead to place an ammunition-wagon without horses in rear of No. 2 and No. 5 guns, or in rear of each division. As in this case the intervals between the guns of each half-battery or of each division can be also diminished, in order to lessen the distance through which the shell must be brought up, it will thus be possible to obtain cover for the teams without prejudicing the service of the guns.

I propose to consider again our familiar situation on the battlefield of Königgrätz, which we have so frequently selected as a practical example ; if the defender has determined to fight his decisive action at Lipa, he would do well to dispose his batteries in accordance with the foregoing plan. The assailant also will have an opportunity of making use of it if he takes up a position which he apparently will be able to occupy for a long time, and which will not be affected by accidental changes in the situation of of the action. This would be the case with his artillery on the Roskos-berg, as soon as he is securely posted there, owing to his infantry having seized the Bistritz, and also while it is re-establishing the passages. But that artillery of the assailants which crosses the river at the Skalka wood, in order to take up a precarious position on the other side, with the object of suddenly bringing about a revolution in the artillery duel by its energetic fire, would not dare to risk placing its limbers at a greater distance from the guns than that which is prescribed by the regulations.

It is a well-known fact also that it is desirable to make some artificial cover for the guns. But I cannot neglect this opportunity of telling you of a very unpleasant experience which I once went through in action. We were in the habit at manœuvres, etc., whenever time permitted, of excavating cover for the guns. The first time that I made use of this plan in war, the wheels on the recoil sank so deep into the freshly-disturbed ground that after the third round the trail stood high in the air, while the wheels and the muzzle stuck deep in the earth, so that we had nothing left to do but to abandon the gun-pit, and to post ourselves in front of it on the natural level. In peace-manœuvres these experiences are never met with, since the ammunition then used does not give so strong a recoil. If these gun-pits are made on wet ground (and this is generally the case), platforms of planks must be laid down for the guns ; otherwise such positions cannot be used for long.

For these reasons it is always better to place the guns on the natural surface of the ground, and to use existing cover, such as undulations of the ground, brushwood, hedges, etc.

7. On Horse Artillery.

With reference to your question concerning the necessity for Horse Artillery, I must first tell you that before the war of 1870-71 an opinion was frequently expressed among senior officers of artillery, that Foot Artillery (as unmounted Field Artillery was then called) could discharge all the duties of Horse Artillery, since, owing to the axle-tree seats, it was now possible to carry all the detachments of a battery on the carriages, while the Horse Artillery, with its mounted detachments, offered too many targets to the accurate shooting of rifled guns. It was considered better to give up Horse Artillery altogether, and to supply its place with Field Artillery carrying its detachments on the carriages. This opinion was shared by persons who had considerable influence in high places. The experiences of the war of 1870-71 entirely silenced these suggestions. I have told you already (in Letter VI.) how Von Dresky relates that he on the 6th of August, after a march with the corps artillery of 16 miles in a hilly country, was called to arms and moved off at 3 P.M. His Horse Artillery took only three hours to reach the battlefield, which was at a distance of 20 miles, while his Field Brigade took an hour and a half longer, and thus arrived too late.

On the 16th of August he received an order to advance as quickly as possible to the field of battle. The Horse Artillery arrived three-quarters of an hour earlier than the others, after a march over nearly 8 miles of hilly road. His Horse Artillery Brigade *only* reached the battlefield of Beaune-la-Rolande in time to take part in the action, and that by a march of 32 miles.

As far as regards the battle of Sedan, I can tell you that the Field Brigade of the corps artillery of the Guard was called to arms an hour earlier than the Horse Artillery, which had been for the night attached to the cavalry division. The Horse Artillery obeyed the order to come up and join the corps artillery for the day of battle so quickly that they arrived (after a march of 11 miles) exactly as the Field Brigade took up its position.

The enormous marches made by some Horse Artillery batteries, and even by some entire Horse Artillery Brigades which were attached to cavalry brigades and divisions, and of which I have already given you some examples, would have been impossible for unmounted Field Artillery. As I told you when I wrote about cavalry, I am of opinion that in future still greater exertions will be demanded from the cavalry, and in this I believe that every cavalry officer will agree with me. When, therefore, cavalry have been trained to make such exertions, the unmounted Field Artillery will be less able than ever to follow them. There can then be no doubt but that the artillery which is attached to cavalry must be Horse Artillery.

But the corps artillery also needs Horse Artillery in cases where it has to move quickly into position. The ideal corps artillery would consist entirely of Horse Artillery. If it be said that the supply of horses in the country would not, after furnishing the number required by the cavalry, suffice to mount the whole of the corps artillery, it would at least be desirable to mount it as far as this supply will permit.

8. On the abolition of corps artillery.

I have heard the cry for the abolition of the

corps artillery, and for its equal division between the two divisions of the army-corps. It was caused by some articles in military papers and pamphlets. I have up to the present paid no attention to this desire. But since you ask me about it, I will give you my opinion.

The wish for this change originated entirely and specifically among the artillery. It is very disagreeable for the officer commanding a regiment of divisional artillery to see his regiment at the moment of mobilisation divided into two parts, and to have nothing whatever to say to it ; while the unity of the regiment, which is so important, is broken up just at the most critical time. But this is the only good reason for the abolition of the corps artillery. Now this is really not at all an artillery question. I see that you are astonished at this apparently paradoxical assertion. But nevertheless I am right. If the corps artillery be abolished, an army-corps, now that the independent cavalry divisions are placed directly under the command of the officer commanding the army, will consist of two equal parts—the divisions. Thus the unity of the corps ceases to be a necessity. The Staff of the army would dispose of it entirely by divisions, and the unity of the corps and its Staff would be abolished. I may add that, as a matter of course, the brigade command of Field Artillery would also be done away with. We should then have army divisions, or small corps of about the strength of our present divisions, which comes to the same thing. But whether such a change shall be made is a question for the officers entrusted with the direction of the army, for those who are to lead it in battle, and not for the artillery. The most skilled and practised leader in battle of all time, since there has been any question of artillery, Napoleon I., held that the division of an army into corps was necessary.   In 1806 we introduced army-divisions, and this organisation was found to be unpractical.   In the year 1866, in the 1st army, four divisions were placed directly under the officer commanding the army.   This experiment, after greater experience of war, has not been repeated. I therefore think that we shall retain the unity of the corps.

I should be very sorry on tactical grounds if the corps artillery were abolished.   It produces, in combination with the divisional artillery, a tremendous effect wherever the General in command may please to use it ; and thus prepares the way for the main decisive action.   The very existence of a corps artillery points out that the effect of artillery should not be dispersed, but should be concentrated on the decisive point.   I think I have already told you how among the Staff of the Guard corps in 1870 the employment of the corps artillery was so distinctly taken to be a sign of energetic action, that when we played whist (as often happened in the long evenings during the siege of Paris) we used to say, when any one played a trump, " He is sending his corps artillery into action."   The young officers at head-quarters declared jokingly that the General in command, whenever he received a report which obliged him to mount his horse, used to call for " My boots and the corps artillery ! "

Jests like these mark the character of the situation.

I feel as deeply as do the officers commanding regiments the disadvantage of breaking up the regiments of divisional artillery into two parts. But I think that I could thoroughly remedy it in a better way.

We have less Field Artillery than the neighbouring States. I consider then that we, unless we are prepared to experience disaster, must increase our Field Artillery. An augmentation of two field batteries per army-corps would place us in a position to form two regiments of divisional artillery (one for each division) of 2 brigades of 3 batteries, and a regiment of corps artillery of 3 brigades of 3 batteries. Such an organisation would answer the purpose, and would no longer necessitate the breaking up of the regiment on mobilisation.

Some voices have been raised loudly against any increase of the artillery, saying that it would be a serious thing to further augment the train of the army. Now I absolutely refuse to argue with any one who, after the deeds which were done and the results which were obtained by the artillery in the years 1870 and 1871, can continue to consider it as "train," and not as a combatant arm.

LETTER XVI

ON THE DRILL REGULATIONS

I DO not agree with your last remark that I contra-
dict myself when, though I constantly advise the
observation of the drill regulations, yet I also
sometimes suggest opinions which are not in accordance with the prescriptions of those regulations. It
is easy to obey the prescriptions of the regulations
with the greatest exactness, even though one is
quite persuaded that they ought to be altered. I
felt thus when I commanded a regiment, and I was
then quite determined that the very letter of the
regulations should be followed, though our then
regulations were very much out of date, and I was
endeavouring by all legitimate means to get them
altered ; at last a committee, over which I was set
as president, was appointed to draw up new regulations. After the experiences of the war of 1870-
1871, I should have proposed that they should be
still more simplified, in order to give the troops time
to practise these simple things with still greater
precision. The last regulations, of the 23d August
1877, have made full use, as no one can deny, of
the war-experiences of 1870-71, and they are,
taken as a whole, most excellent. But they still

include a by no means small number of artificial movements and formations which, so long as they remain in the regulations, must be practised and thus cost time, but which cannot be used in war, and are pernicious, inasmuch as they make men think that they are applicable to war ; so that those who are inexperienced in war will, on first going into action, try to use them, and thus some loss will be caused.

Drill regulations must certainly contain much which is of no use in war ; for example, the whole of the 1st Part, dealing with instruction on foot, and also many movements in the 3d Part, dealing with mounted drill. On this matter I might, for the artillery, also join in the wish of Colonel von Rosenberg, which he has expressed in his *Zusammengewürfelten Gedanken*, that the regulations for the cavalry might point out the movements which are to be used in peace, and those which are possible in war. But the new regulations of 1877 include also some movements which, in my opinion, are unnecessary for artillery in time of peace, and which needlessly occupy time during the drill season. Everything which is in the regulations must be continually practised. On the other hand, some formations are omitted from the regulations which are so practical and useful in war that I am inclined to call them indispensable.

Before I enter into details, may I once more bring to your notice the statement of Colonel von Dresky ? He writes, with reference to his first appearance on the scene at the battle of Vionville, as follows : " I might here relate to you an experience which I met with on this occasion.

"The drill regulations for Field Artillery of 1877 (4th Part, paragraph 193, the Advance and the Occupation of a Position for Action) lay down the column of divisions at close interval[1] as the formation for flank movements. The formation of my brigade of Horse Artillery, in which it made the previously described movement to the flank, was column of route. This formation was not selected beforehand as one particularly suitable to the given conditions, but it was chosen because under most circumstances of war it is the simplest and the most natural. If the brigade had been formed in the prescribed column of divisions, it would have been obliged to halt at the bridge, which was only wide enough for one gun, in order to form column of route, and would probably have suffered heavy loss from the hot fire of the enemy.

"The experience which I obtained on this occasion caused me, in later actions, always to make flank movements under the enemy's fire in column of route, and this formation preserved me from all loss. When you have to present your flank to the enemy, the length of the column is of no importance, since the enemy will always shoot straight enough, but his shot will be short or over ; it is the width of the column which matters, and two guns side by side (whether at full or at close intervals) afford a deeper target than one gun. At Beaune-la-Rolande, on the 28th of November 1870, I had to make with my Horse Artillery Brigade a flank march of about 1500 paces in front of two batteries of the enemy, and I suffered no loss while doing it. The enemy's shell

---

[1] Close interval is 5 paces. Full interval is 20 paces. Both measured from muzzle to muzzle.—*N.L.W.*

(for the most part) struck close to us, either short or over, but none directly hit us, while the very soft ground saved us from the splinters.

"At Chilleurs-aux-Bois, on the 3d of December 1870, I had also, in order to reach my intended position, to make a flank march of over a mile. The whole of the corps artillery was collected here, and on account of the condition of the ground (which was slightly frozen, but was still so soft that the horses' feet broke through the crust) could move only at a walk. Three French batteries fired on me, but I suffered no loss ; the column of route and the wet ground saved me.

"On· the 11th of December, at Le Mans, the Horse Artillery Brigade received orders to fire on some French troops which showed themselves on the heights of Champagné. General von Bülow and I rode on in front of the brigade in order to look for a position for it. But all search for even a moderately practicable position was useless, owing to the quantity of very thick brushwood with which the ground was covered. We had to give up any idea of using artillery. The brigade, which had followed us, had to get into a small field surrounded by bushes in order to reverse, for the road was too narrow, being also shut in by a hedge. As we retired we came suddenly under a flank fire. It was impossible to find out the position of the enemy's artillery. The shells fell close round about us, but not one hit. The column of route was not deep enough for that."

Recalling my own experiences, I may add that in the three campaigns of 1866, 1870, and 1871, the whole of my collected batteries never used any formation but the column of route and the advance in line. I must except, as I have already told you, the commencement of the battle of Königgrätz and that movement at Sedan by which the 2d brigade of Field Artillery took up its last position of the day. It limbered up to advance, wheeled to the left by divisions at close interval, passed in this formation through the narrow wood-road, and then moved by the rear of the 1st brigade, which was already in action, and came up on its left. I certainly myself ordered the formation in column of divisions, but I think that the column of route would have been better. The brigade suffered no loss at all, but this would have been equally the case if it had adopted the other formation.

From this it follows (forgive me the repetition of my former letters) that the column of route and the advance in line are the only formations which regulations for the movement of batteries in war ought to lay down as available for use. We adopted during the war two kinds of formations in the case of the column of route: the "formation for rapid march," and the "formation in lines."[1] The former was always used as the ordinary march formation, since when on the march it was impossible to say at what moment the "formation for rapid march" might not become necessary, in which case the detachments found themselves already close to those carriages on which they were to be carried. In a

---

[1] The "formation for rapid march" is simply our column of route with the detachments mounted. In the "formation in lines" (*mit formirten Staffeln*) the guns moved first, followed by the 1st line of 3 ammunition-wagons and a store-wagon, while the 2d line consisted of the remainder of the wagons.

similar manner the wagon belonging to each gun formed a permanent sub-division with it, and the battery thus consisted of eight sub-divisions, of which the seventh and eighth, under the command of the quartermaster - sergeant, included the two supply-wagons, the field-forge, the baggage-wagon, and the spare horses. We only formed lines shortly before the battery came into the sphere of action.

If the battery advanced in line into action the wagons of the 1st line, as I have already said, followed it immediately, and only those of the 2d remained in rear; these were collected from the whole brigade, and placed under an officer. When the battery was halted or on the move in line outside the field of battle, each wagon followed its gun, and the wagons which were under the quartermaster-sergeant followed as a 3d line in rear of the five wagons on the right of the battery; the spare horses followed No. 5 wagon. This was also the formation in which the batteries paraded, and a very good formation it was, since the captain could inspect the whole of his command, of which the front was 100 paces and the depth 3 carriages, or not quite 100 paces. Line with full intervals was preferred to line with close intervals, since with the former it was more easy to move about between the guns. However, it sometimes happened that there was not sufficient space for this, and then we used close intervals. This formation can also be used in war by a battery which has formed line. All the other drill formations of a battery, and all movements, which are not required as a means of passing from one of these formations to another, must in my opinion be considered as belonging to those drill formations and movements which can only be used in time of peace.

I would especially recommend that long distances be covered at a trot in column of route and in line (Horse Artillery should practise long gallops in line), and that such movements should form the principal part of the drill. It is of the greatest importance that during these lengthened and rapid movements steadiness of pace and perfect quiet should be preserved, so that the horses may not be annoyed by constant checks, nor be tired out by being suddenly started. This is very difficult to manage, since, especially at curves and corners of the road, intervals are apparently soon lost, and then the guns bound on, and any rebuke of the officer is unheard on account of the deafening noise of the carriages. In war, as I have already said, many miles must often be passed over at a trot in column of route. Wherefore we must in time of peace practise trotting at least four and a half miles without exhausting the horses. We also ought to practise forced marches of at least thirty miles in the day, so that all may learn how this is to be done without injuring the horses. We shall then be able in war to get over sixty miles, when we are ordered to do so at whatever cost. That artillery should be able to do this as an ordinary thing is more important than the execution of the most elegant drill-movements.

While I am of opinion that artillery, wherever it is in any way possible, should fight in brigade in order that they may always be employed in sufficient masses, yet I consider that drill-movements in brigade are seldom possible in war, nor will they ever be necessary. I have already taken an opportunity to tell you that, in consequence of the inclination of the 2d Field Brigade at Königgrätz to make brigade movements at the moment of their arrival on the field, the whole of their ammunition-wagons were separated from them, so that we, at the most decisive period of the battle, suffered seriously from want of ammunition. In most cases a drill-like movement of the brigade is of itself impossible. Four batteries can perfectly well fight in conjunction, without being capable of being moved into position as a drill. Very often they will be separated from each other by ravines, farms, etc. If they are posted in echelon (on account of the direction of the wind) a drill-like advance is at once out of the question. Moreover, you must remember that a battery on war-footing contains as many carriages and horses as a brigade on the peace establishment, and thus you may imagine the difficulty which is found in directing a mass of four batteries at war strength with the voice. If you are moving fast, even at a trot, there can be no possibility of commanding a battery with the voice on account of the rattle of the carriages, and even trumpet calls are of no use, but are as often misunderstood as comprehended. Thus a drill-movement of a brigade at war strength is seldom possible, and when it is possible it is generally wrong. I thoroughly agree with the opinion of the author of the pamphlet which I have already mentioned on *The Conduct of Artillery*, when he says that the brigade should not be taken into action in any other way than the following, namely, the officer commanding the brigade should give personal instructions to each individual captain of a battery, or should send them such instructions by his adjutants.   As a rule, he will direct the advance of the first battery into the position, and will order the other batteries to unlimber on the right or left of this.

You will, perhaps, quote against me the movement which I have before mentioned, of the 2d Field Brigade of the Guard at Sedan, since it moved up in column of divisions in rear of the 1st brigade and took up its position on its left flank.   But this movement was not carried out, like a drill-movement, by the personal word of command of the officer commanding the brigade, but solely according to orders sent by him and under the personal guidance of Major von Krieger. The brigade was beforehand in a position in which only three batteries could find room, and which was further divided into two parts by a ravine.   By order of the officer commanding the brigade, in accordance with my direction, the three batteries limbered up to advance, and wheeled to the left by divisions at close intervals.   The battery on the right, which was separated from the others by the ravine, had to retire to cross this ravine in order to join them.   The battery which for the moment had been kept out of action received an order to join also.   The officer commanding the brigade then ordered the head of the column to trot and directed it through the wood-road.   As he was passing the dangerous space over which he had to make a flank march 500 paces in rear of the 1st brigade, receiving the missiles which had passed over it, he behaved exactly as if he had

been only at drill, rode out to the front where the
enemy's bullets were whistling, and gave directions
to the head of the column as if he had been on parade,
such as: "A steady pace!" "Keep your distance,
2d Division!" "Centre driver of No. 5 gun, don't
gallop!" "No. 1 of No. 6 gun, keep your dressing!"
"Eyes right!" etc. Then he cried to the captain of
the battery, "Captain, it is time to wheel into line;
align yourself with the 1st brigade!" then he galloped
off to the next battery, led it in the same manner
over the dangerous zone, and so on. Thus it was no
regulation drill-movement with which this brigade was
moved as a whole; the batteries went to their proper
position according to his orders, and were not man-
œuvred by the regulation word of command of the
officer commanding the brigade.

You may think, perhaps, that I shall now say that
what the artillery cannot use in war is not necessary
for it in peace. In that case I should have to abolish
the whole of brigade-drill in time of peace. But in
this case deductive logic would bring us to a false
conclusion. Since a brigade at its peace establishment has as many carriages and horses as has a
mobilised battery in time of war, it taken as a whole
gives the best possible example of the difficulty of
directing such a mass; yet it is easier to command
than a battery at war strength, since the officer commanding the brigade has the captains of batteries and
many more officers to help him than has the captain
of a mobilised battery. Again, as I have already
remarked, the superior officers, who are over the
officer commanding the brigade, such as the Inspector,
the Inspector-General, and the General in command,

have not time to inspect each individual battery. They must form their judgment from the brigade-movements, and there must thus be regulations to lay down these movements.

But I am of opinion that with regard to this the very simplest formations only are needed, and that in the new regulations very complicated evolutions have been introduced which have not been shown to be necessary either in war or in peace. The simpler the regulations are, the more accurately can the evolutions which they contain be carried out.

Allow me to specify some of the movements to which I have alluded; I will do so as shortly as I can, in order not to weary you with details.

In the 1st Part of the regulations, which concern instruction on foot, I do not wish to abolish or to change anything, since it has borrowed from the infantry field-exercise only so much as is necessary for artillery.

I have noticed with great pleasure the short, concise, and correct construction of the 2d Part, concerning standing gun-drill. Only I should like to strike out paragraph 84 (which belongs properly to the 3d Part, mounted instruction), since it is there laid down what a Horse Artillery gunner has to do when the gun moves off at a trot, before the detachments are mounted. I have already told you once what mischief must result if this manœuvre, which is so beautiful to look at in peace, were ever to be attempted in war.

Again the drill-regulations which were drawn up after the war of 1866 lay down absolutely that "*All movements to the rear are, as a matter of principle, to commence at a walk.*" This rule, which is on page 170, paragraph 195, is in direct contradiction with para graph 84 before mentioned.

As you will have anticipated from what I have already said, I have most to say about the 3d Part, on mounted instruction.

In the 2d chapter of this part I find the "half-column "[1] introduced ; I cannot see any necessity for this. It is taken from the cavalry drill-regulations. For cavalry it was found useful, in order to move them over considerable distances to the right or left front, since the troopers crush and press each other, and thus get out of order when they ride long dis tances at half-right or half-left. But this is not the case with artillery. For its movement half-right or half-left is effected by a half-wheel of each gun, which afterwards moves straight to its front ; we have thus, to a certain extent, a half-column of guns, and thus the half-column of divisions appears to be superfluous. We cannot do without the movement half-right or half-left, and this differs so little from the half-column, which is formed by the half-wheel of divisions, that I cannot help thinking that by retaining both forma tions the regulations are unnecessarily complicated.

If the half-column were abolished many other complicated movements of the 2d chapter of the 3d Part would also be done away with. I cannot omit to remark that many officers of importance (for example, Von Rosenberg) have said that the half-column is undesirable for cavalry, as it is very

---

[1] " Half-column " is an echelon of divisions, moving to the former right or left front, and is formed by the wheel half-right (or half-left) of divisions. The distance between divisions is 10 paces ; the interval 8 paces.—*N.L.W.*

difficult to carry out, and thus absorbs much time at drill.

In the 3d chapter of the 3d Part I find the battery-columns[1] and the brigade-column introduced. Both formations are taken from the cavalry drill-regulations. But I see no use for either for artillery. Battery-columns, they say, adapt themselves better to the ground than does a deployed line. But nothing adapts itself better to the ground than a deployed line of artillery, for it is not, like a line of cavalry, an unbroken wall, but is calculated, since there are intervals of 20 paces between the guns, to pass with ease small obstacles which may be in its way. And an artillery line can also easily pass through other troops. I remember to have seen in a battle a cavalry brigade, which sought to avoid the fire of the enemy, pass in extended order through the intervals between the guns of my batteries as the latter were trotting forward. But if a line of artillery meets with an extended obstacle which can be passed in only a few places (such as a river, a broad ditch, etc.) it must then form column of route, either by batteries or by brigade (as Von Dresky did at Vionville), and for that also the battery-column will be of no use. Again, when under fire the "battery-columns" offer so deep a target that it cannot be missed, while when out of the enemy's fire we march in column of route or in line. Therefore there is no necessity for the use of "battery-columns."

The brigade-column, in which the batteries stand

[1] "Battery-columns" is a line of batteries in columns of divisions with intervals of 60 paces (100 paces at war strength, with 6 guns); a brigade-column is a similar formation with the intervals reduced to 20 paces.—*N. L. W.*

at close interval in column of divisions, serves, so
they say, especially well for a formation for assembly,[1]
since it furnishes, in the most simple manner, every
facility for movement in all directions. Whoever
agrees with me that a brigade can be commanded in
war only by means of instructions or orders to individual batteries, and under no circumstances by an
actual word of command from the officer commanding it, will also acknowledge that the case can scarcely
arise in which a mass of artillery formed in assembly
formation will suddenly find it necessary to extend
in any direction. Masses of artillery can stand in
assembly formation only when they are at a considerable distance from the field of battle, and must
always have a long distance to traverse before arriving at the place where their services will be required ;
and therefore it does not matter whether the advance begins by a wheel of the head of the column,
or whether the flank battery wheels in column of
divisions. Even in peace manœuvres a mass of
artillery cannot be kept in assembly formation at such
a short distance from the enemy that any sudden
movement to the flank can be necessary.

Again, quarter-column of batteries is a much
more practical and natural assembly formation for
large masses of artillery than is the new brigade-
column. It is more practical, especially for a battery
at war strength, since in it each captain can easily
look after his battery. The battery forms, as I have
already said, when it is in line at full intervals, and
the wagons are in two lines in rear of the guns,

[1] " *Rendezvous-Stellung*," the formation in which a brigade falls in on
being called to arms.—*N.L.W.*

a mass nearly as deep as it is wide, and thus the
captain can at one glance see the whole of it. But
when in brigade-column, the battery, being in column
of divisions, has a front of 20 paces and a depth of
nine carriages, that is to say, of 180 paces, and is
thus much more difficult to superintend. We often
have to stand during many hours in assembly formation ; for example, the Guard corps had to do so on
the morning of Saint-Privat and during the battle of
Beaumont. The men thus get weary and must be
looked after. Again, this is the time at which
everything is inspected, and all mistakes in harness-
ing, packing, etc., are corrected, especially when it
has been necessary to march before daybreak, and
when the march of the previous day has lasted until
dark. It is thus important that the captain of the
battery shall have everything close to his hand, and
shall not have to wander here and there as he makes
the required inspection. It is true that paragraph
196 allows the use of the quarter-column as an
assembly formation, but no mention is made of it in
the whole of the 3d Part of the regulations. This
appears to be rather a serious omission.

The quarter-column is also of great practical use
for the movement of large masses beyond the zone
of action. At the beginning of the battle of Saint-
Privat, Scherbening trotted with the whole of the
corps artillery from Doncourt to beyond Anoux-la-
Grange, passing along the crest of the heights on the
left of the 1st Division of the Guard, a distance of
over two miles. Each battery was in line, and the
wagons in two lines in rear of the guns. He did
not allow the formation in lines of wagons until he

had arrived within reach of the enemy's shells ; he then led forward the foremost battery himself, after having given orders to the others to come up on the left of it in echelon, each battery coming into action 200 paces nearer to the enemy than that which preceded it.

I should propose also to strike out of the regulations the deployment of a large column of artillery to a flank, since it, as we have already said, can never happen that a great mass of artillery will have suddenly to extend to a flank from its assembly formation in order to come into action. I should except the coming into action to a flank from the column of route, which is often of use in taking up a position which can be approached under cover.

Let us then erase the " half-column," the " battery-columns," and the " brigade-column " from our regulations, and content ourselves with the column of route, the column of divisions, and the quarter-column ; we shall thus make the regulations very much more simple, and so gain more time to practise correctly all the movements contained in them. To be sure, many most elegant manœuvres would thus disappear from sight. But these would only be such movements as none but cavalry can use with advantage. Much as I wish that artillery should be assimilated to the other arms, I yet consider it very undesirable that it should waste its time in practising evolutions which have nothing to do with its special duty as artillery.

I regret that the 3d Part of the regulations, from paragraph 106, is drawn up only for a battery on the peace establishment, while the instructions con-

cerning a battery on a war-footing, with its ammunition-wagons and other carriages, are relegated to the
4th Appendix ; even here the formation for a rapid
march is not mentioned, nor are any instructions
given here as to how and where the carriages are to
march or to stand under various circumstances ; for example, when the battery is in assembly formation, etc.

The 4th Part of the regulations, regarding the
fighting of Field Artillery, is, with the exception of
a few matters on which I have before remarked,
unsurpassable both as regards its form and its contents.   Each individual officer of artillery ought to
be required to know it by heart, since it gives as
briefly as possible the most important artillery truths,
as they have been deduced from the experiences of
the last war.

A novelty in the regulations which gives me much
pleasure consists in the appendices.   The instructions
which they contain were formerly published in a
separate form, and the task of the instructor is much
simplified, since all the regulations are now in one
book.

The instructions in the 1st Appendix, which relate
to the sword-exercise, are taken from those of the
cavalry, and call for no remark.

The 2d Appendix, which relates to gun-carriages
and others, has divided those of the arm who are
skilled in these matters into two camps, those who
consider that a gun should take ground on a radius of
8 paces, and those who hold that it should do so on
a radius of 2 paces.[1]   As long as I have been in the

---

[1] "*Bogenwendung*" or "Bow-turn" on a radius of 8 paces ; "*Haken-
wendung*" or "Hook-turn" on a radius of 2.—*N.L.W.*

service these systems have been changed every ten years, according as the direction of such matters was in the hands of a partisan of one or the other. The new regulations order, as a principle, in the case of changes of front that a radius of 8 paces is to be used (the "*Bogenwendung*"), which can be more easily carried out with horses which are not perfectly trained; but in special cases it permits the use of the "*Haken-wendung*," or even of wheeling a gun on its own ground ("*Scharfe Wendung*"). I think that it is of very little importance which of these modes of taking ground is preferred, so long as the system is not too frequently changed, and the principle may thus be ground into all instructors, whether senior officers, lieutenants, or N.C. officers.

The 3d Appendix relates to the charge of detachments of Horse Artillery when the guns retire. You know that I strongly desire that this charge shall be declared obsolete. I have already said so much as to my reasons for this, that I should only repeat myself if I again gave these reasons. The time and the trouble which were formerly expended on this system would be much better employed in teaching the gunners the use of the sword on foot and when mounted, and in practising them in single combat, for this is the only sort of fight, whether it be on the march or in quarters, when there will ever be any necessity for them to draw their swords.

The 4th Appendix contains instructions for the direction of the wagons of a battery, or brigade, and for the renewal of ammunition. These instructions are founded on the experiences of the last war, and I have only a few remarks to make on them.

These refer first to paragraph 318. The formation which, in sub-paragraph 2, is given for ordinary marches is that which in 1870 was called "The formation for rapid march." It was always used until the battery went forward into action; it was then formed in lines. Sub-paragraph (b) directs that lines shall be formed at the commencement of a march during which an engagement may be expected; the second line of wagons will thus from the first be at the tail of the column of march of the other arms, and I consider that this system is faulty, since thus the battery is to its detriment divided too early into two parts. I have already expressed myself so freely about this that I will say no more about it. I should like to see it laid down that a battery is to retain its "formation for rapid march" up to the moment when it receives the order to advance into position; and that then it should form lines.

With regard to paragraph 321, I should propose to order that the ammunition should be replaced as soon as it begins to be expended, and that every effort of the captains of batteries must be given to as far as possible keep their limbers full, and with this object, to draw ammunition direct from the wagons, so that the latter may be empty before the limbers. I would entirely omit the instruction that the renewal of ammunition is to begin "at the latest before half the common shell in the gun-limbers have been shot away." It inclines the captain of a battery, if he has not yet been in action, to think that there is no need for haste to renew his limber-ammunition until this stage is reached. But it is always necessary to be in haste to renew ammunition so long as it is possible to renew it at all; for no one can tell whether the next moment of the battle may not bring about some critical condition which will make a renewal of ammunition impossible, and will also demand a great expenditure of ammunition.

The rules for the practice of the Field Artillery given in the 5th Appendix bring the regulations to a very satisfactory end.

I have left to the last something which I have to say about the 5th Part—the Grand Parade. Not that I have most fault to find with this part. On the contrary, I do not care in the least what instructions are given for the Grand Parade. But it is most important that these instructions, let them be what they may, should be conscientiously obeyed. The Grand Parade is of very great importance for the artillery. But no arm is so much inclined as the artillery to consider this parade as of secondary importance. An arm in which one man finds it his duty in battle to sponge out a gun, another to fire it, and a third to bring up a shell, etc., and in which in action no man ever stands in line with another, is thus too much inclined to consider the parade as a mere accessory and as useless play. But the parade is the best touchstone for the discipline and the obedience of the troops. On ordinary days of drill we have here and there to shut our eyes to some little irregularities. But the parade-day is that on which the troops show that they try, and are able, to do all that is ordered in the most accurate manner; and to put the dot over every *i*. The more the special character of the arm inclines it to care little for the precision and the accuracy of the parade, the

greater importance ought the senior officers to attach
to it, in order that the troops may thus be reminded
that obedience to orders, even to the least important
of orders, is with discipline the first essential of an
army.

In the last century our enemies ridiculed the
Potsdam Guard-parade. But the discipline of the
army, kept up by this " gaiter-button " system, enabled
it under the Great Frederic to win the victory over
an enemy far superior in number. The Potsdam
Guard-parade is the genesis of the Prussian army,
even of the German army, which astonished the
whole world by its last successes. Therefore the
artillery, if it wishes to remain the equal of the other
arms, must attribute the very greatest importance to
the Grand Parade, as being the touchstone and the
expression of discipline.

LETTER XVII

THE ANSWER OF THE CORRESPONDENT, GIVING A
SUMMARY OF THE PRECEDING LETTERS

I HAVE waited three months before answering your last letter of September. This is because I have several times re-studied your sixteen letters on Field Artillery. Your ideas wander from one subject to another, like a hunter seeking for game, who follows it as he finds it. I have therefore taken the trouble to make extracts from, to recapitulate, and to summarise what you have written. Will you kindly tell me if I have rightly expressed your meaning in the arrangement of the following list of contents :—

I. Concerning the CLAIMS WHICH WE MAKE ON THE ARTILLERY AT THE PRESENT DAY.

1. The first may be said in three words. The artillery must in the first place *hit*, in the second place *hit*, and in the third place *hit*. In this is included all that has to do with the most correct service of the guns, the most accurate observation of the fire, and the most exact correction of the elevation and deflection.

2. It must next be in a condition *to come into position at the right moment*, and, with this object, it

2 C

must practise itself in getting over distances of many miles, and even forced marches of a day or so, at a rapid pace.

If it can satisfy these claims, it will give us everything which is needed as to its fitness for employment in battle.

II. With regard to the CONDUCT OF ARTILLERY IN ACTION the following rules are laid down :—

1. General rules.

(*a.*) Artillery can produce its full effect only on condition that it always remembers that *it is an auxiliary arm to the other troops.*

(*b.*) It must use every effort to avoid all ineffective cannonades, and must thus *always go in as close as possible to the enemy.*

(*c.*) Nevertheless it will, on account of the present condition of the improvements in ordnance, be as a rule necessary *to begin the artillery fight outside of the zone of effective shrapnel, and thus at ranges over* 3800 *yards.*

(*d.*) *But the decisive artillery duel will be fought out at a range of from* 2200 *to* 2700 *yards.*

(*e.*) Artillery must also *always fire at the other arms* as soon as they are seen within the zone of its effective fire. But, since the other troops of the enemy will get as much cover as possible from the nature of the ground, and will, even if they be once visible, soon disappear behind cover, *the combat of artillery with artillery will occupy, during the greater part of the duration of a battle, the attention of this arm.*

(*f.*) *Artillery must not hurry when it opens fire*, and must adhere exactly to the regulation system, *so that the captain of a battery may have full command of his fire.* It must avoid refinements, such as salvoes (except as range-finders), finding the range from a position in rear, and diagonal fire, etc.

(*g.*) Artillery must endeavour *to fight as a rule by entire brigades.* The use of single batteries must be exceptional. Nevertheless, entire brigades must not be taken into action by one word of command or by the sound of one trumpet, but should be guided *by orders or instructions given personally by the officer commanding the brigade to the captains of batteries.*

(*h.*) *Artillery must never be without ammunition.* The punctual renewal of ammunition is a condition of its existence. It must therefore use every endeavour *to keep its limbers always full.* The limber ammunition must be considered as the *last reserve of ammunition*, and must thus, whenever possible, be filled up.

If nevertheless ammunition fails, artillery must remain in position (silent, until it can succeed in procuring a fresh supply), so long as it receives no order to retire.

2. On the offensive.

(*a.*) Artillery, after it has silenced the enemy's artillery, must not as a rule approach *nearer than from* 1600 *to* 1700 *yards to infantry of the enemy which is as yet intact*, and is not engaged with other troops.

(*b.*) *If the enemy's infantry is held in check* by another force of artillery, or by infantry, it is not only advisable, *but it is the duty of artillery*, to advance to a range of from 1100 *to* 1200 *yards.*

(*c.*) *At the most decisive moment of the action artillery must not shun the very closest range.*

(*d.*) As soon as the main attack has proved successful, the artillery must hasten up to secure the captured position by its fire. At such a moment *its proper place, in most cases, is in the line of skirmishers.* •

3. On the defensive.

(*a.*) The normal post for artillery in a defensive position (though this may be modified by the character of the ground) is 500 *yards in rear of the foremost infantry position*, provided always that the latter leaves the field of fire of the artillery open.

(*b.*) Artillery must *never abandon* its position, even if the enemy come up to the muzzles of the guns, *unless the officer commanding the troops has given orders for a general retreat.* But this does not imply that artillery, acting on the defensive, are forbidden, if the assailant begins to get the advantage in the artillery duel, to cease firing for a time and to withdraw their guns under cover, with the object of suddenly coming into action again at the most critical moment.

(*c.*) If the order to retreat is given, the only possible moment at which it can be commenced is *either when the enemy has not yet advanced to the attack, or when he is preparing a second attack after having been repulsed in the first.*

4. Horse Artillery in a cavalry action.

(*a.*) As a rule, *the Horse Artillery should go in at once to a decisive range for the artillery duel*, since the considerations which compel artillery when engaged with infantry to fight at longer ranges, lose their force in this case, owing to the speed at which cavalry can move. From this position it will silence the enemy's artillery, and immediately afterwards, or as soon as it can see them, it will turn its fire on the enemy's cavalry.

(*b.*) *During the charge* of its own cavalry, it will fire on that of the enemy, or, if that be not possible, on his artillery. If it has nothing to fire at, *it will remain in position with loaded guns* (common shell and not shrapnel should be used), in order, in case of the failure of the charge, to give support to its retiring cavalry, and to show them where they are to rally.

(*c.*) The Horse Artillery requires a *special escort* on that flank of its position only on which the cavalry fight is not taking place, and even there it requires it merely for the purpose of scouting. A section will therefore be sufficient.

(*d.*) *If the charge succeeds, the Horse Artillery must gallop up to the spot where it took place*, in order to secure its possession with its fire, and to assist in the pursuit.

III. ORGANISATION.

The following appears to be a very desirable organisation for the artillery :—

Each army-corps to have 3 regiments of artillery ;

of these 2 to be of Field Artillery, and to consist each of 2 brigades of 3 batteries ; the 3d to be a regiment of Horse Artillery, and to consist of 3 brigades of 3 batteries.   If with this organisation we find that we are weaker in field guns than the neighbouring States, I should propose to increase the number of batteries in a brigade of Field Artillery to 4.[1]

On mobilisation one regiment of Field Artillery would be attached to each infantry division, and a brigade of Horse Artillery to each cavalry division. The remainder of the regiment of Horse Artillery would form the corps artillery.

IV. THE EMPLOYMENT OF ARTILLERY BY LEADERS OF TROOPS.

(*a.*) It must be laid down as· a first principle that any serious *artillery action* (I except of course skirmishes, slow cannonades, feints, etc.) *must be opened with a number of guns superior from the first to that of the enemy.*   The excess over his strength will always be employed in outflanking the enemy, with the object of enfilading him.   The improvement of artillery fire has increased the weight of the reasons against the retention of an artillery *reserve,* which even in 1870 *appeared undesirable.*

(*b.*) If this principle be observed, the distribution of the artillery will be as follows :—

1. *The advanced guard of an army-corps* which consists of a brigade [2] of infantry will have a brigade of Field Artillery attached to it.   The other brigade

---

[1] This would give 21 or 25 batteries per army-corps, of which 9 would be Horse Artillery.   We have 15 batteries, of which 4 are Horse Artillery.—*N.L. W.*   [2] Of 6 battalions.—*N.L. W.*

of artillery will remain with the second brigade of infantry.

2. *A complete infantry division* will receive a regiment of Field Artillery.

3. *The corps artillery* will, as a rule, come into action *as a whole*.

4. *The advanced guard of an infantry division*, of the strength of a regiment,[1] will be given *one battery*.

5. The artillery belonging to *a cavalry division will, as a rule, remain massed with the main body*. But as an exception, when it has been foreseen that the advanced guard brigade will be required to fight as well as to scout, artillery will be given to it. Under these circumstances it may happen, especially when it is necessary to force defiles which are occupied by the enemy, that the whole brigade of artillery will be sent forward to the advanced guard.

If the cavalry division is present at a battle, it will send its Horse Artillery into the fighting line of artillery, in order to assist the latter in attaining a numerical superiority.

6. *Rear-guards* will be supplied with artillery on the *same principles* as obtained in the case of advanced guards. But if a rear-guard is intended to delay the enemy, it may happen that considerably more artillery may be attached to it, possibly even the whole of the corps artillery.

7. For *detachments* the same principles as for advanced guards will apply, having regard to their strength and numbers.

[1] Of 3 battalions.—*N. L. W.*

8. *The breaking up of a battery* is to be avoided as far as possible. Detached divisions may very exceptionally be employed in street - fighting, in expeditions against an armed civilian population, etc. A single gun is no gun at all.

(*c.*) *The position of artillery on the march* is closely connected with its distribution among the tactical units. Thus the artillery of the advanced guard of a division or of a corps will march in rear of the leading battalion or regiment of the main body of the advanced guard. The artillery of a division will march in rear of the leading regiment, or at the latest in rear of the leading brigade of the division. The corps artillery will march in rear of the leading brigade of the main body, or at the latest in rear of the leading division. The Horse Artillery of a cavalry division will march in rear of the leading regiment of the main body.

In retiring, the same rules will be followed, except of course that the troops will be supposed to have turned about.

V. The wishes which you utter with regard to the DRILL REGULATIONS may be expressed in one word—SIMPLICITY.

With this object all evolutions in the instructions for mounted drill which are not necessary for the object of artillery in war ought to be abolished, in order thus to save time, which may be employed in practising carefully and exactly all the other instructions contained in the drill regulations.

LETTER XVIII

ANSWERS TO VARIOUS QUESTIONS

YOU do not know me well if you imagine that I could possibly lose my temper on account of the objections, arguments, and questions which your letter contains. On the contrary, I am very glad to have seen them; for they prove to me how carefully you have once more read the whole of my letters on Field Artillery, with the object of forming a general idea of my opinions with regard to that arm. These opinions would have but poor bases, if I could not endure the statement of adverse arguments. It would be a terrible acknowledgment of the poverty of my ideas. I reply to your objections and questions with yet greater pleasure, as the former arise merely from a mistaken comprehension of the statements which I have made, and from insufficient care on my part in expressing my meaning. Your questions afford me an opportunity of filling up many gaps. You must be indulgent in your judgment with regard to the existence of such gaps, on the ground that I wrote these letters on no settled plan and in a chatty manner, in order not to weary you too much with a system divided and subdivided in pedantic style.

1. *Your opinion is decidedly against opening fire at a range of* 5500 *yards.*

I grant you that this number is founded upon no particular grounds, being solely due to deduction, and I acknowledge that I have never yet seen Field Artillery practise at 5500 yards. But I have also no reason to doubt the correctness of the range tables, which are given in the regulations of 1877. I find there that 50 per cent of the shots will hit a horizontal target 9.3 yards wide and 60 yards long. Until this fact has been practically disproved, I feel myself compelled to state, as I did at the beginning of my twelfth letter, that the effect of artillery will be noticeable even at a range of 5500 yards.

If the country in front of the enemy's artillery position is entirely open, so that it is impossible to approach any nearer under cover, it is then surely conceivable that we might be compelled to commence the artillery fight at even 5500 yards. I wish to guard expressly against any assumption that my words could mean, that I should *desire* to order my whole force of artillery to come to the front at a range of 5500 yards. I feel that I have protected myself from this charge by the general tendency of my statements, for I have said over and over again that the first artillery position *should be taken up as close to the enemy as circumstances will permit.* But I have also repeatedly stated that under certain circumstances it will be impossible to refrain from beginning the artillery fight at these long ranges. I considered that it was desirable to draw attention to this fact, in order that no one should be surprised when the necessity for doing so should arise on active service. If this necessity does arise, the number of hits must be increased by the use of a large number of guns, in order to be able, after a short interval, to advance to nearer and more decisive positions. In the days of smooth-bore guns the hitting power of artillery was no greater at 1200 paces than it is now at 5500 yards. Yet in the wars between 1813 and 1815, cannonades of huge masses of artillery sometimes took place at a range up to 1800 paces. The conviction is thus forced upon me that in these days similar cannonades will take place at 5500 yards; and I feel myself compelled by the above facts to state this conviction. I acknowledge that I might have expressed myself more cautiously, and have said, " in these days, when the deadly shrapnel has a range of 3800 yards, it will be *sometimes* necessary, on perfectly open and commanded ground, to prepare the artillery fight at a range of from 4400 to 5500 yards," instead of omitting, as I did, the word " sometimes." I beg of you not to cling to the letter of what I say, but to regard only the sense and the spirit of the whole.

2. You remark to me a little farther on that I lay down the principle that *as much artillery as possible should be brought early into action,* and that you do not think it right to take their artillery from the divisions which are marching in rear, in order to push it forward early into action at long ranges. So far as the last point goes, I am quite of your opinion. But I do not contemplate the " possibility " of taking their artillery from the infantry divisions. The artillery of a division forms with it an integral whole. The General in command has never any right to separate them.

"As much as possible" means that the artillery of the leading division, which is already in action in the front, should be reinforced by the corps artillery.

In my opinion, any separation between the infantry divisions and their artillery must be always avoided. It is only when the officer commanding the division is convinced that his artillery is as distinctly a part of his " I " as any infantry battalion that he will be inclined to use it properly, and not as a mere semi-detached appendage, about which he need not trouble himself. Under such circumstances only will the artillery really learn to work usefully in conjunction with the infantry.

It may happen here and there in the course of a battle that a divisional artillery may find itself altogether separated from its infantry. But this is always a misfortune, which must be provided against as much as possible, just as it is a misfortune when a battalion in the course of the combat becomes separated from its division.

Thus in the battle of Saint-Privat the artillery of the 1st Division of the Guard were separated from their infantry. This could not be avoided. The 1st Division of the Guard had sent forward their artillery to commence the action and they were under fire. I had to reinforce them with the corps artillery, and was obliged to come up on their left, as the Hessian Artillery occupied all the space on their right. During the artillery fight which now developed itself nearly the whole of the infantry of the corps were withdrawn in rear of the artillery into the ravine towards Sainte-Marie-aux-Chênes. When General von Pape attacked that village, and also later on, when he wished to advance against Saint-Privat, he felt the want of his artillery, and I lent him some batteries of the corps artillery to do his work. This was a misfortune, since, especially in the first case, loss of time was caused by the necessity that he should apply to me. I might have sent him his own artillery from the right wing. But this would have caused a yet greater loss of time, for they were the farthest away of all. Such misfortunes will arise. But, because they are misfortunes, they must be avoided whenever it is possible to do so.

3. In a similar manner you have entirely mis-understood me when you blame me because I allow *the artillery of the defence*, if the assailant begins to gain the upper hand in the artillery duel, *to cease firing from time to time* and to withdraw their guns under cover, with the object of surprising the enemy by bringing them forward again at the critical moment. For you are anxious lest this should have an unfavourable moral effect upon the infantry of the defence. Well, I thought that through the whole of my statements there ran one golden rule, that artillery is never to leave infantry in the lurch. Besides, if I wanted to draw back the artillery of the defence under cover at the proper moment for doing so, I could never dream of selecting the time when the infantry of the defence was hotly engaged, and when every sort of assistance, tactical and moral, was due to them. It is obvious, and I have said so many times, that in such a case the artillery must hold its ground up to the moment when the General abandons the position. The time of which I spoke can be none but that when only an artillery fight is going

on, and when the infantry are not as yet engaged. When at a later hour the infantry take up the defence, then that phase of the battle begins, in which the artillery must come to the front again, and must use every effort to assist them, holding their ground with them down to the last man.

I once saw such a retirement and fresh advance. It was at Saint-Privat. We had about 60 French guns opposed to us. After an artillery fight, which lasted a long time, they ceased firing and disappeared. When our infantry advanced to the attack and masked our guns, the French batteries reappeared and united their fire with that of their infantry. They indeed surprised us by doing so, for we thought that we had silenced them.

You think that it would not always be possible to find cover so near, that the artillery could come at the right time into position for the critical moment. In that case the artillery must certainly have chosen their position badly, and must not be allowed to withdraw. For I expressly said that if the guns be drawn back a couple of paces in rear of the crest on which they are standing, this will, as a rule, be sufficient. Everything else must give way to the necessity of having the artillery at the right moment in the position in which it will have to support the other arms ; if it is not there it is good for nothing. All other matters, such as their own protection, comfort, or security, are secondary considerations.

4. Your objections to my opinion regarding the employment of *Horse Artillery in a cavalry action*, prove to me that on the ground which you take there is really no difference between our ideas. Words, at

least such words as I write, are too feeble to express everything, to leave nothing unsaid, and to prevent the possibility of some construction being put upon them which may be quite different from what I intended.

You object to the assertion which I have made in my twelfth letter, that it is absolutely necessary that the Horse Artillery should first cripple the enemy's artillery, saying that to show your artillery prematurely is not the way to surprise your enemy. You are certainly quite right, if there is any chance of surprising him. If that is possible, we should advance as close as we can to him, keeping our cavalry and artillery under cover, and should beat him down (that is to say, his cavalry) with fire, making use of the disorder which will be thus caused for a charge, of which the success will be certain, and in which the enemy's guns must fall into our hands. It is even easy to imagine a case where the cavalry, bent upon a surprise, would dispense with the effect of their artillery, in order not to warn the enemy. But I cannot ground my principles upon such rare cases, or upon any faults so entirely opposed to principles as those which the enemy would have committed on such an occasion. I have had in my mind only the ordinary and usual cases, and cannot consider exceptional situations, since there would be no end to them. especially with regard to cavalry actions, of which the constantly changing conditions afford room for an infinite number of combinations. I must take it that the enemy discovers us in time, as we so discover him. He will then conceal his masses in folds of the ground, and we shall do the same with ours ;

and thus the engagement will commence with a fight between the two artilleries, with the object of finding an opportunity of breaking out with their cavalry masses from the cover afforded by the ground.

You object also to my saying, "This will not prevent at least a part of the artillery from being used to fire on the enemy's cavalry, wherever they may be visible within effective range." You found your objection upon the fact that no words are too strong to reprobate such a division of fire. In this you speak to my very heart. I also cannot endure a division of fire. But you have not noticed that I wrote "with *at least* a part": this implies that as a rule the whole of the artillery should fire on the cavalry as soon as their fire is likely to be effective. The sentences in my letter which follow say the same, as also do the general principles for all artillery which are laid down in my seventeenth letter (subdivision II., 1 [*e*]), which state that artillery is always to fire on the other arms as soon as the latter are visible within the zone of effective fire. When I wrote the words "at least a part" I was thinking that the enemy might, during the cannonade, show somewhere on his flank some small detachment of cavalry, perhaps a squadron or so ; in such case it might be worth while to break them up and disperse them with a couple of good shells, without its being necessary to interrupt the artillery fight along the whole line.

I will now turn my attention to answering the questions which you have asked me, and which give me an opportunity of filling up such gaps as I may have left.

(a.) *How far should the authority of the generals commanding troops extend, and is it necessary to allow greater independence to the spontaneous action of artillery than would be permitted to the other two arms?*

I consider that it is a most serious matter to define exactly how far the authority of generals should extend. Discipline might be endangered by such a definition, as indeed used to be the case in the artillery. I mentioned this in my seventh letter when I was writing about the Spirit of Caste. Moreover, the artillery itself would find this disadvantageous, since the general would dislike it, if obedience to his orders was forbidden by such a definition. The harmonious co-operation of the different arms, and punctual tactical support reciprocally rendered, must suffer from it. Nothing but the closest possible union of the artillery with the other arms can enable the former to do all that is expected of it, and only by the closest union within itself can it develop its whole power in battle. It must yield absolute obedience to what the general orders, and he must have power, if he wishes it, over every detail. It must not only obey the letter of the order, but must also assist the designs of the general by meeting them half way, and by even forestalling them.

When the officer commanding the artillery of a body of troops, whether a division or an army-corps, has won the confidence of his general by his obedience, by his readiness to act, and by fully supporting the action of the other troops, then the two factors, the readiness of the artillery and the

2 D

confidence of the general, will settle of themselves
how far the authority of the general should extend.
This extent will vary with the character of each
individual. If, however, there is a want of harmony
between these two persons, if the subordinate stands
upon his dignity, if he holds back and waits for
orders instead of seeking for them, if he finds fault
with these orders at decisive moments and carries
them out unwillingly, or if he presumes to override
them on his own responsibility, in that case a good
understanding must be brought about, and definitions
are of no use for that purpose.

In the whole course of the war of 1870-71 I
never found any necessity for any defined limit being
placed to the authority of the general, with the object
of preventing hindrance to the spontaneous action of
artillery. But in this respect individuals differ very
much. In the 1st Division of the Guard the general
commanding had the very greatest confidence in the
commander of his artillery brigade. This confidence
grew in course of time, owing to the personal charm
of both, to a sort of intimacy. General von Pape used
only to say to his Lieutenant-Colonel, von Bychel-
berg, " My object is so and so, work the batteries
accordingly." But in some cases he gave an order,
" Bring the batteries here as quickly as you can."
And this was done. Lieutenant-Colonel von Bychel-
berg had already commanded the same batteries of
the same division in 1866, and possessed the fullest
confidence of the other arms.

It was very different in the other division. The
officer commanding the artillery was several times
changed in consequence of casualties which had to

be filled up. General von Budritzky knew very little as to their military qualifications. Moreover, this general took a great interest in the details of the artillery, in which he had formerly served for a year. For this reason he interfered a good deal in these details. During the siege of Paris I often met with him seeking carefully for positions for his batteries, of which he superintended and watched the very construction. He often personally pointed out the target, and directed the rate of the fire. I never heard, however, that any difficulty as to working together arose from this. Certainly no quarrel arose about it. The general ordered and the artillery obeyed. On the contrary, I on one occasion (it was after the storming of Le Bourget on the 30th of October 1870) saw the general embrace a field-officer of artillery and thank him for his assistance.

It is much easier to tell you my opinion with respect to the general in command of an army-corps. The officer commanding the artillery of an army-corps has really nothing to do with leading troops. He is, tactically speaking, only the adviser of the general in artillery matters, and passes on his orders. If he gives an order he can do so only so far as he is authorised to give it in the name and as the representative of his general. He does not take over the real command of the artillery line in action, unless more than half of the artillery of the army-corps is engaged ; and then only by the order of the general. I always used to ride up to the Prince of Wurtemberg and wait there. This made the management easy. The prince asked my opinion with regard to the place and the time at which the batteries should be employed ; he then gave his orders either agreeing with or differing from it, and I sent my adjutants to carry them in his name. I could naturally make suggestions as to the employment of the batteries whenever he had time to listen to them. He agreed to, or he differed from, these according as to whether they were, or were not, in accordance with his intentions. As time went on these suggestions were more rarely declined, as I gradually grew to understand more distinctly the object of the prince. But every now and then he differed from me. For example, at Sedan, where I at 11 A.M. already wished to advance closer to the enemy with the whole of the corps artillery in conjunction with that of the 1st Division. The prince did not agree, since at that time it was necessary to push the 2d Division of the Guard farther to the left, in order to support the 12th army-corps. On the contrary, he ordered the brigade of Horse Artillery to move to the centre in order to fill up the interval between the two divisions. This order was carried out more quickly than the prince had considered possible. This increased his confidence in the artillery. At a later date consequently ordinary orders concerning the artillery only were left to me. Thus, at the time of the sortie of the 21st December 1870, the prince, who was in my quarters, allowed me to say that I should at once take a battery from such and such a body of troops to Dugny, and should show them there the point on which to form ; this I carried out immediately.

I need not therefore say any more with the object of pointing out precisely the bounds of the authority of the general. If I were told to define this limit, I should be exceedingly puzzled as to how to decide upon it. You will say perhaps that it is all quite simple ; the general decides upon all tactical matters, but does not interfere with technical artillery details. That would be quite wrong. One general says to the commander of his artillery, " I am going to attack that village, prepare the attack "; another says, " Bring up your batteries here on to this hill and fire on that village, I am going to attack it when you are ready." The general must be allowed to judge as to how far he can rely upon his artillery officers. He must not be forbidden to interfere even in artillery details. He must be able to say, " Concentrate the whole of your fire against that flank of the enemy ; I have received a report that troops are being massed there for an attack." Or he must be permitted to order the artillery to change from column of divisions to column of route, if he wants them to give him more room. Or he must be able to order the ammunition-wagons of the 2d line to move from the position which has been selected for them, if he requires that spot for other troops. I could mention many such cases.

It seems to me that the present regulations are quite sufficient, and I do not wish anything changed in them. They may be summed up as laying down the absolute dependence of the commander of artillery upon the general, and as directing that the proper position of the former is with the general, up to the moment when half or more than half of his batteries are in action. The moment when independent action can begin is thus precisely laid down.

I cannot see that the spontaneous action of artillery

requires more independence than that of the two
other arms. On the contrary! During most battles
the artillery is posted on or near the points whence
the best view can be obtained, and these also the
general naturally selects for his position. As for
individual bodies of infantry in battle, they are
generally so far away that they are compelled to rely
upon their own action, in exchange for which they
can at any time hold on to the artillery. Now as to
the cavalry! They are always far away, whether
they are reconnoitring miles to the front, or whether
they are during a battle halted under cover in rear
of a flank looking for a favourable moment to make
a charge; for this, moreover, they will be too late, if
they are not allowed any independence.

It was thus in the last war. The Prince of
Wurtemberg generally stood near the corps artillery,
or even (as at Sedan) between the guns, unless he
could find some better point of view, or, as at Saint-
Privat, advanced and rode through the ranks of the
infantry to encourage the men. Generals von Pape
and von Budritzky were always to be found near
their guns, except at the crisis of an infantry fight, as
at Saint-Privat, or as when Budritzky went on with
the stormers into Le Bourget.

But, you may perhaps say, supposing that the
general knows nothing about artillery? I will ask
you: "Supposing he knows nothing about infantry,
being a cavalry man?" No instructions can be
grounded on such exceptional cases, any more than
they could be founded on the case where, like the
unfortunate Kaminskoy in 1806, the general might
suddenly go mad, or on the case where the general is

a raw ignorant butcher, as was the Jacobin Legendre in the war against La Vendée at the time of the French Reign of Terror. The case where a general knows nothing of artillery, infantry, or cavalry, must be an exceptional one, since divisions and corps will not be intentionally entrusted to generals who know nothing about the employment of the three arms.

(*b.*) *What are the details of the formation of a mass of artillery ; what will be the sequence of command in it ; and what form will its direction by the brigadiers of artillery take ?*

I can give you no especial rules in answer to these questions. But I can tell you what was done in the battles and actions at which I was present. Owing to the order of march which we adopted in the war of 1870-71 (the corps artillery following the leading division), the formation of masses of artillery was tolerably easy even on the offensive. When the head of the corps was received at Saint-Privat by the fire of the enemy, the general in command, after the enemy's position had been reconnoitred, asked for the opinions of the Chief of the Staff and of the artillery brigadier. We both agreed to push in the corps artillery, since we could count 60 guns opposed to us. Whereupon the 4 batteries of the leading division (the 1st) trotted forward by batteries into action.

I have already (in Letter VI.) said that Colonel von Scherbening had trotted up of his own accord on hearing the first gun, and appeared upon the spot just as the general in command had issued the order to summon him. He simply formed line with his

batteries to the left of those of the 1st Division. The
rear battery (the 2d Horse) galloped up into line. I
do not think that more than a quarter of an hour
elapsed between the first shots of the leading battery
(the 1st Light) and that of the last (the 2d Horse).
There were altogether 9 batteries, which arrived
almost simultaneously in position. The Prince of
Wurtemberg stood and allowed them all to march
past him. When the 8th battery drew near him, I
reminded him that I, according to the regulations,
ought now to go to the front (we had 15 batteries in
the corps), in order to take over the command. He
gave me his permission, and I went forward with the
2d horse battery. I informed General von Pape
(commanding the 1st Division), by one of my adjutants, that I had received the order to take up the
command of the line of artillery. Upon this his
brigade of artillery passed for the time being from
that general's command, and came under mine.
Later on the 2d Division of the Guard sent an
infantry brigade and 3 batteries on to the field of
battle ; one brigade and one battery had been sent
to support the 9th corps. General von Budritzky
sent the 3 batteries into line on the left of Saint-
Ail, and thus on the left flank of the 9 batteries
which were already engaged. At a later hour still
the general in command ordered the cavalry division
to send up both the horse batteries, which were
attached to it, and these took up a similar position
on the left flank. There were thus 14 batteries
engaged at this point, the whole in one mass under
one command ; they were, naming them from the
right, the 1st Field Brigade, the 2d Brigade, the

Horse Brigade, and on the left the three batteries of the 3d Field Brigade. I selected a small undulation of the ground as a position from which I could superintend the guns ; it stood about 20 paces in rear of the leaders of the limbers, about opposite to the right flank of the corps artillery and to the left of the 1st Field Brigade. From thence I sent my orders to the field-officers, and went in person hither and thither according as it became necessary. After the storming of the hill in which I had taken part with the 2d heavy battery, I stood, as I have already told you, behind the captain of No. 4 heavy battery, Captain Seeger, and took part in the details of ranging the battery ; after that I sent my adjutants right and left to inform the other batteries of the ranges, and ordered the target for each.

After the end of the battle I sent back the 1st brigade to their division, having had to keep them with unlimbered guns in the foremost line up to daybreak.

The close connection between the artillery combat and that of the infantry is for the moment more difficult, when the commander of the artillery is not actually with the general in command. On this account I sent one of my adjutants from time to time to the general, in order that I might remain acquainted with his intentions. He and his Staff stood a little to our rear on a hill which formed a better post for observation than did the artillery position, but which was too far away to be occupied by the guns.

I should have done better if I had left all my adjutants with the Staff, with the simple order to bring me instantly information of any change in the intentions of the general.

At Sedan the task was yet easier and more simple. We were called out of our cantonments and bivouacs at 3 A.M. The divisions used different roads for their advance. The 1st moved to the right by the Ardennes, the 2d to the left of the road by the river Chiers. As we started from Carignan the general ordered the corps artillery to trot at once at the head of the column as far as Pouru Saint-Remy. The Horse Brigade had been, during the previous days, attached to the cavalry division which had been working in our front, and had bivouacked with it in rear of Carignan. I proposed to the Prince of Wurtemberg to re-attach the Horse Brigade to the corps artillery for that day's battle. This was sanctioned, and I sent the order. For this reason the Horse Brigade moved from Carignan considerably after the 2d Field Brigade. When the general, who hurried on ahead, had reached the height to the east of Villers-Cernay, whence he could obtain a good view, the corps artillery was ordered thither by Francheval. The 2d Field Brigade came up to these heights with their horses all in a lather, just as the advanced troops of the 1st Division of the Guard had completed their dispositions for clearing the enemy's skirmishers out of the opposite woods (the Bois de Villers-Cernay). At my request the general allowed me to order the 2d Field Brigade to dismount that the horses might get their wind, and to go myself to the front in order to reconnoitre ; it thus came about, as I have already told you, that I met General von Pape. At his wish I hurried on the advance of the artillery belonging to his division, and obtained the permission of the general in command to reinforce them with the corps artillery. The deployment this time was a little slower than it had been a fortnight before, owing to the steep slopes and the heavy ground. But when the batteries were in action, it was easier to direct them, since the general in command stood between or in the batteries. I was constantly in movement between him and the brigades, and carried orders to the divisional artillery "in the name of the general in command." It was not until the latter allowed me to advance all the 90 guns into their last position (and I was about to carry out that rather risky manœuvre of which I have told you, and which fortunately succeeded) that I "took over the formal command." I then personally informed the generals commanding divisions that I had received an order to lead on the artillery; they *released* their commanders of brigades *from their command,* and *gave them over to my orders.*

Such an arrangement as this is absolutely necessary, and I strongly recommend that this formality be always gone through, since otherwise it may easily happen that the artillery will receive different orders from two commanders. This must certainly be avoided. When troops have more than one commander, confusion generally ensues, or, at the least friction, the conflict of authority and uncertainty. No man can serve two masters.

At Sedan, when I took over the command of the line of artillery, the necessary close connection with the general and the generals of divisions was much easier to keep up than at Saint-Privat, since they

henceforth remained near or between the guns, and
I could thus constantly communicate with them
and receive the orders of the general in command.

I have never taken part in any defensive action
as brigadier of artillery, for at the sorties of Le
Bourget, etc., we always acted strongly on the
offensive against the troops making them ; but I
think that the employment of artillery masses on the
defensive would be much easier than the development,
when on the offensive, from the order of march to
the order of battle.   At least, when I picture to
myself the case where a sortie against our block-
ading position might have compelled us to defend
that position, it seems to me that the command of
the artillery would have been a very simple matter.
The batteries would be posted in positions, selected
by the artillery commanders and sanctioned by the
generals commanding, which, moreover, would have
been gradually more and more strengthened by art ;
these positions they would take up as soon as a sortie
was reported, and would, in the case of an attack by
the enemy upon them, have nothing to do but to
fire on the hostile troops.   Since we actually always
advanced on the offensive against the attacking
troops, and fought every time *in front* of our defensive position until the enemy fell back under shelter
of his forts, these were really all offensive actions, so
far as it was a question of the activity and the influence of the various departments.   In them the
formation of masses of artillery, the sequence of
command, and the directing powers of artillery
brigadiers were the same as in the battles of Saint-
Privat and Sedan.   A detailed description of matters

which I have already touched upon would only weary you, as it would be a mere repetition.

It once happened that during a battle I came up into a line of artillery belonging to a division who were in action, without the command of this line being given over to me. In this case I did not dare to interfere by giving orders, and had to content myself with advice. If the officer commanding the artillery had met my counsels with an order from his divisional general which was opposed to them, I should have had to give way.

During the march I used to ride, as a rule, with the general in command. Such functions as I had to discharge according to regulation—for example, the supply of officers, men, horses, and ammunition—were carried out in writing from my quarter or bivouac after the march, and formed a part of the daily orders. These daily orders were issued by the chief of the staff of the corps immediately at the end of the march, before he dismounted, and before the troops had taken up their quarters or cantonments ; with this object he previously ascertained the wishes of the general commanding. Our Chief of the Staff had held the same position in the campaign of 1866, and was thus thoroughly experienced in his duties. He always dictated the orders directly to the adjutants who wrote them down. Finally, before what he had dictated was read through and collated, he used to ask the several departments, the divisions, the artillery, the train, etc., whether they had still any other question to ask him. At this invitation I used, when necessary, to suggest my instructions for the artillery. Of course in doing so I passed over the fact that the Chief of the Staff was my junior in rank. In war every one must consider the interests of the whole rather than such questions of etiquette.

It, moreover, often happened that in the course of my duty, or in order to look after the artillery details of the batteries and ammunition-columns, I had to visit them myself. This, of course, I could not do without the permission of the general in command, and then only on those days when, according to the reports of our advanced cavalry, there was no possibility of a battle.

On such occasions I either stayed behind or I rode on in front during the march. But after the march was over I generally rode on a fresh horse to the troops which I desired to see.

An order was given by the general in command (whom I had asked to give it) to the officers commanding the several divisions, to allow me to inspect the artillery which was by the organisation of the army told off to their divisions. No conflict of authority nor any friction ever arose on this ground.

There were no special regulations on this point. But the custom arose naturally from the " Ordre de bataille."

All this proved much simpler and easier in practice than one would have expected, judging by the written order for the sequence of command, since, as a rule, I found the officers commanding the divisional artillery riding with the divisional generals.

(*c.*) *Which is the most desirable position in the various forms of attack for the main mass of the artillery ; and what is there to be said with regard to artillery firing over the heads of infantry ?*

It is no easy matter, even in theory, to point out
some distinct position which the artillery must take
up if they are intended to support the action of the
other arms. This is equally true, whether it is a
question of a single battery which is attached to a
regiment or a brigade, or of the artillery of a division,
or of the main mass of the artillery of an army-corps ;
while if any such theoretical position is to be laid
down, the case of absolutely open level ground, such
as is never found in practice, can alone be considered.
Thus results may be arrived at which are of no use in
any real case, and which, if they be employed for
the purpose of drawing up rules, will only tend to
confuse one's ideas. To any one who is even only
moderately acquainted with the tactics of the different
arms, the positions of the artillery are in practice so
clearly, and even imperiously, pointed out by the
character of the ground, in connection with the general
situation of the action, that there can be no doubt
upon the subject.

That artillery should fire over their own infantry
is always an evil, since it has a bad influence on the
latter, especially if they are not as yet inured to
battle, but it *cannot be always avoided.* Infantry get
accustomed to it when they have seen a little service.
During the bombardment of Montmédy, after the
battle of Sedan, on the 5th of September 1870, I
pushed forward a line of skirmishers, as cover to the
batteries, to the farther edge of the plateau on the
east of Thonelle and close up to the fortress. These
infantry laughed and joked at the shell which whistled
backwards and forwards over their heads. They
were tired, for they had made a night-march, and

they fell asleep in the sun on the stubble so soundly that I was obliged to post sentries, in order that they might wake the skirmishers in case the enemy should advance. This shows how entirely the men had grown accustomed to fire passing over their heads.

It is very easy to say that artillery should always be posted on a flank. But it is often impossible to do so, especially when it is fighting between two army-corps. I have already mentioned how desirable it is to post the wagons of the 1st line on the same front as the batteries. This will necessitate a front of 200 paces per battery, and thus of 3800 paces for the 19 batteries of a corps, if the ground allows all the batteries to stand close to each other. The fighting front of an army-corps cannot be allowed to be much longer than this. The space within which the Guard corps had to fight at Saint-Privat, from the left gun of the Hessian division to the right gun of the Saxons, measured 3800 paces (see the map in the official account, for 5 P.M.); while at Sedan, from the right flank of the Saxons to the right flank of the Guard corps, it was about the same distance (see map of Sedan, afternoon). At many places it was necessary to fire over their own infantry; for example, about Givonne, of which the low ground was held by the fusiliers and jagers of the Guard.

I have already written something to you on this subject, and then said that there is in this no real danger for the infantry, unless the shell break up in the bore and thus act as case shot, or except when the artillery are posted so far to the rear that they cannot distinguish friend from foe. For these reasons artillery which has to fire over its own infantry must not stand too close to them (they should be at least 500 paces from them), and must not be too far from them, not farther, I think, than 1000 yards.

If infantry when attacking have to advance through the guns, the latter must consider themselves masked, and remain silent until the infantry have pushed on some hundreds of yards to their front. Even though this cannot be avoided, it still remains an evil, which must be taken into account ; it is also a factor which cannot be ignored when the question of the attack is under consideration. For this will be the moment in which the defender will again bring his artillery into action, if he has for a time allowed it to remain silent.

I can here answer yet another of the questions which you ask me : concerning the position of the great mass of artillery which hurried forward to the aid of the infantry of the Guard and the 12th corps, when they were for a time unable to make a further advance.

In many places the batteries stood from 600 to 700 paces in rear of the lines of infantry, which were lying down and firing. But where the infantry lines were very thin, the batteries unlimbered in the line of skirmishers, so that the latter lay between the guns. As an example I may name the 2d and 4th heavy batteries of the Guard, with which I was present (see map of Saint-Privat, 7 P.M.)

(*d.*) *How far is it advisable to "lay back" ?*

I have not been accustomed to this sort of practice. According to the description, it is intended to be used when it is impossible to see the target, since the guns are kept under cover (of woods, brushwood,

2 E

rising ground, etc.), in order that, when within the
zone of effective shrapnel, they may not be put out
of action immediately after unlimbering. The gun
is then laid from the trunnion-sight over the tangent-
scale upon some point in rear. Elevation is given
by the quadrant. Observers posted on high ground
report the effect of fire, and the laying is corrected
accordingly.

I can very well imagine a case in which this
mode of procedure might be useful; and it must
then produce considerable effect, for the enemy will
receive a very efficient fire, cannot tell where it
comes from, and can neither see nor fire on our
artillery. I have a lively recollection how unpleasant
some of the enemy's guns were to us at the siege of
Paris ; they were posted so entirely under cover that
we could not see them, and thus remained long in
doubt in what direction and with what elevation we
were to reply to their fire.

But we must not overlook the fact that it will be
more difficult and take longer to " range " the guns
from such a covered position than it would if they
could be laid directly on the target, and that when
firing in this manner a change of target and fire
against moving targets would become impossible in
war. Thus such completely covered positions can
be used only for the commencement of the artillery
fight at short ranges, and must soon, when the enemy's
fire has been somewhat reduced, be abandoned for a
position which affords a good view, in order to be
prepared for all eventualities, and especially in order
to be ready for infantry who may push forward to
within a short distance. There is further a chance

that, owing to the difficulty of " ranging " the guns by laying back, so much time may be lost that this second position on the crest may be taken up too late. In that case this process will have done only harm.

I think myself that it is a complicated mode of working which will only in very rare cases fulfil the expectations formed of it.

Finally, here are two answers to the parts of your letter in which you mention some points which you dislike.

In the first place, you find that I have contradicted myself, in that I said in my ninth letter that I as a rule formed line with the 1st line of wagons (3 ammunition-wagons and 1 store-wagon) on the left of the battery and in line with it ; and then asserted that I placed one wagon in rear of No. 2 gun and another in rear of No. 5, in order that the shell might be taken directly from them. I acknowledge that this might be taken for a contradiction. In order to explain this matter I must add the following words :—

When a battery took up a position, the above-mentioned four wagons formed line on the left of it at full intervals, and on the same front as the battery, with the horses' heads towards the enemy. The captain then gave his orders with regard to the description of fire, corrections, etc. As soon as the fire was regularly established, he had to trouble himself about the supply of ammunition, and then ordered a wagon to be placed in rear of No. 2 and No. 5 guns. The third ammunition-wagon remained on the left flank of the battery with the store-wagon. I think that it is better to place an ammunition-

2 E 2

wagon in rear of each half battery, rather than in rear of each division, for otherwise it may happen that all the three wagons of the 1st line may be empty at the same time, and may be all obliged to fall back to fill up.   Then the battery would be left without wagons, and would be compelled to use the ammunition out of the limbers until the wagons sent from the 2d line had come up.

Lastly, you blame me because I did not name the late General von Podbielski, though I said so much about General von Hindersin.

Forgive me if I honestly confess that I laughed when I read this.   Have you then not read the first page of my first letter?   In that I wrote about the development of our artillery in the seventh decade of this century, and about the rules which were drawn up for the future from the experiences of the wars of 1864, 1866, and 1870-71.   General von Podbielski became a gunner in the year 1872, and had thus nothing to do with it, any more than Tempelhof, Holzendorff, Prince August, or Prince Adalbert of Prussia, who are nevertheless acknowledged and renowned authorities on artillery.

INDEX.

Printed by R. & R. CLARK, LIMITED, *Edinburgh.*

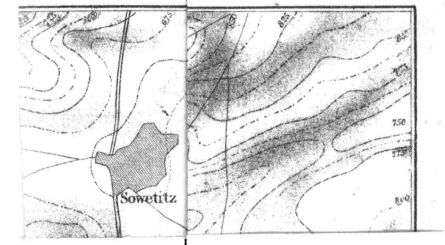

Sowetitz

IE BATTLEFIELD OF KÖNIGGRÄTZ.

N

Vincent Brooks Day &

PLAN III.

LEFIELD OF VIONVILLE.

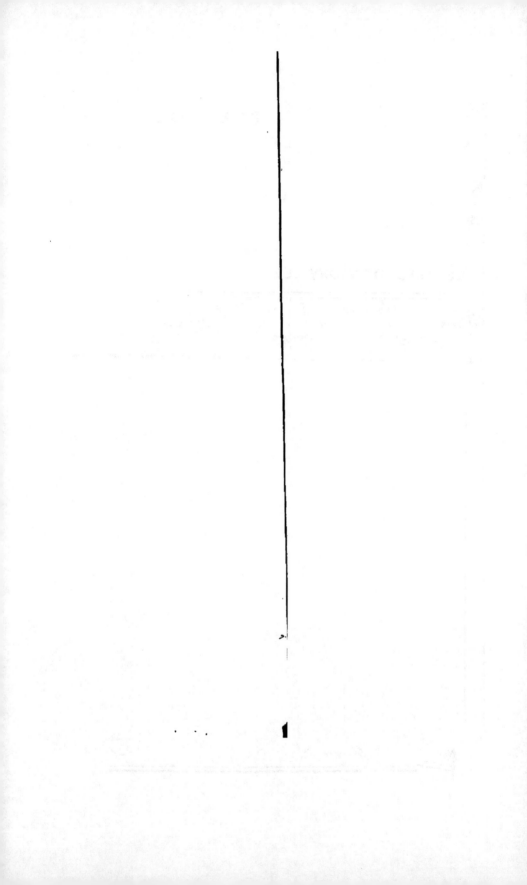

THE BATTLEFIELD OF GRAVELLOTE.

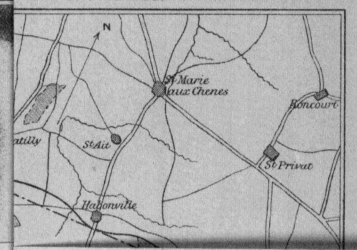

AND T
5.000

rvals of

PLAN V.

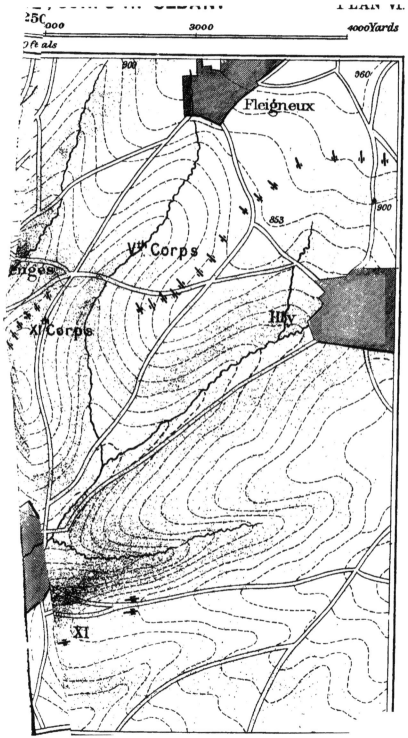

9 781340 962180